CENTRAL ASIA: TRAVELS IN CASHMERE, LITTLE THIBET AND CENTRAL ASIA

CENTRAL ASIA: TRAVELS IN CASHMERE, LITTLE THIBET AND CENTRAL ASIA

TAYLOR, BAYA

GYAN

Published by

GYAN

Gyan Publishing House
5, Ansari Road
Daryaganj, New Delhi-110002
Phone: 011-47034999, 9811692060
E-mail: books@gyanbooks.com

Distribution Network
gyanbooks.com
India, USA, Canada, UK, Australia, France

ISBN : 978-81-212-3201-2 (PB)

2nd Impression 2020

Printed at: Gyan Press, Delhi.

Central Asia: Travels in Cashmere, Little Thibet and Central Asia
Author: Taylor, Baya

TRAVELLING IN THE ASIATIC DESERTS. LIGHT IN THE DARKNESS.

ILLUSTRATED LIBRARY OF TRAVEL, EXPLORATION, AND ADVENTURE.

CENTRAL ASIA.

TRAVELS IN

CASHMERE, LITTLE TIBET,

AND

CENTRAL ASIA.

COMPILED AND ARRANGED BY

BAYARD TAYLOR.

NEW YORK:
SCRIBNER, ARMSTRONG, AND COMPANY.
1874.

CONTENTS.

LIST OF ILLUSTRATIONS.

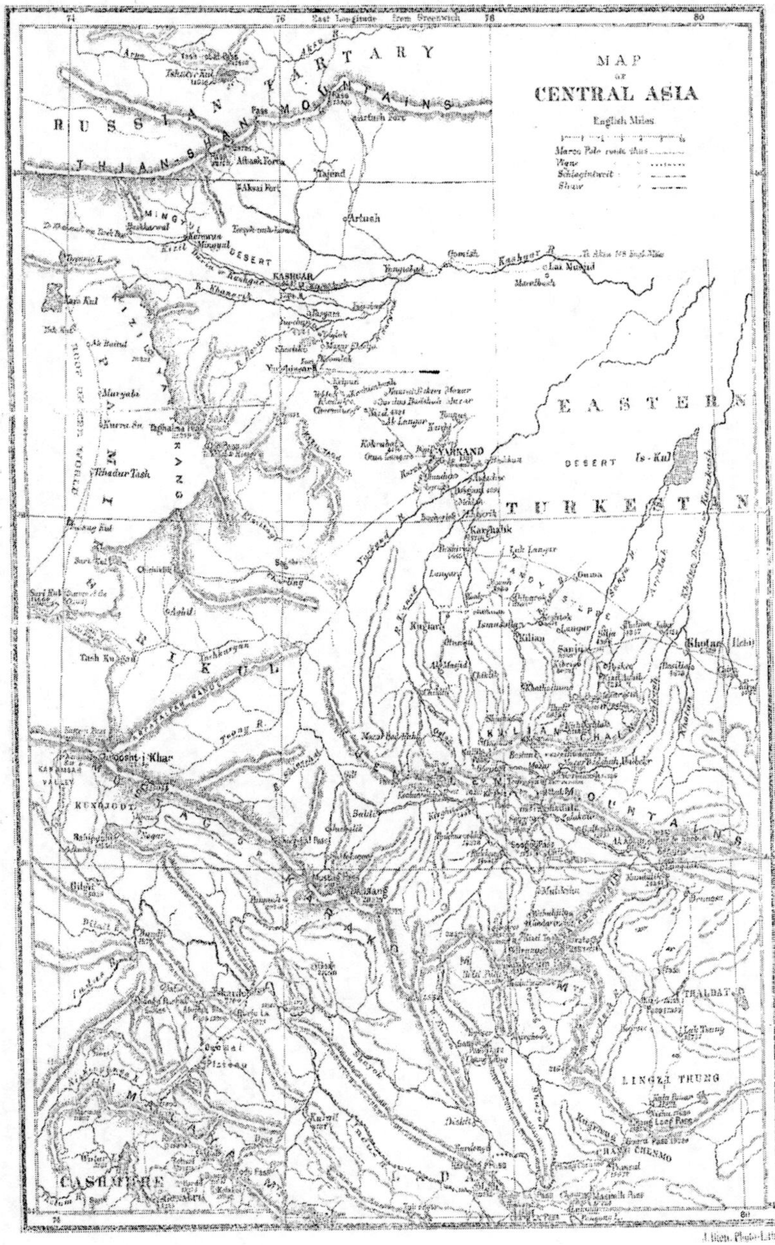

J. Bien, Photo-Lith.

TRAVELS IN CENTRAL ASIA.

CHAPTER I.

THE COUNTRIES OF CENTRAL ASIA.

THE name "Central Asia" correctly describes, in a geographical sense, the heart of that continent. It is separated from the river-system of the Aral and Caspian Seas, on the west, by almost impassable mountain-ranges; from the affluents of the Indus and Ganges, on the south, by the chain of the Küen-lün, the rival of the Himalayas, and from the rivers of China to the eastward, by the great Desert of Gobi. A line drawn from Constantinople to Peking, and another from the latitude of Cape Comorin to that of the Polar Sea, bisecting the former line, would very nearly indicate the central portion of the region, as also of the continent.

Here,—partly, perhaps, on account of its remote and nearly inaccessible situation, and also partly from concurrent traditions—many ethnologists have placed the original cradle of the Aryan race. India was undoubtedly colonized by tribes descending from the high plateaus to the northward, and the legends of the earlier Aryan inhabitants of Europe have been traced backwards, step by step, until they lose themselves among the labyrinth of mountains from which descend the Oxus and the Jaxartes. The remarkable physical features of the region must have impressed themselves upon even the primitive inhabitants. The three inclosing mountain-chains, which form almost three sides of a square, rise to such an elevation that few of their passes are less than 18,000 feet above the sea. Above the western wall lies the table-land of Pamer, or Pamir, called by the natives, *Bam-i-doonia* or "Roof of the World." The fertile lands beyond those upper realms of rock and snow and scanty summer pastures, can only be reached after many days of dangerous travel, where beasts of burden find no food, where water is rarely to be had, and where, even in summer, hurricanes of intense cold threaten to destroy all life in a few hours.

Scarcely anything is known of the early history of this part of Asia. The armies of Alexander reached its western and southern frontiers, but neither crossed them nor brought back any satisfactory report of the land beyond. It was no doubt settled by one of the branches of the large Tartar family, and its primitive communications must have been with the region known as Soongaria, on the north, and the countries of Turkestan, or Independent Tartary, on the west. It formed part of the temporary empire of Genghis Khan, and its later subjection to China was probably a result of his conquest. Afterwards it was possessed by Tamerlane, and by his great grandson, Baber, the founder of the Mogul dynasty in India. Its subsequent history very much resembles that of western Turkestan, to the inhabitants of which its own are most nearly allied by blood, religion and habits. Small states, governed by petty chiefs, arose after the dismemberment of the Tartar empires, and continued to exist, with the usual episodes of jealousy, assassination and war, until about a hundred years ago, when the whole region was again brought under Chinese rule. The recent revolution by which this rule was overthrown, has been the direct means of opening Central Asia to explorers.

A more than geographical interest, however, is now directed towards this region. For twenty years past Russia has possessed the whole of Soongaria, even to the grand dividing ridge of the Thian-Shan, and since 1867 she has added the former Khanate of Khokand on the west, beyond the table-land of Pamir, to her territory; while England, extending her sway from the south, over Cashmere and Ladak, virtually governs as far as the passes of the Karakoram and Küen-lün chains, and the loftier peaks which feed the rivers of Yarkand and Khoten. Between these two rival powers lies a warm and fertile land, commanding the roads to China and great Tibet. Hence the Russian merchants from the north and the English officials from the south have lost no time in attempting to secure an influence, which has no great present importance, but may affect the character of future events. Affghanistan and the little independent states scattered among the fastnesses of the Hindoo-Koosh still intervene between England and the advance of Russia in Western, or Independent, Tartary: but here, in Central Asia, by a sudden and most unexpected internal revolution, the interests of the two great powers are for the first time brought face to face.

This first encounter will have the character of a military reconnoissance. It may either lead to, or entirely avert, the great and final struggle for political supremacy in Asia, which the thoughtful statesmen of both countries seem to anticipate. It will, at least, bring into sharper contrast the difference between the systems of annexation and government, which each employs; and these differences are inherent in the character of the two races. Lieutenant von Heller, in an article entitled "The Russians in Central Asia"—the most exact and impartial statement of the present situation which has yet appeared*—makes this parallel: "The Anglo-Saxons cannot be surpassed, where their task is to colonize virgin soil and create new cities and states by a free course of organization; but the art of rendering barbaric and semi-barbaric tribes completely subject to them, to blend themselves with such tribes by a strict and thorough

* Published in the *Austrian Military Magazine*, 1869.

process of amalgamation, as the Russians have accomplished with so much success along the whole southern frontier of their Asiatic possessions—this art is alien to the English nature. The Anglo-Saxon colonizes as did the Greek, the Russian as did the Roman. The pioneers of the latter are military colonies, not those squatters who, conscious of their free, unrestricted individual force, feel at home beyond the limits of the civilization for which they break the way. Through a system of military colonies, the nomadic Tartars, Kalmucks and Kirghizes are forced into the organization of the Russian state, accustomed to taxes and military service, and thus gradually Russianized. Within 25 years, the descendants of those fierce Sultans, who less than half a century ago still led the life of robbers, at the head of their hordes, along the Chinese and Siberian frontier, will be seen among the pliant military and court nobles of the Czar.

Thus far, the English rule in India is based simply upon force, and by force sustained. Notwithstanding the comparative order and security which have been established, the physical development of the country, the building of canals and railroads, the extension and protection of trade in every quarter, the native population has learned no loyalty to the Government under which they live. The English officials are strangers and exiles, who never forget their homes. Even the commercial or agricultural colonists are only temporary, and few of them manifest, if they feel, any interest in having native ignorance enlightened or native wrongs abolished. There is like intermixture of the races, and even less social intercourse than an intelligent policy would dictate. India, thus, is an extraneous possession, while Russian Tartary is grafted upon the national stock.

On both sides also the means of communication are approaching each other. The English railways now extend from Bombay and Calcutta to the Upper Indus, while the Russians have projected a line from Oxenburg, on the Ural River, across the steppes into Turkestan. It is possible that a few years more may see an unbroken line of rail from St. Petersburg to the Oxus and the northern base of the Hindoo-Koosh. Although there is no near probability of any direct conflict, the natural impulsion, which both nations are compelled to follow, will gradually lead them to that point where their different systems of annexation will stand in direct opposition, and one must give way to the other.

The tremendous mountain-chains which for so many centuries have shut out Central Asia from intercourse with the world, form nearly three sides of a square. The northern range, called the Thian-Shan, stretches eastward from the right angle which it makes with the western range or Belur Dagh, dividing the rivers which .lose themselves in the desert of Lob from those which flow into the detached lakes of Russian Tartary. It is a great natural barrier, with passes 16,000 feet, and summits more than twenty thousand feet. The

Belur Dagh, upholding the great table-land of Pamir on the west, has an equal if not greater average elevation. At its southern extremity, where it merges into the Hindoo-Koosh, it makes nearly a right angle with the Karakoram range which divides the waters of the Indus from those of the rivers of Yarkand and Khoten. Many peaks of the Karakoram have an elevation of over 24,000 feet, and one of them, the Dapsang, rises to the great height of 28,278 feet. The summit ridge of this chain, further to the eastward, sinks into an uneven table-land, about 19,000 feet above the sea, which attaches it to the parallel range of the Küen-lün, which latter chain thus forms a continuation of the southern wall of Central Asia.

The physical features of the region are thus described by Mr. Shaw: "East Toorkestan [the name now generally used] resembles an immense bay, open to the eastward, but inclosed by gigantic mountain ranges on all other sides. A desert thirty days' journey in width lies before its mouth and divides it from China, which until recently possessed the country. In this desert all the rivers of Toorkestan are swallowed up; they end in marshes or lakes, or gradually disappear under the sand in broad jungles. At the north-western corner, between the Thian-Shan and the plateau of Pamir, there is a secondary bay, at the opening of which lie the cities of Yang-hissar and Kashghar, the latter the political capital of the country, as Yarkand is the commercial capital. The great bay of Toorkestan also stretches out two long arms to the eastward, at the foot of the northern and southern mountain-chains, between them and the great desert, forming the province of Khoten in the south, and the provinces of Usch-Turfan, Aksu, Kutsha, &c., in the north. The inhabited territory has therefore the general form of a cresent, with its convex side to the mountains and its concave towards the desert. It has an average elevation of four to five thousand feet above the sea.

"The northern and southern boundaries of East-Turkestan are by no means simple chains of mountains, like the Alps or Pyrenees, which may be crossed by single passes; they are agglomerated mountain-systems, consisting of many chains, and embracing considerable regions, such as Little Tibet and Cashmere, in their valleys. In travelling from India to Toorkestan on the usual path of trade, there are not less than *eleven* lofty passes to be surmounted, only two of which are lower than the summit of Mont Blanc.

"The rivers which have their rise in the southern mountain-system exhibit the singular feature, that they do not directly find their way to the plains, but often flow for many hundred miles in long valleys, lying between the chains and parallel with them, before they finally collect their strength, and burst forth from their imprisonment through a cleft in the mountain-barrier. The most remarkable example is the Indus, which, rising on Chinese soil, flows northwestward behind five distinct ranges of the Himalayas before he reaches his turning-point, and then must break through all these ranges before he issues upon the plains of India. Within this great curve he embraces the entire courses of his five large tributary rivers, which give a name to the Punjab. Each of the latter imitates his example on a lesser scale, and the gorges which they break through the mountain-walls constitute the wildest scenery of the Himalayas. It is interesting to note that this peculiarity is repeated on the northern side of the great watershed. The Karakash flows for eighty miles along the southern side of the Küen-lün, before it suddenly turns and breaks through the gorge of Shahidoolla; and the river of Yarkand, rising in the Karakoram pass, describes a great arc behind another part of the same Küen-lün before it turns towards Yarkand. It commences with an almost western course, and ends in the desert after a long journey to the east. This feature of the country occasions the principal difficulty of travel, for the routes of commerce are led directly across all the intervening chains, instead of following the long wanderings of the rivers.

"The northern mountain boundary of East Toorkestan is almost equally complicated, with the exception of one point at its western extremity, where a single Alpine wall divides the territory of Kashghar from the upper valleys of the Jaxartes. We see, therefore, that East Toorkestan is a very compact state, cut off from all neighboring lands by lofty mountains and tremendous deserts. The physical result of this is the almost entire absence of rain. All the clouds laden with the moisture of the Indian Ocean exhaust themselves on the outer ridge of the Himalayas, where the rain-fall occasionally amounts to three hundred inches in a year. The second and third chains receive much less, and beyond them lies the sterile region which is called Tibet. The other inclosing mountains present similar obstacles to the clouds from the north and west, while the immense distance of the China Sea acts as a barrier, in that direction.

"Therefore, although the first view of Central Asia, as seen from the crest of the Küen-lün, reminds us of the open plains of India which we have left behind us, nevertheless we remark an important difference in the country as soon as we begin to descend. Here no forests deck the mountain slopes, no green refreshes the eye, weary of gazing continually on naked gravel and stones; even the plain, at first, is as barren as the mountains we have left. So much the more surprising is the appearance of the rich cultivation, with which the soil has been clothed by the hand of man. From the edge of the desert border, which sinks away at a distance of ten or twelve miles from the foot of the mountains, the traveller enters a cultivated land, where in spring a sea of green fields of grain spreads to the right and left, dotted with scattered farms and villages which are buried in groves of fruit trees. The orchards are so numerous that they restrict the view to a few hundred paces. Their productions are much the same as in Cashmere: apples, pears, apricots,

PRIMITIVE AGRICULTURE OF THE EAST.

peaches, mulberries, walnuts, melons, and even wine; while the chief harvests of the fields are wheat, barley, maize and lucerne, together with some cotton, flax and hemp."

The dry climate, which makes a desert of the greater portion of the land, in fact, allowing habitation only in the neighborhood of the mountains, has given rise to a singular arrangement of the settlements. In the absence of periodical rains, the inhabitants are obliged to rely upon the streams which come from the mountains in spring and summer, for the fertilizing of their fields. They therefore construct long canals and ditches from the gorges of the streams to their fields, and thereby, notwithstanding the rudest agricultural implements, they obtain regular and excellent harvests, unless there happens to be an unusually scanty snow-fall upon the mountains, and the supply of water is diminished in consequence. The resemblance, in this respect, to Utah, and other parts of our American "Great Basin," will strike the reader.

On account of this dependance of the crops on the rivers, the towns and villages of East Toorkestan are all situated upon or very near the latter. The entire population of the country is thus concentrated upon strips of territory, stretching in parallel lines from the mountains towards the desert, with other strips of bare, waste soil lying between. The latter are mostly open plains, crossed by low ridges of shifting sand, or sometimes marshes interspersed with sandy steppes.

In journeying from one city to another, the traveller is obliged to cross these desert tracts, but it rarely happens that he does not find a good camping-place every night. All the roads in the lower country are practicable for vehicles, and regularly travelled by two-wheeled carts. The beasts of burden are the ass and the camel, while the Tibetan yak is used in the mountains.

The population of the country is principally of Turanian blood. The country people are called "Moguls" by the inhabitants of the towns. In addition, there are also Chinese who have been forcibly converted to Islam, and some few Calmucks: also, among the merchants, emigrants from Tartary and Affghanistan. Most of the civil and military offices are filled by Uzbek and Kiptchak Tartars. The mountains are inhabited by wandering Kirghiz tribes, which pasture their great herds of goats, sheep, yaks and camels during the summer months on the high Alpine meadows, but in winter descend into the lower and warmer valleys.

The principal cities, each the capital of a province, are Yarkand, Kashghar, Khoten and Aksu. The population of the first two of these has been variously estimated at from 50,000 to 120,000 each. There are said to be from sixty to seventy other towns and large villages, containing, all together, about one-half the entire population of the country, which, according to the most recent estimates, is not more than 600,000.

CHAPTER II.

MARCO POLO IN CENTRAL ASIA.

THE only European traveller, from the most remote period down to the present age, who ever visited the high table-land of Thibet and the countries beyond, was Marco Polo of Venice. Although his narrative was dictated from memory, long after his return from a series of travels so extensive and adventurous that they have scarcely their parallel in the annals of exploration, the exactness of his statements has been wonderfully confirmed by all recent discoveries. The latest and by far the most complete and satisfactory edition of his work is that by Sir Henry Yule, from which we take those passages which refer to the subject of this volume.

The Polos were a noble family of Venice, who, early in the thirteenth century, engaged in trade with the East. Nicolo, the father of Marco, with his elder brother Maffeo, appear to have been settled in Constantinople in the year 1260: the boy Marco, then four years old, had been left behind in Venice. A branch of their house appears to have been already established in the Crimea, whither

Nicolo and Maffeo went, in the year above named. The prospect of successful trade carried them far to the northward along the Volga, thence to Bakhara in Tartary, and finally eastward through Central Asia to the court of Kublai Khan, at Cambalu (Peking), the capital of Cathay.

"Kublai," says Sir Henry Yule, "had never before fallen in with European gentlemen. He was delighted with these Venetians, listened with strong interest to all they had to tell him of the Latin world, and determined to send them back as his ambassadors to the Pope, accompanied by an officer of his own court. His letters to the Pope, as the Polos represent them, were mainly to desire the dispatch of a large body of educated missionaries to convert his people to Christianity. It is not likely that religious motives influenced Kublai in this, but he probably desired religious aid in softening and civilizing his rude kinsmen of the Steppes, and judged, from what he saw in the Venetians and heard from them, that Europe could afford such aid, of a higher quality than the degenerate Oriental Christians with whom he was familiar, or the Tibetan Lamas on whom his patronage eventually devolved when Rome so deplorably failed to meet his advances.

"The brothers arrived at Acre in 1269, and found that no Pope existed, for Clement IV. was dead the year before, and no new election had taken place. So they went home to Venice to see how things stood there after their absence of so many years. The wife of Nicolo was no longer among the living, but he found his son Marco, a fine lady of fifteen.

"The Papal interregnum was the longest known, at least since the dark ages. Two years passed, and yet the Cardinals at Viterbo had come to no agreement. The brothers were unwilling to let the Great Khan suppose them faithless, and perhaps they hankered after the virgin field of speculation that they had discovered; so they started again for the East, taking young Marco with them. At Acre they took counsel with an eminent churchman, Tedaldo (or Tebaldo) Visconti, Archdeacon of Liege, whom the book represents to have been Legate in Syria, and who in any case was a person of much gravity and influence. From him they got letters to authenticate the causes of the miscarriage of their mission, and started for the further East. But they were still at the port ot Ayas on the Gulf of Scanderoon, which was then becoming one of the chief points of arrival and departure for the inland trade of Asia, when they were overtaken by the news that a Pope was at last elected, and that the choice had fallen upon their friend, Archdeacon Tedaldo. They immediately returned to Acre, and were at last able to execute the Khan's commission, and to obtain a reply. But instead of the hundred able teachers of science and religion whom Kublai is said to have asked for, the new Pope, Gregory X., could supply but two Dominicans; and these lost heart and drew back when they had barely taken the first step of the journey.

"Judging from certain indications we conceive it probable that the three Venetians, whose second start from Acre took place about November, 1271, proceeded by Ayas and Sivas, and then by Mardin, Mosul and Baghdad, to Ormuz at the mouth of the Persian Gulf, with the view of going on by sea, but that some obstacle arose which compelled them to abandon this project, and turn north again from Ormuz. They then traversed successively Kerman and Khorassan, Balkh and Badakhshan, whence they ascended the upper Oxus to the plateau of Pamer, a route, not known to have been since followed by any European traveller except Benedict Goes, till the spirited expedition of Captain John Wood of the Indian Navy, in 1838. Crossing the Pamer steppe, the travellers descended upon Kashgar, whence they proceeded by Yarkand and Khotan and the vicinity of Lake Lob, and eventually across the great Gobi Desert to Tangut, the name then applied by Mongols and Persians to the territory at the extreme north-west of China, both within and without the Wall. Skirting the northern frontier of China, they at last reached the presence of the Khan, who was at his usual summer residence at Kaipingfu, near the base of the Khingan Mountains, and about fifty miles north of the Great Wall. If there be no mistake in the time (three years and a half) ascribed to this journey in all the existing texts, the travellers did not reach the Court till about May of 1275.

"Kublai received the Venetians with great cordiality, and took kindly to young Marco, who must have been by this time one-and-twenty. The 'Young Bachelor,' as the story calls him, applied himself to the acquisition of the languages and written characters in chief use among the multifarious nationalities included in the Khan's court and administration; and Kublai, after a time, seeing his discretion and ability, began to employ him in the public service. M. Pauthier has found a record in the Chinese annals of the Mongol Dynasty, which states that in the year 1277, a certain Polo was nominated a second-class commissioner or agent attached to the Privy Council, a passage which we are happy to believe to refer to our young traveller.

"His first mission apparently was that which carried him through the provinces of Shansi, Shensi and Szechuen, and the wild country on the east of Tibet, to the remote province of Yunnan, called by the Mongols Karáján̈g, and which had been partially conquered by an army under Kublai himself, in 1253, before his accession to the throne. Marco, during his stay at court, had observed the Khan's delight in hearing of strange countries, their marvels, manners and oddities, and had heard his Majesty's frank expressions of disgust at the stupidity of his commissioners when they could speak of nothing but the official business on which they had been sent. Profiting by these observations, he took care to store his memory or his note books with all curious facts that were likely to interest Kublai, and related them with vivacity on his return to Court. This first journey, which led him through a region which is still very nearly a *terra incognita*, and in which there existed and still exists, among the deep valleys of the Great Rivers flowing down from Eastern Tibet, and in the rugged mountain ranges bordering Yunnan and Kweichan, a vast ethnological garden, as it were, of tribes of various race and in every stage of uncivilization, afforded him an acquaintance with many strange products and eccentric traits of manners, wherewith to delight the Emperor.

"Marco rose rapidly in favor, and was often employed again on distant missions, as well as in domestic administration, but we gather few details as to his employments. At one time we know that he held for three years the government of the great city of Yangchan, though we need not try to magnify this office, as some commentators have done, into the viceroyalty of one of the great provinces of the Empire ; on another occasion, we find him with his uncle Mafieo, passing a year at Kanchan in Tangut ; again, it would appear, visiting Karakoram, the old capital of the Khans in Mongolia ; on another occasion in Champa, or Southern Chocin-China ; and again, or perhaps as a part of the last expedition, on a mission to the Indian Seas, when he appears to have visited several of the southern states of India. We are not informed whether his father and uncle shared in such employments ; and the story of their services rendered to the Khan in promoting the capture of the city of Siangyang, by the construction of powerful engines of attack, is too much perplexed by difficulties of chronology to be cited with confidence. Anyhow they were gathering wealth, and after years of exile they began to dread what might follow old Kublai's death, and longed to carry their gear and their own gray heads safe home to Venice. The aged Emperor growled refusal to all their hints, and but for a happy chance we should have lost our mediæval Herodotus.

"Arghun Khan, of Persia, Kublai's great nephew, had lost his favorite wife, the Khatun Bulughán; and, mourning her sorely, took steps to fulfil her dying injunction that her place should be filled only by a lady of her own kin, the Mongol tribe of Bayant. Ambassadors were dispatched to the Court of the Great Khan to seek such a bride. The message was courteously received, and the choice fell upon the lady Kukáchin, a maiden of seventeen. The overland road from Peking to Tabreez (in Persia) was not only of portentous length for such a tender charge, but was imperilled by war, so the envoys desired to return by sea. Tartars in general were strangers to all navigation; and the envoys, much taken with the Venetians, and eager to profit by their experience, especially as Marco had just then returned from his Indian mission, begged the Khan as a favor to send the three Franks in his company. He consented with reluctance, but, having done so, fitted out the party nobly for the voyage, charging the Polos with friendly messages for the potentates of Europe, including the King of England. They appear to have sailed from the port of Zayton (as the Westerns called Chin-chan, in To-kien) in the beginning of 1292. It was an ill-starred voyage, and involved long detentions on the coast of Sumatra, and in the south of India, to which, however, we are indebted for some of the best chapters in the book; and two years or upwards passed before they arrived at their destination in Persia. The three hardy Venetians survived all perils, and so did the lady, who had come to look on them with filial regard; but two of the three envoys, and a vast proportion of the suite, had perished by the way. Argun Khan, too, had been dead even before they quitted China; his brother, Kaikhatu, reigned in his stead, and the latter's son, Ghazan, succeeded to the lady's hand. We are told by one who knew both the princes well that Arghun was one of the handsomest men of his time, while Ghazan was, among all his host, the most insignificant in appearance. But in other respects the lady's change was for the better. Ghazan had some of the highest qualities of a soldier, a legislator and a king, adorned by many and varied accomplishments; though his reign was too short for the full development of his fame.

"The princess, whose enjoyment of her royalty was brief, wept as she took leave of the kindly and noble Venetians. They went on to Tabreez, and after a long halt there proceeded homewards, reaching Venice, according to all the texts, sometime in 1295."

We now take from Ramusio's edition of Marco Polo's travels (published in Venice, in 1553), the account of the return of the three, father, uncle and Marco, to Venice :

"And when they got thither the same fate befel them as befel Ulysses, who, when he returned, after his twenty years' wanderings to his native Ithaca, was recognized by nobody. Thus also these three gentlemen, who had been so many years absent from their native city, were recognized by none of their kinsfolk, who were under the firm belief that they had all been dead for many a year past, as indeed had been reported. Through the long duration and the hardships of their journeys, and through the many worries and anxieties that they had undergone, they were quite changed in aspect, and had got a certain indescribable smack of the Tartar both in air and accent, having indeed all but forgotten their Venetian tongue. Their clothes too were coarse and shabby, and of a Tartar cut. They proceeded on their arrival to their house in this city, in the confine of St. John Chrysostom, where you may see it to this day. The house, which was in those days a very lofty and handsome *palazzo*, is now known by the name of the *Corte del Millioni* for a reason that I will tell you presently. Going thither, they found it occupied by some of their relatives, and they had the greatest difficulty in making the latter understand who they should be. For these good people, seeing them to be in countenance so unlike what they used to be, and in dress so shabby, flatly refused to believe that they were those very gentlemen of the Ca' Polo, whom they had been looking upon for ever so many years as among the dead. So these three gentlemen,—this is a story I have often heard, when I was a youngster, from the illustrious Messer Gasparo Malpiero, a gentleman of very great age, and a Senator of eminent virtue and integrity, whose house was on the canal of Santa Marina, exactly at the corner over the mouth of the Rio de San Giovanni Chrisostomo, and just midway among the buildings of the aforesaid Corte del Millioni, and he said he had heard the story from his own father and grandfather, and from other old men among the neighbors,—the three gentlemen, I say, devised a scheme by which they should at once bring about their recognition by their relatives, and secure the honorable notice of the whole city ; and this was it :

"They invited a number of their kindred to an entertainment which they took care to have prepared with great state and splendor, in that house of theirs ; and when the hour arrived for sitting down to table they came forth of their chamber all three clothed in crimson satin, fashioned in long robes reaching to the ground, such as people in those days wore within doors. And when water for the hands had been served, and the guests were set, they took off those robes and put on others of crimson damask, while the first suits were by their orders cut up and divided among the servants. Then after partaking of some of the dishes they went out again and came back in robes of crimson velvet ; and when they had again taken their seats, the second suits were divided as before. When dinner was over they did the like with the robes of velvet, after they had put on dresses of the ordinary fashion worn by the rest of the company. These proceedings caused much wonder and amazement among the guests. But when the cloth had been drawn, and all the servants had been ordered to retire from the dining-hall, Messer Marco, as the youngest of the three, rose from table, and, going into another chamber, brought forth the three shabby dresses of coarse stuff which they had worn when they first arrived. Straightway they took sharp knives and began to rip up some of the seams and welts, and to take out of them jewels of the greatest value in vast quantities, such as rubies, sapphires, carbuncles, diamonds and emeralds, which had all been stitched up in those dresses, in so artful a fashion that nobody could have suspected the fact. For when they took leave of the Great Khan, they had changed all the wealth that he had bestowed upon them into this mass of rubies, emeralds, and other jewels, being well aware of the impossibility of carrying with them so great an amount in gold, over a journey ot such extreme length and difficulty. Now this exhibition of such a huge treasure of jewels and precious stones, all tumbled out upon the table, threw the guests into fresh amazement, insomuch that they seemed quite bewildered and dumbfounded. And now they recognized that in spite of all former doubts these were in truth those honored and worthy gentlemen of the Ca' Polo that they claimed to be; and so all paid them the greatest honor and reverence.

"And when the story got wind in Venice, straightway the whole city, gentle and simple, flocked to the house to embrace them, and to make much of them, with every conceivable demonstration of affection and respect. On Messer Maffeo, who was the eldest, they conferred the honor of an office that was of great dignity in those days; while the young men came daily to visit and converse with the ever polite and gracious Messer Marco, and to ask him questions about Cathay and the Great Khan, all which he answered with such kindly courtesy that every man felt himself in a manner in his debt. And as it happened that in the story, which he was constantly called on to repeat, of the magnificence of the Great Khan, he would speak of his revenues as amounting to ten or fifteen *millions* of gold; and, in like manner, when recounting other instances of great wealth in those parts, would always make use of the term *millions*, so they gave him the nickname of 'Messer Marco Millioni:' a thing which I have noted also in the public books of this republic, where mention is made of him."

We will now quote those portions of Marco Polo's narrative which relate immediately to Central Asia. After the disappointment of the travellers at Ormuz, and their change of plans, they crossed Persia in a north-easterly direction, and reached Balkh, in Tartary. Thence their course was up the valley of the Oxus to the great central table-land of Asia. Balk has been visited in recent times by English travellers. Beyond that place, Polo passed through Taican [the modern Talikan] and Casem [Kishm] to the province of Badashan [now Badakhshan], which he thus describes :

"Badashan is a province inhabited by people who worship Mahomet, and have a peculiar language. It forms a very great kingdom, and the royalty is hereditary. All those of the royal blood are descended from King Alexander and the daughter of King Darius, who was Lord of the vast Empire of Persia. And all these kings call themselves in the Saracen tongue, *Zulcarniain*,* which is as much as to say 'Alexander ;' and this out of respect for Alexander the Great.

"It is in this province that those fine and valuable gems, the Balas rubies are found. They are got in certain rocks among the mountains, and in the search for them the people dig great caves underground, just as is done by miners for silver. There is but one special mountain that produces them, and it is called Syghinan. The stones are dug on the king's account, and no one else dares dig in that mountain, on pain of forfeiture of life as well as goods ; nor may any one carry the stones out of the kingdom. But the king amasses them all, and sends them to other kings when he has a tribute to render, or when he desires to offer a friendly present ; and such only as he pleases he causes to be sold. Thus he acts in order to keep

* Arabic, signifying "two-horned," from the horned head of Alexander on many of his coins.

the Balas at a high value; for if he would allow everybody to dig, they would extract so many that the world would be glutted with them, and they would cease to bear any value. Hence it is that he allows so few to be taken out, and is so strict in the matter.

"There is also in the same country another mountain, in which azure [lapis lazuli] is found; it is the finest in the world, and is got in a vein like silver. There are also other mountains which contain a great amount of silver ore, so that the country is a very rich one; but it is also (it must be said) a very cold one! It produces numbers of excellent horses, remarkable for their speed. They are not shod at all, although constantly used in mountainous country, and on very bad roads. (They go at a great pace, even down steep descents, where other horses neither would nor could do the like. And Messer Marco was told that not long ago they possessed in that province a breed of horses from the strain of Alexander's horse Bucephalus, all of which had from their birth a particular mark on the forehead. This breed was entirely in the hands of an uncle of the king's; and in consequence of his refusing to let the king have any of them, the latter put him to death. The widow, then, in despite, destroyed the whole breed, and it is now extinct.)

"The mountains of this country also supply Saker falcons of excellent flight, and plenty of lanners likewise. Beasts and birds for the chase are there in great abundance. Good wheat is grown, and also barley without husk. They have no olive oil, but make oil from sesamé, and also from walnuts.

"In the mountains there are vast numbers of sheep—400, 500, or 600 in a single flock, and all of them wild; and though many of them are taken, they never seem to get aught the scarcer.

"Those mountains are so lofty that 'tis a hard day's work, from morning till evening, to get to the top of them. On getting up, you find an extensive plain, with great abundance of grass and trees, and copious springs of pure water running down through rocks and ravines. In those brooks are found trout and many other fish of dainty kinds; and the air in those regions is so pure, and residence there so healthful, that when the men who dwell below in the towns, and in the valleys and plains, find themselves attacked by any kind of fever or other ailment that may hap, they lose no time in going to the hills; and after abiding there two or three days, they quite recover their health through the excellence of that air. (And Messer Marco Polo said he had proved this by experience; for when in those parts, he had been ill for about a year, but as soon as he was advised to visit that mountain, he did so and got well at once.)

"In this kingdom there are many strait and perilous passes, so difficult to force that the people have no fear of invasion. Their towns and villages are also on lofty hills, and in very strong positions. They are excellent archers, and much given to the chase; indeed, most of them are dependent for clothing on the skins of beasts, for stuffs are very dear among them. The great ladies, however, are arrayed in stuffs, and I will tell you the style of their dress! They all wear drawers made of cotton cloth, and into the making of these some will put sixty, eighty, or even one hundred ells of stuff. This they do to make themselves look large in the hips, for the men of those parts think that to be a great beauty in a woman.

"You must know that ten days' journey to the south of Badashan there is a province called Pashai, the people of which have a peculiar language, and are idolaters, of a brown complexion. They are great adepts in sorceries and the diabolic arts. The men wear earrings and brooches of gold and silver, set with stones and pearls. They are a pestilent people and a crafty; and they live upon flesh and rice. Their country is very hot.

"Now let us proceed and speak of another country which is seven days' journey from this one towards the southeast, and the name of which is Keshimur [Cashmere].

"Keshimur also is a province inhabited by a people who are idolaters and have a language of their own. They have an astonishing acquaintance with the devilries of enchantment; insomuch that they can make their idols to speak. They can also by their sorceries bring on changes of weather, and produce darkness, and do a number of things so extraordinary that no one without seeing them would believe them. Indeed, this country is the very original source from which idolatry has spread abroad. In this direction you can proceed further until you come to the Sea of India.

"The men are brown and lean, but the women, taking them as brunettes, are very beautiful. The food of the people is flesh, and milk, and rice. The climate is finely tempered, being neither very hot nor very cold. There are numbers of towns and villages in the country, but also forests and desert tracts, and strong passes, so that the people have no fear of anybody, and keep their independence, with a king of their own to rule and do justice.

"There are in this country Eremites (after the fashion of those parts), who dwell in seclusion and practice great abstinence in eating and drinking. They observe strict chastity, and keep from all sins forbidden in their law, so that they are regarded by their own folk as very holy persons. They live to a very great age.

"There are also a number of idolatrous abbeys and monasteries. (The people of the province do not kill animals nor spill blood ; so if they want to eat meat they get the Saracens who dwell among them to play the butcher.) The coral which is carried from our parts of the world has a better sale there than in other parts of the country.

"Now we will quit this country, and not go any further in the same direction ; for if we did so we should enter India ; and that I do not wish to do at present. For on our return journey I mean to tell you about India, all in regular order. Let us go back, therefore, to Badashan, for we cannot otherwise proceed on our journey.

"In leaving Badashan you ride twelve days between east and northeast, ascending a river [the Oxus] that runs through land belonging to a brother of the Prince of Badashan, and containing a good many towns and villages and scattered habitations. The people are Mahometans, and valiant in war. At the end of these twelve days you come to a province of no great size, extending indeed no more than three days' journey in any direction, and this is called Vokhan. The people worship Mahomet, and they have a peculiar language. They are gallant soldiers, and they have a chief whom they call None, which is as much as to say *Count*, and they are liegemen of the Prince of Badashan.

"There are numbers of wild beasts of all sorts in this region. And when you leave this little country, and ride three days north-east, always among mountains, you get to such a height that 'tis said to be the highest place in the world! And when you have got to this height you find a great lake between two mountains, and out of it a fine river running through a plain clothed with the finest pasture in the world; insomuch that a lean beast will fatten there to your heart's content in ten days. There are great numbers of all kinds of wild beasts; among others, wild sheep of great size, whose horns are good six palms in length. From these horns the shepherds make great bowls to eat from, and they use the horns also to enclose folds for their cattle at night. (Messer Marco was told also that the wolves were numerous, and kill many of these wild sheep. Hence quantities of their horns and bones were found, and these were made into great heaps by the wayside, in order to guide travellers when snow was on the ground.)

"The plain is called Pamier [Pamir, or Pamere], and you ride across it for twelve days together, finding nothing but a desert without habitations or any green thing, so that travellers are obliged to carry with them whatever they have need of. The region is so lofty and cold that you do not even see any birds flying. And I must notice also that because of this great cold, fire does not burn so brightly, nor give out so much heat as usual, nor does it cook food so effectually.

"Now, if we go on with our journey towards the east-north-east, we travel a good forty days, continually passing over mountains and hills, or through valleys, and crossing many rivers and tracts of wilderness. And in all this way you find neither habitation of man, nor any green thing, but you must carry with you whatever you require. The country is called Bolor [Belur, or Bielor Dagh, the White Mountains]. The people dwell high up in the mountains, and are savage idolaters, living only by the chase, and clothing themselves in the skins of beasts. They are in truth an evil race.

"Cascar [Kashgar] is a region lying between north-east and east, and constituted a kingdom in former days, but now it is subject to the Great

Khan. The people worship Mahomet. There are a good number of towns and villages, but the greatest and finest is Cascar itself. The inhabitants live by trade and handicrafts ; they have beautiful gardens and vineyards, and fine estates, and grow a great deal of cotton. From this country many merchants go forth, about the world, on trading journeys. The natives are a wretched niggardly set of people ; they eat and drink in miserable fashion. There are in the country many Nestorian Christians, who have churches of their own. The people of the country have a peculiar language, and the territory extends for five days' journey.

"Yarcan [Yarkand] is a province five days' journey in extent. The people follow the law of Mahomet, but there are also Nestorian and Jacobite Christians. They are subject to the same Prince I have mentioned, the Great Khan's nephew. They have plenty of everything, particularly of cotton. The inhabitants are also great craftsmen, but a large proportion of them have swollen legs, and great crops at the throat, which arises from some quality in their drinking water. As there is nothing else worth telling, we may pass on.

"Cotan [Khoten] is a province lying between north-east and east, and is eight days' journey in length. The people are subject to the Great Khan, and are all worshippers of Mahomet. There are numerous towns and villages in the country, but Cotan, the capital, is the most noteworthy of all, and gives its name to the kingdom. Everything is to be had there in plenty, including abundance of cotton, with flax, hemp, wheat, wine and the like. The people have vineyards and gardens and estates. They live by commerce and manufactures, and are no soldiers.

"Pein [Pima ?] is a province five days' in length, lying between east and north-east. The people are worshippers of Mahomet, and subjects of the Great Khan. There are a good number of towns and villages, but the most noble is Pein, the capital of the kingdom. There are rivers in this country, in which quantities of jasper and chalcedony are found. The people have plenty of all products, including cotton. They live by manufactures and trade. But they have a custom that I must relate. If the husband of any woman go away upon a journey and remain away for more than twenty days, as soon as that term is past the woman may marry another man, and the husband also may then marry whom he pleases.

"I should tell you that all the provinces that I have been speaking of, from Cascar forwards, and those I am going to mention, as far as the city of Lop, belong to Great Turkey.

"Charchan [Chachan] is a province of Great Turkey, lying between north-east and east. The people worship Mahomet. There are numerous towns and villages, and the chief city of the kingdom bears its name, Charchan. The province contains rivers which bring down jasper and chalcedony and these are carried for sale into Cathay, where they bring great prices. The whole of the province is sandy, and so is the road all the way from Pein.

and much of the water that you find is bitter and bad. However at some places you do find fresh and sweet water. When an army passes through the land, the people escape with their wives, children and cattle, a distance of two or three days' journey into the sandy waste; and knowing the spots where water is to be had, they are able to live there, and to keep their cattle alive, whilst it is impossible to discover them; for the wind immediately blows the sand over their track.

"Quitting Charchan, you ride some five days through the sands, finding none but bad and bitter water, and then you come to a place where the water is sweet. And now I will tell you of a province called Lop, in which there is a city also called Lop, which you come to at the end of those five days. It is at the entrance of the Great Desert, and it is here that travellers repose before entering in the Desert.

"Lop [Lob] is a large town at the edge of the Desert which is called the Desert of Lop [Gobi, or Shamo, on modern maps], and is situated between east and north-east. It belongs to the Great Khan, and the people worship Mahomet. Now, such persons as propose to cross the Desert take a week's rest in this town to refresh themselves and their cattle; and then they make ready for the journey, taking with them a month's supply for man and beast. On quitting this city they enter the Desert.

"The length of this Desert is so great that 'tis said that it would take a year and more to ride from

A WELL IN THE DESERT.

one end of it to the other. And here, where its breadth is least, it takes a month to cross it. 'Tis all composed of hills and valleys of sand, and not a thing to eat is to be found on it. But after riding for a day and a night you find fresh water enough, mayhap, for some fifty or a hundred persons with their beasts, but not for more. And all across the Desert you will find water in like manner, that is to say, in some twenty-eight places altogether you will find good water, but in no great quantity; and in four places you find also brackish water.

"Beasts there are none; for there is nought for them to eat. But there is a marvellous thing related of this Desert, which is that when travellers are on the move by night, and one of them chances to lag behind or to fall asleep or the like, when he tries to gain his company again he will hear spirits talking, and will suppose them to be his comrades. Sometimes the spirits will call him by name; and thus shall a traveller ofttimes be led astray so that he never finds his party. And in this way many have perished. Sometimes the stray travellers will hear, as it were, the tramp and hum of a great cavalcade of people away from the real line of road, and taking this to be their own company they will follow the sound; and when day breaks they find that a cheat has been put on them and that they are in an ill-plight. Even in the day time one hears those spirits talking. And sometimes you shall hear the sound of a variety of musical instruments, and still more commonly the sound of drums. Hence in making this journey 'tis customary for travellers to keep close together. All the animals, too, have bells at their necks, so that they cannot easily get astray. And at sleeping time a signal is put up to show the direction of the next march.

"So thus it is that the Desert is crossed."

This is Marco Polo's brief, yet remarkably correct account of his journey from Badakhshan, on the Oxus, in Independent Tartary, to the western extremity of the Great Wall, in China. It is remarkable that there is not a single custom or superstition which he mentions, that does not exist at the present day, or has been discovered to have existed, by later travellers. When we consider that his account was dictated from memory, unassisted by notes, at least twenty-five years after he made the journey, and after such a quantity of intervening adventures and experiences, his character as a veracious narrator is wonderfully vindicated.

Still more remarkable is it, perhaps, that nearly six hundred years should have elasped since this journey through Central Asia, before any portion of the region was again trodden by the feet of a European explorer.

CHAPTER III.

MODERN ATTEMPTS AT EXPLORATION.

TWO centuries after Marco Polo's journey, the discovery of Vasco de Gama completely changed the course of the commerce between Europe and the Indies. The long, toilsome and perilous routes of overland travel were relinquished, with all their opportunities for interior exploration; the knowledge of the civilized world commenced anew along the coasts of the great Eastern continent and slowly forced its way inwards.

The English conquests in India gradually advanced the line of exploration, first to the base of the Himalayas, then westward along the range to the Indus, and finally to Cashmere and Affghanistan. From 1830 to 1840, when the East India Government concerned itself much more than was necessary in the affairs of the latter country, and with such disastrous results, the cities of Cabul, Ghuznee, Kandahar and Herat were reached by English officers, and even some of the passes traversed in the Hindoo-Koosh, dividing Affghanistan from Tartary.

One of these officers, Lieut. John Wood, in the

autumn of 1837, reached Balkh on a mission to the ruler of that Tartar principality. The lateness of the season obliged him to remain all winter there, before returning to Cabul, and he planned an expedition to the source of the Oxus, as daring in conception as it was successful in the result. Leaving Balkh with a very small party and only the most necessary supplies, he made a winter journey on the track of Marco Polo, up the valley of the Oxus, visiting the celebrated ruby and turquoise mines of Fyzabad, on the way. In spite of the hardships of the road and the severity of the weather, in February, 1838, he reached the source of the Oxus, the lake Sir-i-kol, on the table-land of Pamir, at an elevation of 15,630 feet above the sea. The lake was hard-frozen ; the meadows, inhabited in summer by the wandering Kirghizes, were deserted and covered with snow, and it was impossible to extend his exploration beyond that point.

Lieut. Wood was the first European of modern times, to stand upon "the Roof of the World." It was at first supposed that this famous plateau was of moderate extent, and formed only by the uniting ridges of the Belor Dagh, Hindoo-Koosh and Karakoram ranges ; but later researches show that it forms a broad, enormous table-land, nearly two hundred miles from north to south, and varying from 16,000 to 18,000 feet above the sea. Its exact breadth has not been ascertained, but it is probably between 60 and 70 miles.

Mr. Hayward, who accompanied Shaw to Yarkand and Kashghar, and was murdered, in 1870, in the wild mountain region of Chitral (lying to the north-west of Cashmere), thus describes the eastern front of the Roof of the World, as seen from Yang-hissar, in East Toorkestan: "Contrary to the usual supposition, that the eastern edge of the plateau of Pamir falls gradually down to the plains of Toorkestan, the mountain-chain, which forms this eastern edge, rises to a series of peaks near 21,000 feet in height, the flanks of which fall sheer and steep to the plain below. The chain thus presents a precipitous front towards the lowlands of East Toorkestan, and it seems very improbable that any of the Pamir lakes have an outlet towards the East: all the waters of the table-land must flow westward, into the valley of the Oxus. It is not possible for any landscape to surpass in sublimity this mountain-chain, as it towers aloft like a gigantic wall, and prints the sharp outlines of its snowy peaks and glaciers upon the deep blue of the sky."

At the same time that Lieutenant Wood made his expedition, Mr. G. T. Vigne, Fellow of the Geographical Society, was employed in a series of explorations in Cashmere, Baltistan and Little Tibet. Cashmere had been twice or thrice visited before, by officials of the East India company or travellers from Europe, but none before Mr. Vigne penetrated to Iokardo (the capital of Baltistan), on the Upper Indus, or advanced so far into Tibet. As the most interesting portions of his narrative are given in the following chapters, we need only allude to him, in the order of research, at present.

After the conquest of Ladak, or Little Tibet, by the Sikhs, in 1834, and its transfer, through English influence, to Golab Sing, the Rajah of Cashmere,—of which country it still forms the largest province—the facilities of exploration were greatly increased. An English resident was stationed at Leh, the capital of Ladak, and the road thither over the tremendous passes of the Himalayas became tolerably safe. No extensive exploration of the country, however, was undertaken, until the journey of the Brothers Schlagintweit, in 1856.

Hermann, Adolf and Robert Schlagintweit, natives of Bavaria, devoted themselves, as young men, to the study of geology and physical geography. Their works, especially that of Hermann upon the physical geography of the Alps, attracted the attention of Humboldt, and in 1854, principally upon his recommendation, they were commissioned by the King of Prussia to make a scientific exploration of India. Their services were also accepted, and their plans materially assisted by the East India Company. Reaching Bombay towards the close of the year 1854, they first traversed the Deccau to Madras, by various routes. At the latter place, the brothers separated, the following spring. Adolf and Robert proceeded to the north-western extremity of India, and devoted themselves to the examination of the passes, glaciers and mountain-system of the Himalaya ranges. They penetrated into Ladak, and there attempted to reach the summit of the Ibi-Gamin, one of the loftiest peaks. Although the attempt

ROBERT. HERMANN. ADOLPHE.

THE BROTHERS SCHLAGINTXEIT.

was unsuccessful, they succeeded in climbing to the height of 22,000 feet, an altitude never before attained by man, on the surface of the earth. In the mean time, Hermann made extensive journeys into Sikkim and Assam, and all the region lying between the Brahmapootra and Burmah, both in the tropical lowlands and almost unexplored mountain regions.

The three brothers met again at Simla, in Northern India, in May, 1856, and then set out together for Cashmere. They afterwards visited Iskardo, made several excursions into the wild regions lying between the Upper Indus and the table-land of Pamir, and then explored the southern slopes of the great Karakoram range, in Little Tibet. They ascertained that the peak of Dapsang, in this range, which has an elevation of 28,278 feet, is the second highest mountain of the globe. Finally, crossing the Karakoram by a pass nearly 19,000 feet above the sea, they were the first Europeans to behold the great range of the Küen-lün,—the last mountain-barrier guarding the countries of Central Asia. They still pushed forward and succeeded in crossing the Küen-lün also ; but here, at the threshold of the most tempting field of exploration, they found it prudent to return. All then together made their way back to India, where Hermann and Robert embarked for Europe in the spring of 1857.

Adolf Schlagintweit, however, determined to take up the thread of discovery where it had been relinquished, and to cross Central Asia to the

Russian possessions lying north of the Thian-Shan. Reports o the suceessful Tartar rebellion against Chinese rule had already reached Little Tibet, and the time seemed to be propitious for such an attempt. He passed the Karakoram and the Küen-lün in safety, made his way to Yarkand, but was not allowed to enter its walls, and then pushed onward towards Kashghar. Although deserted by his Indian secretary and interpreter, and menaced with increasing danger as he advanced, he reached Kashghar and presented himself to Wallé Khan, the insurgent chieftain, who was then besieging the Chinese fort. What happened then can never, perhaps, be correctly ascertained : the simple fact is that the unfortunate traveller was executed by Wallé Khan's order. All attempts to recover his papers have proved fruitless.

CHAPTER IV.

VIGNE'S JOURNEY TO CASHMERE.

MR. G. T. Vigne, one of the first and most thorough explorers of the valley of Cashmere, and the wild and difficult mountain regions of the upper Indus, on the borders of Central Asia, left England in 1832, and travelled leisurely, by way of Constantinople, Armenia and Persia, to India. His time and means seem both to have been ample; he visited the principal cities of India and made a journey into Affghanistan, before commencing those excursions which led him into remote and only partially explored lands.

In the summer of 1835, finally, he set out from Loodiana, in northern India, on his way to Cashmere. Travelling slowly, by way of Bilaspore and Sultanpore, he gradually penetrated into the mountain country of the upper Sutlej; which at that time was under the dominion of Runjeet Sing. The Punjab was then outside of the British territory, but the temporary success of English arms in Affghanistan gave a partial security to travel.

The first part of the journey lay through those

open valleys, among the lower Himalayas, which are called *Dhoons* in India. The parallel and ever ascending chains of the mountains were divided by spaces a few miles in width, where the rich bottom-lands were dotted with hillocks of sandstone, covered with forests of firs, and occasionally seamed with deep and stony ravines, down which the little streams foamed and sparkled on their way to add their tributes to the classic flood of the Indus. The path, which in many places showed the remains of a pavement made by the Mogul Emperors, during the golden days of Delhi and Cashmere, wound among the hollows and eminences of the jungle; sometimes direct, smooth and practicable for horses, then so rough and slippery that the traveller was obliged to dismount and make his way on foot.

"The view," says Mr. Vigne, "was incessantly changing. The land mark of any description that I had noticed in the distance was often lost when I had sought for it from the opposite side of the dell; one mountain-top was quickly hidden by another, and the recess between was often shut up by some unforeseen but nearer object. A view such as I had reason to expect would not always be seen from the summit of an inviting ridge, and, on the contrary, after passing over a foreground of less promise, I would suddenly emerge upon a prospect of startling and extensive magnificence. The place of exit from the hills of one or other of the Punjab rivers could generally be pointed out to me; the straths and gorges that opened upon the plains would often afford a peep into the interior of the mountains, and the snowy ranges would be seen at the end of them. From one place the crests of the Palum Himalaya sank down upon the horizon behind me, or those of Chumba and Budrawar were extended in front, or the isolated Brihma was hiding itself among the distant clouds.

"The noble Trekotar, frowning over the castle of Rihursi, and the debouchure of the Chunab river, would now become conspicuous, on account of its triple summit, and an elevation far exceeding what is usual among the lower hills upon the borders; and the southern portion of the snowy Panjal of Cashmere would now come in sight, bounding the prospect to the northward, and circling, like a mighty wall, around the celebrated valley beyond it, where

> "'Summer, in a vale of flowers,
> Lay sleeping rosy at its feet.'

"Upon the loftier divisions of the long, extended ridges of sandstone that crept along the plain parallel to the lower range, at a varying distance of five, ten or fifteen miles, were frequently to be seen the ruins of an ancient fortress, originally the residence of some chieftain, who probably owned no authority but that of the Moguls; or the less picturesque but somewhat more scientifically built strongholds of the Sikhs, with towers, curtains, loopholes, and embrasures, an inaccessible precipice beneath them, with a thick jungle or a torrent at its foot.

"The country had frequently been cleared to a very considerable extent, and large open spaces in the valleys were occupied by numerous corn-fields and rice-grounds, continued in plateaux up the slope, in order to obtain the benefit of irrigation from the descending stream. The residence of the *zemindar*, or farmer, would often consist of a group of two or three cottages, built of mud and stones, or wood and bamboos, in some places flat-roofed, in others thatched with rice straw, and so neatly as to remind me of England. The path that led to them was often enclosed by hedgerows, and the dwelling was thus surrounded by a thick profusion of cactus, milk-plants, jujubes, acacias, plantains and bamboos. Conspicuous *topes*, or clusters of the larger trees, were scattered over the country; the sacred peepul marked the locality of the Devi, or Hindoo shrine; the cattle chewed the cud in security around it; the dark-green and massive foliage of the mango trees threw a perpetual and grateful shade upon the village and the village well; while the banyan, so beautifully described by Milton, dropped its dusty and fantastic branches within the clefts and interstices of the antiquated masonry by which the latter was encircled.

"But the indications of collective dwelling were not to be gathered only from the eye; for, as I approached a village, I frequently heard a loud and discordant sound of voices in advance of me, and soon found that it proceeded from a dozen or two of old women, who were drawn up in line, linked together by their arms thrown around each other's necks, and who in this manner screamed forth (I cannot call it singing) a chorus, the words of which, I believe, contained a greeting to the passing stranger, and an appeal to his humanity for relief."

After a further journey of four or five days, passing by some small but beautiful lakes, which are considered holy places by the Hindoos, Mr. Vigne approached the town of Jamu, on the borders of Cashmere. The Rajah, Golab Sing, sent him a palanquin for the last stage of the road, but he preferred entering the place on horseback. On arriving at Jamu, quarters were assigned to him in a garden below the hill on which the palace is built. "In the evening," he writes, "Urjum Sing, the eldest son of the Rajah, came to pay me a visit. He seemed to have an inclination to corpulency, had regular features, but a round full face, and a heavy look. He was, nevertheless, said to be a young man of excellent abilities; but an assumed and stupid air of indifference was upon him during our interview, though I attempted, through the medium of my interpreter, to draw him out in conversation. It is often observable in the East, that an imperturbable countenance, and an apparent carelessness of what is going forward, do duty for greatness and dignity; and I have usually remarked that, among men in power, those who laugh and talk like Europeans, and are the least constrained in their deportment, are the best and most superior men.

"The next morning I ascended to the palace, by a long paved way that led up the hill. The town of Jamu is built upon the summit of the first wooded sloping ridge that rises from the plains of the Punjab, and at the place where it is divided by a narrow ravine, which allows an exit to the river Tani, on its way to its junction with the Chenab. The town is built upon the right bank of the ravine, and the white buildings of the palace, and of the fort, which is on the opposite side, are seen glistening in the sun, from a great distance on the plains.

"The court-yard of the palace was alive with the crowds of officers and attendants, gorgeously apparelled in red and yellow shawls and silks, and armed with spears, swords, shields and matchlocks. Two guns were discharged close to me, just as I entered, by way of salute; and Golab Sing received me in the open pillared hall of the palace, and excused himself for not having called upon me, by saying that he had caught a rheumatism and stiffness in the limbs, in consequence of marching with Runjeet Sing to Peshawur; all of which he supposed I should believe, as well as the assertion which he shortly afterwards made, that his ancestors had reigned at Jamu for five thousand years!

"He afterwards asked me whether it was true that the king of France paid tribute to the king of England, and some other questions equally absurd, by way of ascertaining whether I was disposed to deceive him. He exhibited his arms and discussed their various merits. Amongst them were some bell-mouthed blunderbusses, one of which he loaded and fired in the usual manner. It cannot be rested against the shoulder, as it carries a heavy charge, but it is held low, at arm's length, by both hands, one grasping the barrel and the other the stock, so that it may swing as it recoils ; the right leg being kicked up behind in a very ridiculous manner, at the same time. The Rajah fired, and thinking that he had astonished me, looked at me for applause, spoke of the number of men that such a weapon could wound at one discharge, and seemed a little disconcerted at my not expressing great wonder."

The next place which Mr. Vigne reached was Rihursi. It is a town of little importance, built on a level space at the foot of the mountains. Near it rises the Trekotar, which is visible for a great distance to the south ; it is divided, as its name implies, into three peaks, and towers in one steep slant to a height of 5,000 feet above the valley. On its summit, it is said, is a Hindoo shrine, at which cocoanuts are offered. The pass by which the mountains are first entered, on the way to Cashmere, is about four miles beyond Rihursi. It has an elevation of only a thousand feet above the plain ; on the other side the road descends to the Chunab river, across which the traveller and his party were drawn upon a rope bridge, the horses being forced to swim.

The country rapidly became more wild and broken ; the precipitous ascents and descents made the road very fatiguing, and there were frequent chasms which must be crossed by rope bridges. Mr. Vigne attempted to sketch three women whom he met ; but no sooner had he commenced than they ran away, climbed some trees with the activity of monkeys, and could not be induced to come down again. He gives the following description of the native villages : "They are clusters of flat-roofed huts, the poorer kinds looking very dirty, with smoke marks on the walls, and cakes of cow-dung sticking to them, for the purpose of being dried and used as fuel. The better kind of hut is distinguished by its new and clean mud walls ; the ends of the rafters project neatly from the sides of the building, and the roof itself is free from holes, except the one used as a chimney. The windows of these huts are mere chinks in the walls, and the doors are not above five feet high ; while the chief man's house is recognized by the doorway being of greater height, the windows larger and more numerous, and it sometimes boasts of an up-stairs room, from which he can see over the whole village.

"On the roofs, and around and below, are to be seen men scarcely clothed, sitting, sleeping, cooking and eating ; women spinning, knitting and kneading, or combing and braiding their own black and well-oiled hair. Children amuse themselves with quarrelling and grovelling in the dust, in company with dogs and poultry. The best-dressed man in the village is usually the shopkeeper, who may be seen sitting on his shop-board, with his bowl of copper and cowries for small change, and heaps of flour, Indian corn, red-pepper, spices and other articles of Indian cookery. On the plain, at a short distance from the village, will be seen the carcase of a horse or cow, and some ten or twenty vultures sitting on and around it, and keeping other animals at a respectful distance. Monkeys chatter, doves coo, jackdaws caw, and kites scream as they whirl about incessantly in search of offal; while half-starved cattle remain in groups near the well, under the banyan and mango trees.

"The common wants of travellers, of whatever faith, country or calling, oblige them to halt near a well for the night. There the itinerant merchant cooks his supper, places a guard over his merchandise, and lies down to rest; and the sepoy on leave, the robber by profession, and the Thug disguised as best suits his purpose for the morrow, are soon in a state of repose. The pious follower of Mahomet is seen bending and bowing at his evening prayers, rising from them more probably a better Mussulman than a better man; the Brahmin, distinguished by the string which is a sign of his caste, mutters his prayers as he performs his ablutions; and the Hindoo fakeer, with his person plastered over with mud, and the wild and ferocious expression of his countenance rendered more sinister by the use of hasheesh and opium, is often to be seen for days together in the same place near the well, because he is aware that the sanctity of his character and appearance will secure him alms, or a supply of food, from those who must resort to it."

The next place Mr. Vigne reached was Rajawur, where he was very well received by the Rajah, a strongly-made, intelligent man, who had six toes on each foot. "In the middle of the first night of my stay," he writes, "I was awakened by the intelligence that one of my Hindoo servants was very ill with cholera. He had been eating of some raw roots while we were waiting in the garden. I found him nearly senseless, and to all appearance dying, while the good Rajah and a number of people were standing near his bed. I immediately uncorked the cholera medicine that I had brought with me from Bombay, and was proceeding to administer it, when somebody uttered the word 'wine.' It flew from mouth to mouth; the Rajah himself objected, but mildly, to my giving wine to a Mussulman; and the man himself, although at the last gasp, and a great rascal as I afterwards found, having understood that I was about to give him wine, protested against such a proceeding, by moving his hand before his mouth, and making a grimace as if he had taken the most nauseous medicine. I declared that it was not wine—nor was it (only it contained a large proportion of brandy); he then swallowed it, opened his eyes almost instantly, and said that now he could recognize me. In short, I soon got him round, and the next day he was walking about as if nothing had happened, rather pleased than otherwise at having been an object of so much interest. The Rajah and the others returned to their rest, talking loudly in praise of the wonderful medicine. Having occasion again to refer to the same bottle, in treating another patient, I missed the contents, although it was well corked, and could get no account of it."

Eleven miles beyond Rajawur is the town of Thána, at the foot of the lofty Panjal range, which separates the Vale of Cashmere from the plains of India. Here there is a large caravanserai for travellers, built of red brick, and the work of the Mogul Emperors. The houses of the town are curiously crowded together in tiers, on every available spot, on a precipice overhanging a river, and shaded by walnut and mulberry trees. Every pathway was a gutter, containing running water. The inhabitants are Cashmerians, who gain a subsistence by spinning and weaving. The place is 5,000 feet above the sea, yet early in the morning, on the 13th of July, the mercury stood at seventy-four degrees in the shade.

After leaving Thána, the ascent of the first range soon begins, and the traveller and his path are hidden in the recesses of the jungle. To continue Mr. Vigne's narrative: "The first object I remarked was a well, with some old equestrian reliefs on the stonework around it; then, upon turning a corner, I saw some old and tattered garments by the wayside, and a human foot, the remnant of a body that had been devoured by jackals, vultures and hyenas. I found afterwards that not a day passed while I was on the way to Cashmere, and even when travelling in the valley, that I did not see the bleached remains of some unfortunate wretch who had fallen a victim either to sickness or starvation.

"Two of the largest mountain-eagles I had ever seen were circling in the air, over the hamlet of four or five log-houses on the summit. The khan of Thána was seen as a speck at the foot of the ascent, and the ranges I had passed through were visible as far as the plains. But I only glanced at a view that was comparatively tame, and turned to the prospect of the Panjal range, and the vast depths that were yet to be passed on this side of it. The peak of Tata Koti, reported by the natives to be composed of crystal, rose conspicuously among a line of others, rearing themselves with a grandeur of elevation that, to an eye unaccustomed to mountain scenery, would seem to defy all ascent. I halted to sketch the view, and then commenced the descent to Barumgulu, the 'defile of rains,'—rejoicing in the sight of snow, which was now so near me, and invigorated by the mere reflection that I should cross the Panjal on the third day afterwards. A lofty forest of pines and deodars covered the whole face of the mountains in the foreground. The horse-chestnut tree was also very numerous, and the bark upon its long straight stem was split into flakes, and curled so as to bear a strong resemblance to that of the hickory in the American forests.

"Beyond Barumgulu, the elevation of which above the sea is 6800 feet, the way to Cashmere continues northward, up the bed of a stream which descends the ravine with great impetuosity. It is crossed and recrossed, within a short distance, by at least thirty wooden bridges, each of them about thirty feet in length. Three of them were to be repaired for me, by order of the Rajah. The last was not ready when I arrived, and I sat quietly on the bank with my people, while the villagers of Barumgulu cut down trees of sufficient length for the purpose ; and one of these, which was upraised and allowed to fall to the opposite bank, was made a bridge to one of the party, who crossed upon it and then adjusted a second tree, pushed across by means of the first. Branches were then placed upon them, and made sufficiently secure even for the footing of a horse.

"I halted for the night at the village of Poshiana, which contains about one hundred houses, whose roofs rest against the bank, by which they are in some measure protected from the effects of snow-storms. It lies considerably beneath the limit of forest, but there are very few trees near it. The green slope on the side of which it is built, and the summit of which is seven or eight hundred feet above it, affords a pasturage for sheep and goats ; but cultivation is almost entirely confined to turnips. It is customary, for those who can afford it, to sacrifice a sheep or goat before ascending to the Panjal summit, and the head is carried to the fakeer, who lives in a stone hut close to the tower, during the summer months. I complied with the custom, at the request of the Mahometan part of my retinue ; the priest said a prayer for a safe ascent on the morrow, and the goat was immediately made lawful eating, that is, had its throat cut under a white flag in front of my quarters.

"There was another steep but not very long dip into a valley, and on the opposite side of it commenced an ascent, which hardly ceased until it reached the summit of the Panjal. The path was in very good condition, and I was able to ride nearly the whole distance. An hour's travel from Poshiana brought me to the edge of the lowest snow, which was arched and hardened over a small stream of its own creation. The forest began to be much thinned, but vegetation was still profuse, and roses and many other wild flowers were in full bloom. The hill, near the summit, is bare of trees, but a fine turf is visible where the snow has melted. Another final ascent, and I suddenly found myself on the summit of the Pir Panjal.

"An octagonal tower, twenty feet high, built of small loose fragments of rock, and a wooden frame, rears itself over the very brink of the descent; and close to it, on the opposite side of the path, is the stone hut of the Mussulman fakeer, who usually has by him a small store of flour, bread, tobacco and water, for which travellers are glad to remunerate him in some way or other. He thankfully accepted my offering of the sheep's head, and was still better pleased with a little money which I gave him. He was a good-humored looking person, short and shaven, with a chubby face, but little intellect in his countenance, and a twinkling expression of cunning in his eye. In winter he cannot remain on the Panjal, on account of the snow, and in summer months he presents himself wrapped up in the folds of a large blanket, which envelops him from head to foot and makes him look as broad as he is long.

"The Jesuit missionary, Père Hypolite Desideri, who crossed the Panjal Pass in 1714, says: 'The Gentiles have a profound respect for this mountain; they carry offerings thither, and they offer superstitious worship to an old man, to whom, as they pretend, the charge of the place is confided. This is doubtless a fragment of the remembrance which they have of the fabulous history of Prometheus, which, according to the fictions of the poets, belonged to the Caucasus. Whatever may be indicated by the play of the lightning, and the presence of the vultures,—

> 'On Imaüs bred,
> Whose snowy ridge the roving Tartar bounds,
> Dislodging from a region scarce of prey,
> To gorge the flesh of lambs or yearling kids,
> On hills where flocks are fed, flies towards the springs
> Of Ganges or Hydaspes, Indian streams'—

the little fakeer, whom I saw on the Panjal, was certainly not a person who looked as if he could act the part of Prometheus.

"The view from the Panjal in the direction of the plains, is, of course, magnificent. The different ranges which I had crossed on the way, and even the points where I had crossed them, were visible in the distance. I looked down on the roofs of Poshiana, where I had slept, and could distinguish the situation, and even the buildings and smoke, of Rajawur. Indistinctness pervaded every part of the gray-colored expanse of the plains, and I vainly tried, with my telescope, to detect the minarets of imperial Lahore, which may be perceived with the naked eye in very clear weather, though about 130 miles distant.

"The limit of forest, or the height above which forest-trees will not grow, as laid down by Hodgson and others from their observations in Alpine India, on the east of the Sutlez, is 11,500 feet. The summit of the Panjal Pass is about 300 feet above the limit of forest; my thermometer gave me about 12,000 feet; so that I am justified in laying down its height at 11,800 feet, or thereabouts. The temperature at mid-day, July 16th, was 66°. Birches and firs seemed to contend for the highest place; the birch has the best of it generally. Above this, the only plant that I remember in the shape of a tree is the dwarf juniper, and this is to be seen at different altitudes, up to 12,000 feet, on the mountains around Cashmere and in Tibet. The descent from the Panjal towards the Vale of Cashmere, which is very gentle, commences immediately, and the snow-capped mountain tops are divided by an inclined and verdant plain, on which bloomed numerous varieties of flowers. Amongst them I joyfully noticed many that were common in England; and as I trod the green carpet beneath me, I found myself refreshed by inhaling the cool breeze richly burdened with all the perfume of an English clover-field.

"The defile on the northern side is extremely narrow, and the stream occupies the whole of the space between its banks; but it soon afterwards opens on a splendid view. The valley of the stream suddenly sinks below the level of the path, and I looked down upon a beautiful meadow, from which the precipitous slopes of the Panjal suddenly rose with all their majesty, and clothed with a fir-forest to the very bed of the stream that rushed along their bases. Finally, after crossing the stream by a wooden bridge, I found myself at the small village of Huripore, where the steepness ot the descent ceases. The next morning, after proceeding for two or three miles through the woods, the plains of Cashmere came full in sight. The lofty mountains on the other side of the valley, distant from thirty to thirty-five miles, were shrouded in clouds, and a part only of the snowy ridge, with a few isolated peaks, were to be seen here and there at intervals.

"The first object on nearing Shupeyon, the next town, was a wooden mosque, by the wayside, whence there is a view in the direction of the city of Cashmere. This mosque is of the same pattern as that which I afterwards found to be common throughout the valley. It partakes of the aspect and architecture of the pagodas of China, but the slope of the roof is straight instead of being concave. Its basement, ten to twenty yards square, is of stone or wood, raised a few feet from the ground, and supporting eight or ten pillars deeply grooved, with bases and capitals formed ot fantastically sculptured leaves. The interior is also square, and is generally a beautiful specimen of wood-work. The windows and doors are Saracenic, with rich lattice-worked panels instead of glass.

"Shupeyon is now a miserable place, bearing the impress of having been once a thriving town. Its dwellings, now chiefly in ruins, are but the remains of what once were houses, of two or three or four stories in height, with gable ends and sloping roofs of wood. Large sheets of birch-bark, which is nearly impervious to moisture, are laid over the rafters, and upon them is spread a layer of earth, which is often planted with flowers. The walls are of brick, burnt or sun-dried, and secured in a frame of wood, as a prevention against the effects of earthquakes.

"In the farm-houses, the upper stories are often entirely of wood. The windows are rectangular, numerous, and disposed in rows, as in Europe. Exquisitely finished trellis-work, displaying a great variety of Moorish patterns, usurps the place of a window-frame ; the thin paper of the country is pasted over it and does duty for glass, so that warmth is thus obtained at the expense of light. Some of the rooms have fire-places, but the smoke is always allowed to escape through a hole in the wall above them. The houses are usually separate, with small gardens between them. There are also orchards of standard fruit-trees, and mulberries, apples, pears, peaches, apricots and roses, are to be had in abundance, in their proper season.

MOUNTAIN SCENE NEAR CASHMERE.

"The hill of Shupeyon rises from the plain about one mile from the town: it is composed of trap rock, and its height is about 350 feet. I thence enjoyed a first and excellent view of the valley, which was hardly broken throughout its whole length of ninety miles, and entirely surrounded by snowy mountains. Far to the left, over the extreme north-western end of the valley, rose the snow-peaks of Durawur; the two or three small hills, breaking the level surface of the valley, were distinguished with difficulty; and the whole of the intervening slopes of the Pir Panjal, from the snow downward into the valley, are covered with a magnificent forest of pines, thirty miles in length and from three to seven miles in width. The valley of Cashmere is generally a verdant plain, ninety miles in length aud twenty-five miles in its greatest width, at the southern end, between the cataract of Arabul and the ruius of the great temple of Martund; surrounded on every side by snowy mountains, into which there are numerous inlets, forming glens on a level with the plain, but each with a lofty pass at its upper extremity. There are many elevated points of view from which this extraordinary hollow gave me, at first sight, an idea of its having been originally formed by the falling in of an exhausted volcanic region.

"The interest taken in a view of the Valley of Cashmere would certainly be rather that of the agriculturist than of the prospect-hunter; but nothing can be more truly sylvan than the greater part of the mountain scenery. It has not, however, the verdure of the tropics. The trees, it is true, in many instances, may differ from those of Europe; but with the exception of occasional beautiful masses of deodars, the aspect of the forest, at a little distance, is wholly European. Looking from the hill of Shupeyon, innumerable villages were scattered over the plains in every direction, distinguishable in the extreme distance by the trees that surrounded them: all was soft and verdant, even up to the snow on the mountain-top; and I gazed in surprise, excited by the vast extent and admirably defined limits of the valley, and the almost perfect proportions of height to distance, by which its scenery appeared to be universally characterized."

CHAPTER V.

THE VALLEY OF CASHMERE AND THE RUINS OF MARTUND.

MR. VIGNE is a confused and somewhat perplexing narrator. The thread of his journey is constantly lost amid a multitude of small geographical details, and interwoven with the accounts of other journeys, made in other seasons, in the same region. We shall, therefore, endeavor to select those passages which possess the most interest and value, concerning the Vale of Cashmere, and resume the direct narrative when we find the traveller compelled, by the nature of his subject, to confine himself to it.

In passing onward through the valley, Mr. Vigne encountered scenes of ruin and desolation, in striking contrast with its natural beauty and fertility. Earthquake, cholera, famine, and the invasions of Runjeet Sing had terribly devastated the once thickly peopled country. Many of the houses were tenantless and deserted ; the fruit was dropping unheeded from the trees ; the orchards were overgrown with a profusion of wild hemp and wild indigo ; but the graveyards were still covered with blue and white iris-flowers, which are always planted over them, partly for ornament, and partly because the roots being matted together, prevent the turf from falling in. Enough remained, however, to show how neat and comfortable the villages had once been. There was always a clear, rapid brook at hand, with green turf on its banks, shaded by fine walnut-trees, and the *bryn*, resembling the English elm. Around the base of the gigantic chunar-trees, there was always a raised bench of wood or stone, for the village gossips, a few of whom still lingered in their half-deserted homes,—some sleeping, and others praying, or smoking.

The city of Shahbad, the largest place in the southern part of the valley, was a ruin, and there was scarcely anything to be seen of the ancient palace of the Moguls. Its environs were overgrown with nettles and wild hemp. The orchards ot Shahbad, however, still produced the best apples, and the wheat grown there is considered the finest in Cashmere. The people, also, are very fond of bread made of buckwheat flour. A few miles from the city is the celebrated fountain of Vernag, a favorite place of the Mogul Emperors. "The palace," says Mr. Vigne, "is now a ruin with scarcely any of the beauties of a ruin, and the country is overgrown with weeds and jungle. But neither time nor tyranny can make any change in the magnificent spring of Vernag. Its waters are received into a basin partly made by the Emperor Jehangir: the circumference is about 125 yards, and the whole is surrounded by a low octagonal wall, in which are twenty-four niches, each of eight feet in height. The water is beautifully clear, 25 feet deep, and swarming with Himalaya trout.

"In the interior, on the wall, there is the following inscription: 'This place of unequalled beauty, was raised to the skies by Jehangir Shah; consider well. Its date is found in the sentence,—Palace of the Fountain of Vernag.' In the Persian language, letters are also used for the expression of numbers, and the letters in the foregoing sentence are equivalent to the number 1029 (of the Hegira) which answers to A. D. 1619. Over the entrance is written: 'This fountain has come from the springs of Paradise!'

"I have been twice in Cashmere when the new snow has fallen," says Mr. Vigne, *apropos* of a description of some of the other mountain passes. "About the 10th of December the summits of the Panjal are enveloped in a thick mist, and the snow usually falls before the 20th. This is the great fall which usually closes the passes for the winter. It frequently happens that a casual fall takes place a month or three weeks earlier: this remains on the ground for three or four days, and then disappears before the sun. I am now speaking of the snow upon the plains of Cashmere. It occasionally falls on the mountains as early as September, and the cold blasts which it produces do great injury to the later rice-crops.

"They have a custom throughout these countries,

which answers in some respects to what we call making an April fool. When the new snow falls, one person will try to deceive another into holding a little in his hand; and accordingly he will present it to him (making some remark by way of a blind at the same time) concealed in a piece of cloth, or a stick, or an apple, folded in the leaves of a book, or wrapped up in a letter. If the person inadvertently takes what is thus presented to him, the other has a right to show him the snow he has thus received, and to rub it in his face, or to pelt him with it, accompanied by the remark: 'New snow is innocent!' and to demand, also, a forfeit of an entertainment, or a dance, or some other boon, of the person he has deceived. The most extreme caution, is, of course, used by every one upon that day. Ahmed Shah, of Little Tibet, told me that some one once attempted to deceive him by presenting him with a new gun-barrel, and pretending that he wished for his opinion about it; but that he instantly detected the snow in the barrel, and had the man paraded through the neighborhood on a donkey, with his face turned towards the tail."

"Islamabad is the next place to be visited, and is the largest town in the valley, the capital city alone excepted. It is now but a shadow of its former self. It contains but six or seven hundred houses: many of them are ornamented with most elegant trellis and lattice-work, but their present ruined and neglected appearance is placed in wretched contrast with their once gay and happy condition, and speaks volumes, upon the light and joyous prosperity that has long fled the country, on account of the shameless rapacity of the ruthless Sikh.

"Islamabad is situated on the westward of, and under a hill which rises to the height of about three hundred and fifty feet above it, commanding an exquisite view of the plain and the mountains at the southern end of the valley. From its foot flows the holy fountain of Anat Nag, the first waters of which are received into tanks whose sides are built up with stone, embellished with a wooden pavilion, and overshadowed with large chunar-trees. Around them are numerous idlers, Cashmerians, Sikh soldiers, Hindoo fakeers, and dogs, reposing in the enjoyment of a cool air and delicious shade. In the evening two or three aged Pundits were to be seen making their way to the place near which the spring issues from the rock, and afterwards kneeling over the water, and mumbling their prayers as their fathers had done before them, by the glare of lighted pieces of split pine.

"At the village of Mar-tund, or 'the sun,' half an hour's ride from Islamabad, is the most holy spring in all Cashmere. It is said that, after the valley was dried, small hills and caves appeared, and that Kashef Rishi, a holy sage, walked about in the greatest delight; that he accidentally found an egg shining most brilliantly, which he picked up. It broke in his hand, and from it flowed the springs of Maha-Martund, 'The great God of the

Sun,' sacred to Vishnu. Houses and Hindoos surround the small tank which is formed near it, and which swarms with Himalaya trout ; but the superstitious Pundits objected to my catching one with my hand,—which would not have been difficult, on account of the number, and the eagerness with which they are fed.

"On the highest part of the plain, where it commences a rise to its junction with the mountains, are situated the ruins of the Hindoo temple of Martund, or Surya (the Sun), or, as it is commonly called, the 'Pandoo-Koroo,' or the house of the Pandoos and Koroos,—of whom it is not necessary to say more than that they are the Cyclopes of the East. Every old building, of whose origin the poorer classes of Hindoos, in general, have no information, is believed to have been the work of the Pandoos. As an isolated ruin, this deserves, on account of its solitary and massive grandeur, to be ranked, not only as the first ruin of the kind in Cashmere, but as one of the noblest among the architectural relics of antiquity which are to be seen in any country. Its noble and exposed situation at the foot of the hills reminded me of that of the Escurial : it has no forest of cork-trees and evergreen oaks before it, nor is it to be compared in point of size to that stupendous building ; but it is visible from as great a distance, and the Spanish Sierras cannot for a moment be placed in competition with the verdant magnificence of the mountain scenery of Cashmère.

"On the northern side of the temple, at the distance of 150 yards, stand a few apricot-trees, and the residence of a fakeer, whose province is to superintend the existence of a well called the well of Harut-Marut. Harut and Marut, so say the Mussulmans, were two angels who represented to the Almighty that the inhabitants of the earth were plunged in wickedness, and were then sent downwards for the purpose of improving them; but, having descended accidentally upon the house of a courtesan, they were surprised into an unhallowed liking for her society, and neglected the work of reformation to which they were appointed. They were, therefore, punished by being shut up in a well; and the Cashmerians say that this is the place of their imprisonment.

"At present, all that remains of the Pandoo-Koroo, or temple of Martund, consists of a central and rectangular building, surrounded by a court or quadrangle, and a rectangular colonnade, facing inwards. The length of the outer side of the wall, which is blank, is about 90 yards; that of the front is about 56. The remains of three gateways opening into the court are now standing; the principal of these fronts due east towards Islamabad. It is also rectangular in its details, and built with enormous blocks of limestone six or eight feet in length, and one of nine, all of proportionate solidity, and cemented with an excellent mortar. There are, I think, about twenty of the pillars of the colonnade, along the inside of the wall, now remaining, out of more than double the number. The height of the shaft of each pillar is six feet, of the capital twenty inches, and of the base two feet. Between each two pillars are trefoiled niches in the walls. The height of the wall, when the building was perfect, must have been about fifteen feet, and that of the doorway eight feet.

"On the interior of the west front there are six pillars on each side of the gate; the east side is a heap of ruins. The capitals of the larger pillars are ornamented with dentils; the shaft, which is grooved rather than fluted, is surmounted by an ornamented neck of beads. The bases are so disfigured by time that I can scarcely conjecture what they may have been. The form of the arch is trefoil, with the bust of a female figure as an ornament over the top. A bank of stones and rubbish occupies the place where there was originally a flight of steps leading to the doorway. Though not a vestige of them remains, there can be no doubt of the fact, as many of the other old temples in the valley are constructed more or less on the same plan as that of Martund, and have steps, or the remains of steps, in front of them.

"The largest stone in the whole building rests over the entrance to the inner chamber or crypt: it is not less than ten feet in length and about a yard in thickness. The whole of the interior is covered with stones that have been shaken down from the roof, and I was informed that there was a spring in the corner of the inner building, which is now blocked up by them. It was once apparently two stories high; and at all events, if I am to judge from other ruins, particularly that of

Pandrynton, near the city, the upper part was certainly pyramidal. Its height, now about forty feet, has been diminished by earthquakes, even within the memory of man. It needs no living evidence to persuade any one that this was the case, a great part of the quadrangle being strewed with enormous blocks of limestone, of which the building is entirely composed.

"Details, characteristic of different styles, are observable in the architecture of the temple of Martund. The pyramidal top would remind us of Egypt and the fire altar. The flying buttress, by which I suppose the wings to have been connected with the centre buildings, would savor of the Gothic. The horizontal entablature, supported by the columns in the peristyle, would, as Professor Whewell has obligingly remarked to me, have a resemblance to the Grecian ; and also, that, as the columns of the gate rise above the pillars of the wall, without bearing any definite relation to them, that part of the building may be Egyptian, Hindoo, or anything but Grecian.

"The greater part of the old ruins in Cashmere were built between the times of Asoka (250 B. C.) and the end of the reign of Avante Verma, in A. D. 875 ; but the same style is apparent in all of them, and the same formation of the arch has been followed in all. The style of architecture used in the religious buildings in Europe for the first thousand years of the Christian period is the Romanesque ; and much of the description of it by Prof. Whewell appears to me to apply generally to the buildings in Cashmere. Few of these ruins, I should say, if any, were Buddhist; those in or upon the edge of the water were rather, I should suppose, referable to the worship of the Nagas, or snake-gods.

"I had been struck with the great general resemblance which the temple bore to the recorded disposition of the ark, and its surrounding curtains, in imitation of which the temple at Jerusalem was built; and it became for a moment a question whether the Cashmerian temples had not been built by Jewish architects, who had recommended them to be constructed on the same plan, for the sake of convenience merely. It is, however, a curious fact that in Abyssinia, the ancient Ethiopia, which was also called Kush, the ancient Christian churches, as I am informed by Mr. Wolff, are not unlike those of Cashmere.

"As I would conclude from its insulated situation, its climate, and other advantages alone, that Cashmere has been a place of consequence from the very earliest ages, so would I also infer that its architecture, or some of its peculiarities, like that of Egypt, is more likely to have afforded a prototype than to be a copy of any known style; and that it may be pronounced to be peculiar to the valley. I, at least, know of nothing exactly like it in Hindustan, nor anything resembling it in any country to the westward of the Indus.

"Without being able to boast, either in extent or magnificence, of an approach to equality with the temple of the sun at Palmyra, or the ruins of the palace at Persepolis, the Pandoo-Koroo ot Martund is not without pretensions to a locality of scarcely inferior interest, and deserves to be ranked with them, as the leading specimen of a gigantic style of architecture that has decayed with the religion it was intended to cherish, and the prosperity of a country which it could not but adorn. In situation it is far superior to either. Palmyra is surrounded by an ocean of sand, and Persepolis overlooks a marsh; but the Temple of the Sun, or Martund, is built on a natural platform at the foot of some of the noblest mountains, and beneath its ken lies what is undoubtedly the finest and most picturesque valley in the known world. The prospect from the green slope behind it is seen to the greatest advantage upon the approach of evening, when the whole landscape is yet in sunshine, but about to undergo a change; when the broad daylight still rests upon the snowy peaks of the Panjal, but commences a retreat before their widening shadows in the valley beneath them. The luminous and yellow spot in which we recognize the foliage of the distant chunar-tree is suddenly extinguished; village after village becomes wrapped in comparative obscurity; and the last brilliant beams of an Asiatic setting sun repose for a while upon the gray walls that seem to have been raised on purpose to receive them, and display the ruins of their own temple in the boldest and most beautiful relief. With the exception of the fakeer's dwelling, there is not a vestige of human habitation upon the green waste. A solitary villager may be seen passing from one district to another; a few cattle may be grazing in the distance, and a shepherd or two may be seen collecting their flocks for the night, while only the bleating of their charge disturbs the silence.

"Though there are, perhaps, not less than seventy or eighty of these old Hindoo buildings in the valley, yet, after having seen Martund, there are but four or five others of sufficient interest to claim a visit from the traveller."

CHAPTER VI.

SRINAGUR, THE CAPITAL OF CASHMERE,—CITY, ENVIRONS, SHAWLS, AND INHABITANTS.

THE town of Islamabad is situated on the river Jelum, which rises within the valley of Cashmere, and a boat, with good rowers, will descend to the famous city of Srinagur, the capital, in twelve hours. The traveller, however, sees little except mud-banks of ten to twenty feet in height, which effectually shut out any prospect, except that of the mountain-tops.

"Before entering the city," says Mr. Vigne, "it will be best to notice the centre of the valley. Its general features are rice-fields, irrigated in plateaux, open meadows, cornfields, and villages embosomed in trees ; elevated alluvial plains, that, either from position, or from being protected by a rocky base, have escaped being washed away by the large and numerous streams that descend from the slopes of the Panjal to a junction with the Jelum, and have furrowed and divided them, more or less, throughout the whole length of the course of the river. The height of the cliff, or terrace, which they form, varies from sixty to a hundred and twenty feet. Here and there a remarkable hill rises from the plain, crowned with a shrine or mosque, or a tuft of fir-trees, giving a pleasing variety to the landscape, which is comparatively bare of forest.

"As I approached the city, I was struck by the Tukt-i-Suliman (Throne of Solomon), an isolated hill, about three-quarters of a mile in length, and four hundred and fifty feet in height, bare of trees, but covered with long grass where the rock permitted it to grow. It is divided from the mountains by a wide ravine, from which opens a view of the city lake, and through which is constantly blowing a breeze that must tend to prevent stagnation of its waters. This singular hill is called by the Hindoos Sir-i-Shur, or Siva's head, in contradistinction to Huri-purbut, the Hill of Huri, or Vishnu, on the opposite side of the city.

"There are the remains of an ancient Hindoo temple on the summit. The interior has been plastered over and whitewashed by the Sikhs, and it is said that beneath it there is an ancient inscription; there is also one in Persian, which informs us that a fakeer resided there, who called himself the water-carrier of King Solomon, and was in the habit of descending every day to the lake, for the purpose of drawing water. A foot-path leads up the ascent from the city side; while, from the other, a good hill-pony can carry its rider to the summit. I knew the foot-path well, as, for almost every day during a month, I used to go up in order to complete a panoramic drawing of the valley. Softness, mantling over the sublime, is the prevailing characteristic of the scenery of Cashmere; verdure and forest appear to have deserted the countries on the northward, in order to embellish the slopes from its snowy mountains, give additional richness to its plains, and combine with its delightful climate to render it not unworthy of the rhyming epithets applied to it in the East,—

> '*Kashmir, bi-nuzir*,—without an equal;
> *Kashmir, junat puzi*,—equal to Paradise.'

"Beautiful, indeed, is the panoramic view that meets the eye of the spectator from the Throne of Solomon, and which, taken far and near, is one

> 'sweet interchange
> Of hill and valley, rivers, woods and plains,
> Now land, now lake, and shores with forest crowned,
> Rocks, dens and caves.'

"The city, which lies to the north-west, may be said to commence at the foot of this hill; and on the other side of it, two miles to the northward, is the fort of Cashmere, built upon Huri Purbut, whose top is about 250 feet above the level of the lake, which occupies the space that intervenes between these two 'portals of light' and the mountains surrounding the valley.

"The aspect of the city itself is curious, but not particularly striking. It presents an innumerable assemblage of house-gables, interspersed with the pointed and metallic tops of mosques, melon-grounds, sedgy inlets from the lake, and narrow canals, fringed with rows of willows and poplars. The surface of the lake itself is perfectly tranquil, and the very vivid reflections which cover its surface are only disturbed by the dabbling of wild fowl, or the ripple that follows the track of the distant boat. At one glance we have before us the whole of the local pictures described in Lalla Rookh.

"The margin of the lake, which from its northern to its southern extremity is nearly five miles in length, by about two and a half in width, is flat, verdant and open, usually edged with willows, poplars, and other trees, numerous only at intervals, so that the eye is immediately attracted by the thicker masses of foliage which form the gardens of Nasim and Nishat, and the far-famed Shalimar. Among them sparkles the white pavilion on the isle of Chunars, or Silver Island, and another green spot is the Golden Island. The large platform of a ruined building is seen on the southern shore, and on the northern are the terraces of two other gardens, neglected and in ruins. Numerous villages on the edge of the water, surrounded with walnuts and chunars, are taken into the view; a green causeway which extends across it is an object of attraction; but we look on the famed floating gardens of Cashmere without being able to distinguish them from the green and richly cultivated grounds upon that edge of the water which borders the city.

"A precipitous but verdant range of about 2,000 feet in height, circles around the lake to the northward, commencing its rise at about a mile from the shores, until it has surrounded that portion of the circumference which extends between the Throne of Solomon and the Shalimar. There it ceases, and a part of the great range which surrounds the Vale of Cashmere lifts its snowy peaks near at hand.

"It must be remembered that we are upon an elevation in the centre of one of the sides of the valley; that it is ninety miles in length, with a varying breadth, and that it is surrounded on every side by a towering wall of mountains, the summits of a great proportion of which are usually covered with snow. Terraces, cornfields, rice-grounds, meadows and morasses occupy the centre of the valley; they are all brightly tinted in the foreground, but in the distance recede into one uniform blue. Several isolated hills and innumerable villages are scattered over the landscape. The line of beauty was never more faithfully drawn in landscape than by the broad and beautiful Jelum, the *fabulosus Hydaspes* of the Augustan age.

"The river passes within half a mile of the foot of Solomon's Throne, and is nearly two hundred and fifty yards in breadth, before it enters the city. Its banks are fringed with willows, among which is a summer-house, with a white cupola, built by the Sikh governor. An avenue of poplars, nearly a mile in length, runs through the cornfields parallel to it, from the foot of the Throne to the Amir's bridge, close to which is the city fort, or residence of the governor, at the entrance of the city, where the stream narrows to about eighty yards. Beyond the bridge we trace it to the north-west, by occasional glimpses, nearly as far as the Great Lake, which is twenty miles distant. The hoary range of the Panjal, in front, is joined with the mountains of Kishtawar on the south, and on the north-west is continued into the still loftier snow-peaks of Durawar, on the left bank of the Indus, so as to form but one vast mural cordillera, and a fitting boundary for the noblest valley in the world.

"Descending from the Throne of Solomon, we immediately pass over the bridge of the Drogjun, under which runs the canal that connects the lake with the Jelum river; it is called by the people, the 'Apple-tree Canal.' When the surface of the lake, as is usually the case, is higher than that of the river, the floodgates remain open, and when the river becomes full they close of themselves, so as to prevent the lake from being overflowed, and its waters from spreading themselves over the adjacent country. The canal is exceedingly pretty; the water is very clear, and numerous fish play among the long reeds that wave upon its edges. One of the governors had it in contemplation to unite the trees on either bank, by a kind of suspended trellis-work, and then to have planted vines, whose fruit and branches would have been thus supported over the midst of the stream.

"The Hindoo ruins in the city are composed chiefly, if not entirely, of large rectangular blocks of limestone, similar to those at Martund and other places. The largest consists of two platforms raised one above another, one of twenty yards square, resting on another of forty-four by sixty-eight yards. The height of this enormous mass of stone work, which no doubt once supported a temple of proportionate size, is now about twenty-four feet. The Hindoo temples must have been exceedingly numerous ; the foundation of the houses in the city, closing the side of the river, are often formed of large blocks which have been drawn from them. A capital turned upside down, a broken shaft or an injured pedestal, may frequently be observed imbedded in the wall, performing the office of ordinary building stone. The river, in passing through the city, has thus been narrowed to a width of about eighty yards; an immovable barrier is opposed to its expansion, and its stream is consequently more rapid and deeper than in any other part of the valley.

"Noor Jehan (the light of the world), the 'Nourmahal' (light of the palace) of Lalla Rookh, is the most renowned name in the valley, that of her august consort, Jehangir, not excepted. In spite of the more authentic story of her birth, the Cashmerians would have us believe that she was a native of the valley. The new mosque in the city was built by her, and is, in fact, the only edifice of the kind that can vie in general aspect and finish with the splendor of the pearl mosque, at Agra. The interior of the building is about sixty-four yards in length, and of proportionate breadth, the roof being supported by two rows of massive square piers, running through the entire length of the building, the circular compartments between them being handsomely ribbed and vaulted. When I was in Cashmere, it was used as a granary or storehouse for rice.

"The mosque of Shah Hamadan occupies a conspicuous situation on the bank of the river, in the midst of the city. His story, as believed by the Mussulmans, is as follows:—Tamerlane was one night wandering in disguise about the streets of his capital (Samarkand), and overheard an old man and his wife talking over their prospects of starvation; upon which he took off an armlet, threw it to them, and departed unseen. A pretended Syud, or descendant of the prophet, asked them how they came by the armlet, and accused them of having stolen it. The matter was made known to Tamerlane, who very sagaciously decreed that the owner must be the person who could produce the fellow armlet. He then displayed it in his own possession, and ordered the accuser to undergo the ordeal of hot iron, which he refused, and was put to death in consequence. Tamerlane, moreover, put to death all the other pretended Syuds in the country. One named Shah Hamadan, who really was a descendant of the prophet, accused Tamerlane of impiety, told him that he would not remain in his country, and by virtue of his sanctity was able to transport himself through the air to Cashmere. He descended where the mosque now stands, and told the Hindoo fakeer, who had possession of the spot, to depart. The latter refused, whereupon Shah Hamadan said that if he would bring him news from heaven he would then believe in him. The fakeer, who had the care of numerous idols, immediately dispatched one of them towards heaven, upon which Shah Hamadan kicked his slipper after it with such force that the idol fell to the ground. He then asked the fakeer how he became so great a man. The latter replied, by doing charitable actions, and thereupon Shah Hamadan thought him worthy of being made a convert to Islam.

"The Mar canal is, perhaps, the most curious place in the city: it leaves the small lake at the north-east corner, and boats pass along, as at Venice. Its narrowness, for it does not exceed thirty feet in width, its walls of massive stone, its heavy single-arch bridges and landing-places of the same material, the gloomy passages leading down upon it, betoken the greatest antiquity; while the lofty and many-storied houses that rise directly from the water, supported only by thin trunks of deodar, seem ready to fall down upon the boat with every gust of wind. It could not but remind me of the old canals in Venice, and although far inferior in architectural beauty, is, perhaps, of equal singularity.

"In a division of the lake called Kutawal, the far-famed floating gardens of Cashmere are anchored, or rather pinned to the ground by means of a stake. These, however, are very *un*-Lalla Rookish in appearance, not being distinguishable from beds of reeds and rushes. Their construction is extremely simple, and they are made long and narrow, that they may be the more easily taken in tow. A floating garden ten yards long by two or three in width, may be purchased for a rupee (50 cents). Mr. Moorcroft has well described the manner in which these gardens are made. The weeds at the bottom, cut by means of a scythe, rise and float on the surface; these are matted together, secured, and strewed with soil and manure; a protecting fence of rushes is allowed to spring up around them,—and upon this platform a number of conical mounds or heaps of weeds are constructed, about two feet in height. On the tops of these is placed some soil from the bottom of the lake; the melon and cucumber plants are set upon it, and no further care is necessary.

"What has been poetically termed the feast of roses has of late years been rather the feast of *singaras*, or water-nuts. It is held, I believe, about the 1st of May, when plum-trees and roses are in full bloom, and is called the Shakufeh, from the Persian *shakufan*, to blow or blossom. The richer classes come in boats to the foot of Solomon's Throne, ascend it, and have a feast upon the summit, eating more particularly of the water-nuts.

"The average depth of the lake is not more than seven to ten feet, and the water being very clear, the bottom, covered with weeds, is almost constantly visible. At the northern corner are the ruins of a once splendid pleasure-ground, whose walled terraces, rising one above the other, might easily be converted into a botanical garden, for which its extent and aspect seems admirably calculated.

"The Shalimar stands on the eastern margin of the lake. It is a building placed at the upper end of a walled garden seven or eight hundred yards in length, by 280 in width. It is of polished black marble, consisting of a central passage and two rooms on either side. The building is 24 yards square, and the north and south sides are ornamented with Saracenic reliefs. It stands in the centre of a square reservoir, which is also lined with black marble : the sides thereof are 54 yards long, and the whole enclosure contains 147 fountains, which are made to play on holidays, the reservoir being filled by the stream which enters it in the shape of a cascade. The stream then descends from the reservoir by a shallow canal, cut through the centre of the gardens and lined with marble, and falls over an artificial cascade at each of the three lodges through which it passes on its way to the lake. A broad causeway or walk runs on each side of it, overshadowed by large plane trees, while here and there a few turfed walks branch off at right angles into the shrubberries, in which are little else than wild plum-trees, planted for the sake of their white blossoms. The principal lodges are plain but elegantly-fronted Saracenic houses, which were evidently intended for the accommodation of the officers and servants of the Emperor Jehangir. Many plane-trees are planted around, and with their shade, combined with the freshness produced by the fountains, the air is as cool as could be wished, even in the hottest day.

"The lotus, with its noble pink and white flower, is very common, and in fact, the leaves are so numerous that in some places they form a verdant carpet, over which the water-hens and others of the same genus run securely without risk of being immersed. In the hot weather, the children in the boats pick a large leaf and place it on their heads, as a shelter from the rays of the sun, or, by breaking off the stalk close to the leaf, obtain a tube through which they drink of the water poured in from above. The stalks are very commonly eaten by the poorer classes: when dry, the seeds are strung together like beads.

"Five kinds of paper, the best of which is superior to that made in the plains, is manufactured in Cashmere. The dipping-frame is made of a kind of reed, which is found near the Shalimar; it grows to about a yard in height, and is of the thickness of a common bell-wire. Every sheet of each kind is smeared with rice-paste by the hand, encased in goats'-hair, and afterwards spread upon a board of wild pear-tree wood, and polished with a piece of agate. The rose-water of Cashmere is surpassingly fine, but there is nothing extraordinary in the way it is made. The attar is procured from trebly-distilled rose water, which is boiled and poured into an open basin over night. While the rose water is still hot, the basin is placed two-thirds deep in a running stream, and in the morning the attar appears like an oil on the surface of the water, and is carefully scraped off with a blade of grass bent in the shape of a V. It is said that a small bottle of attar is the produce of seven or eight hundred pounds of rose leaves.

"The Cashmerians are very expert as manufacturers of wooden toys, turnery, ornamental carving in wood, inlaid work of different woods, ivory and mother-of-pearl ; and the painting on the pen-cases and work-boxes is alike curious and elegant in pattern. They have no oil colors, but flowers and other ornaments are sometimes raised on the surface by means of a composition paste, then painted and oiled two or three times, until they have the appearance of being varnished.

"There are now but five or six hundred shawl-frames in the city. Formerly they were infinitely more numerous. It occupies six or seven frames, of two men at each for six months, to make a pair of very large and handsome shawls. Runjeet Sing ordered a pair to be made, with patterns representing his victories, and paid down 5,000 rupees, after deducting the duties. Only one of these was finished. The *poshm*, or shawl wool is found upon the goats which are pastured upon the elevated plains of Ladak, or little Tibet. It is undoubtedly a provision of nature against the intense cold to which they are exposed, as it is found not only on the common goat, but also on the yak and the shepherd's dog. Its color is a dark, dull, brownish maroon. The *poshm* is a cotton-like down, which grows close to the skin, under the usual coating of hair. The shawl-goat has produced *poshm* in England, but I believe that the quantity will diminish with each succeeding generation, as the climate is not cold enough to demand such a defence from nature.

"The Cashmerian merchants purchase the wool in Leh, at the rate of eighty small handfuls for a small rupee (35 cents). It is then cleaned on the spot, and only one part in four is fit for the purposes of the weaver. When it arrives in Cashmere the governor takes possession of it, and sells it again to the merchants, at 20 per cent. profit on their whole expenses, he keeping the difference for himself. The white *poshm* may then be purchased in the city at about four small rupees ($1.40) for two pounds. The thread is then dyed of different colors, and of these they use about forty different kinds. Their blues and purples are made chiefly from indigo ; their yellows from an Indian flower and a kind of native grass ; their blacks from iron filings and wild pomegranate skins, from which also a light brown is obtained ; their reds from logwood and a native wood ; a drab from walnut hulls ; and it will scarely be believed that the finest of their greens, and a light blue also, are extracted from English green baize.

"All the thread used in making a large pair of shawls does not weigh more than 15 or 20 pounds, and may be purchased for 120 to 150 small rupees ($40 to $50). After the thread is dyed, it is dipped in rice-water, a process which makes it stronger, and fits it to be more safely moved by the shuttle, and the stiffness is removed by washing. The undyed shawl stuff, which sells at five rupees the yard, is called *ubra*, from *ubr*, a cloud.

When made with colored stripes or flowers on it, the long under-coats of the Persians are made from this stuff. If the pattern be worked with the needle, the shawl is far inferior in every respect to those in which the pattern is woven in.

"As soon as a shawl is made, notice is given to the inspector, and none can be cut from the loom but in his presence. It is then taken to the custom-house and stamped, a price is put upon it by the proper officer, and 25 per cent. on the price is demanded. When it is purchased, and about to leave the valley with its owner, the latter has to pay another four rupees for permit duty, and another seal, which enables him to pass with his property; but he is afterwards subjected to further duties. It is necessary to wash the shawls, in order to deprive them of the stiffness of the rice-starch remaining in the thread, and for the purpose of softening them generally. The best water for this use is found in the apple-tree canal, between the lake and the flood-gates. After being wet and stamped upon by naked feet for five minutes, the shawl is taken into the canal by a man standing in the water: one end is gathered up in his hand, and the shawl swung round and beaten with great force on a flat stone, being dipped into the canal between every three or four strokes. This occupies about five minutes. They are then dried in the shade, as the hot sun spoils the colors.

"Old shawls that require cleaning, and in some instances new ones, are washed by means of the freshly-gathered root of a parasitical plant, called *kritz.* A pound of it is bruised and mixed with three pints of water, and to this is added a quantity of pigeon's dung, mixed and beaten up with about the same amount of water. The shawl is then saturated with the liquor, stamped upon, washed with the hand, and then well steeped in the canal. The colors of a shawl, after it has been washed, are often renewed so well as to deceive any but the initiated, by pricking them in again with a wooden pin, dipped in the requisite tints.

"The broker, who transacts business between the shawl manufacturer and the merchant, is a person of great importance in the city, and the manner in which their transactions are carried on is rather singular. They have correspondents in most of the larger cities of Hindostan, whose business it is to collect and forward every species of information connected with their trade. By their means they seldom fail to hear of any merchant who is about to start for Cashmere, even from such a distance as Calcutta, and, if he be a rich man, the broker will send as far as Delhi to meet him, and invite him to become his guest during his sojourn in the valley. Perhaps, again, when the merchant, half dead with fatigue and cold, stands at length on the snowy summit of the Panjal, or either of the other mountain passes, he is suddenly amazed by finding there a servant of the broker, who has kindled a fire ready for his reception, hands him a hot cup of tea, a dish of food, a delicious pipe and a note containing a fresh and still more pressing invitation from his master. Such well-timed civility is irresistible: his heart and boots thaw together, and he at once accepts the hospitality of the broker, who it may be is awaiting the traveller, with a friendly hug, at the bottom of the pass, two or three days' journey from the city, to which he obsequiously conducts him. He finds himself at home, at the house of his new friend, and himself and servants studiously provided with all they can require. His host, of course, takes care to repay himself in the end. He has an understanding with the shawl manufacturers who frequent his house, so that the guest is at the mercy of both parties, and should he quarrel with the broker, hoping to make a purchase without his intervention, he would find it impossible.

"No shawl-vender can by any possibility be induced to display his stores until the approach of evening, being well aware of the superior brilliancy imparted to their tints by the slanting rays of the setting sun; and when the young merchant has purchased knowledge by experience, he will observe that the shawl is never exhibited by one person only; that the broker, apparently inattentive, is usually sitting near, and that under pretence of bringing the different beauties of the shawl under his more special notice, a constant and freemasonic fire of squeezes and pinches, having reference to the price to be asked, and graduated from one to five hundred rupees, is secretly kept up between the venders, by means of their hands extended under the shawl. When the merchant has completed his purchases, the broker, who was before so eager to obtain him as a guest, pays him the compliment of seeing him safe to the outside of the city, where he takes leave of him at the last houses, leaving him to find his way, as best he may, alone over the mountains.

"Srinagur, the capital, has a population of about 80,000 souls. The Cashmerian peasants differ but little from the inhabitants of the city, but the latter are more civilized and perhaps better looking. There are Mussulmans and Hindoos, the former predominating in the proportion of three to one in the city, and nine to one in the villages. The complexion of the Mussulman Cashmerian is generally not so dark, certainly not darker, than that of the natives of the south of Europe, the Neapolitans for instance, to whom they may also be compared on account of the liveliness and humor of their disposition; but their features are large and aquiline, like those of the Affghans, and I do not know that I can better describe them than by calling them subdued Jewish; while a Hindoo may often be distinguished by the fairness of his complexion. I was also told that this was attributable to their eating a less quantity of animal food than the Mussulmans. I have heard that the natives of the valley ascribe their own beauty to the great softness of the water. I have remarked that the water softens a shawl better than any other; and there is undoubtedly a peculiar softness in the air of the valley. It is remarked that the horns of cattle, sheep and goats never attain there to any great size, and, in fact, are rather small than other-

YOUNG WOMAN OF CASHMERE.

wise. Neither has the tobacco of Cashmere the pungency of that grown elsewhere.

"Many of the women are handsome enough to induce a man to exclaim, as did the Assyrian soldiers, when they beheld the beauty of Judith,—'Who would despise this people, that have among them such women?' Their dress is a red gown, with large loose sleeves, and red fillet on the forehead, over which is thrown a white mantilla. The hair is braided in separate plaits, then gathered together, and a long tassel of black cotton is suspended from it almost to the ankles.

"In Cashmere there is no concealment of the features, except among the higher classes. I do not think that the beauty of the women has been overrated. They have not that slim and graceful shape which is so common in Hindostan, but are more usually gifted with a style of figure which would entitle them to the appellation of fine or handsome women in European society. They have the complexion of brunettes, with more pink on the cheeks, while that of the Hindoo women has often too much of the pink and white in it. Whatever the other features may be, they have usually a pair of large, almond-shaped hazel eyes, and a white and regular set of teeth. The inhabitants of the boats, male and female, are perhaps the handsomest people in the valley."

CHAPTER VII.

JOURNEY TO ISKARDO AND THE UPPER INDUS.

BEFORE leaving the Punjab for Cashmere, Mr. Vigne received information which led him to believe that he might succeed in reaching Iskardo, on the Upper Indus, the capital of Baltistan (sometimes also called Little Tibet), which had never been visited by a European. Ahmed Shah, the Rajah of the country, had expressed a desire to see some Englishman at his court, no doubt in the hope of securing some influence which might be of service to him in the then unsettled state of the country.

Mr. Vigne had been but a short time in the Vale of Cashmere, when he found that it would be necessary to carry out his plan during the brief summer of the higher ranges. The Sikh governor at first refused to allow him to proceed further, without permission from Runjeet Sing, at Lahore ; but this was easily obtained. The officials, nevertheless, endeavored to create obstacles of another kind. "The Kazi (Judge) of Cashmere," says Mr. Vigne, "confessed afterwards that they had tried to bribe and intimidate my servants, and I myself was present when the Sikh captain commanding my guard was terrifying them by solemnly assuring them there were Jews at Ladák, whose favorite food, amongst other horrors, was human flesh.

"But all the offers and assertions of the Sikhs were of no avail against the counter-statement of the faithful emissaries of Ahmed Shah (of Iskardo), who I have no doubt promised them both protection and emolument; and when I told them the contents of Runjeet's letter, they only stipulated for double wages during the time they were absent from the valley,—which of course I instantly agreed to give them. All necessary preparations were made without loss of time, and the next day I was rapidly floating down the broad and burnished expanse of the Jelum, and following its windings on my way to Bundurpore on the Wulur lake, where commences the path over the mountains to Little Tibet.

"The night was spent at the foot of the pass. When all was ready for a start in the morning, I was informed that a messenger from Ahmed Shah, of Iskardo, had arrived, and wished to speak to me. His name was Nasim Khan: he was a singular-looking person, thin and pale-faced, dressed in a black velvet frock, with silver buttons, and wearing a black leathern belt, profusely ornamented with little knobs of the same metal. He approached me bareheaded, with the look and manner of a captive brigand, his small, keen, dark eye glancing suspiciously on my Sikh guards; then, after making a most respectful salaam, he stated that his master had sent him to welcome and attend upon me; that he had also brought with him a good pony, who would carry me in safety to Iskardo; and finally, after handing me a letter of invitation from Ahmed Shah, he drew back and remained stationary, with an aspect and in an attitude that betokened the most profound submission.

"When we had commenced the ascent, and his fears and suspicions were over, his tongue was rarely at rest, and I listened with avidity and delight to the recital of his own adventures, his stories of Great and Little Tibet, and the countries on the north of us, including Yarkand and its Chinese masters:—how they were always at war with the people of Khokand; how they had labored for months to cut through a glacier, in order to form a passage for their army; how the general of the Kokokandees had loaded several wagons with the pig-tails of the Chinese soldiers, slain in action; and how, in return, his celestial majesty had sent back the same number of wagons laden with millet-seed, by way of intimating the countless numbers of his troops;—how a Chinese general, to prove his powers of ubiquity, would start off his whole army in carriages over night, to a distant post, the vehicles being sometimes drawn across the country by paper kites; how the walls of one of their strongholds were of loadstone, and the advancing forces were aghast, when their side-arms flew from their scabbards, and their match-locks struggled in their hands!

"It took half a day to reach the halting-station,

a small open lawn surrounded by a pine forest. Here we slept on the ground without pitching tents, in order to be ready to ascend to the summit, and cross the snow before sunrise, while it was yet hard with the night's frost. The table-land in summer-time is covered with a fine greensward, and at the distance of a mile and a half rises a small eminence on the left, towards which, on our approach, Nasim Khan suddenly started off in a gallop, calling on me to follow, and loudly exclaiming that he would show me a view worth a *lack* of rupees. I quickly followed him, and the stupendous peak of Diarmul, more than forty miles distant in a straight line, but appearing to be much nearer, burst upon my sight, rising far above every other around it, and entirely cased in snow, excepting where its scarps were too precipitous for snow to remain upon them. It was partially encircled by a broad belt of cloud, and its finely-pointed summit, glistening in the full blaze of the morning sun, relieved by the clear blue sky beyond it, presented, on account of its isolated situation, an appearance of extreme altitude, equalled by few of the Himalaya range, though their actual height be greater.

"This peak is called Diarmul by the Tibetans, and Nunga Purbut, or the naked mountain, by the Cashmerians. I should estimate its elevation at nearly 19,000 feet above the sea.* The pass on

* Its actual height has since been ascertained, by measurement, to be 26,679 feet, thus ranking *sixth* among the mountains of the world

which we stood has a height of 12,000 feet; on the south we saw two-thirds of the Vale of Cashmere, with the snowy range of the Panjal, behind it.

"On the north side, the valley of Gurys is suddenly exposed to view, at a depth of about 3000 feet below the pass. The entrance into this valley is exceedingly picturesque, as the river comes dashing along through a rich meadow, partly covered with linden, walnut and willow trees, while the mountains on either side present nothing but a succession of abrupt precipices, and Alpine ledges, covered with fir-trees. I was now about to enter the territories of Little Tibet, and for some days to bid adieu to human habitation, saving the little village of Zean, seven miles distant, and was provided accordingly with an extra number of coolies, so that my party now consisted of forty-five people. The officer in charge of the fort in Gurys was also in attendance upon me, and attracted my attention by being the only person whom I met throughout the East, who tacked on the word '*khurbán*' at the end of any answer he made to me. His meaning was simply one of submission, 'I am your victim, or sacrifice.' I need scarcely remark that the same word is used in the Scriptures, although the application is different.

"The Kishengunga river contains a great many fish, and some of my coolies, as we approached a particular spot where there was a little smooth water and quiet lying for them in a nook, apart from the violence of the torrent, took off their sashes, fastened them together, and then let them drop like a net into the water, while another so placed himself as to drive the fish gently towards and over them: they then lifted the cloth and caught at one haul at least one hundred fish, of about half or quarter of a pound each. Some of them were cooked for dinner, but I abstained from eating the roes, as I was cautioned not to do so, as they are considered poisonous. One of my servants, a Hindoo, who disregarded the warning, became so alarmingly ill that for a time I thought he would have died.

"The way now led aloft upon a table-land called Burzil, or the Birches, where the limestone of the valleys gives way to a granite formation. These regions present as wild and gray a scene as any painter could wish for, made up of a confusion of snowy summits, and hoary precipices, broadly relieved in one place by the deep rust color of the ironstone rock; the chaotic masses with which the whole valley was thickly covered; the streams of the infant Kishengunga dashing over and amongst them, with the milk-white and delicate stems of the birch trees, in full leaf, trembling amidst their descending violence.

"As we were approaching Burzil we met a Little-Tibetan, who had been sent on some errand by Ahmed Shah, and from whom my servants learned that there were robbers in the vicinity, and that Ahmed Shah himself was near at hand, with a large force, for the purpose of destroying them on the following day. Towards nightfall, while sitting by a fire near my tent-door, another

Balti native showed himself for an instant, on the crest of the rocky eminence below which we were encamped, and then hastened away with the intelligence of my arrival. In about an hour afterwards, the loud, distant and discordant blasts of the Tibetan music were heard echoing along the glen: the sound grew louder and louder, and we were all on the tiptoe of expectation. At length the band, which was the foremost of the procession, made its appearance above us, consisting of fifes, clarionets, and five or six huge brazen trumpets, about six feet in length, shaped like the classic instruments which are usually put to the mouth of Fame. After these came a group of thirty or forty soldiers, the wildest-looking figures imaginable, wearing large loosely-tied turbans, and armed with match-locks, swords and shields. After them came one of Ahmed Shah's sons, preceded by a few small red horses, and surrounded by more soldiers. Ahmed Ali Khan, for so the young prince was named, had been sent by his father to welcome me and give me honorable escort. He was a young man, of short and slender make, walking with a lame and somewhat awkward gait, in consequence of his having broken both his legs by a fall, when he was a child. They were cured, by-the-bye, by his swallowing pills of rock asphaltum, and living upon milk at the same time. His handsome features and fine expanse of forehead derived a somewhat effeminate expression from his back hair (the front of the head was shaved) being gathered into two large massive curls, hanging down one behind each ear. All the young men of Little Tibet follow this fashion, and leave the mustaches, but shave the beard until it begins to grow strongly. The long curls are then doffed or neglected, and the beard is allowed to luxuriate.

"The young Khan, after a little pressing, consented to sit where he had never sat before—on a chair,—and then gave me a very friendly welcome in the name of his father, the Rajah, or Gylfo, or, as he generally termed him, his *Kiblah-Ghah*, which is, I suppose, equivalent to calling him not only his father, but his 'Father in God.' After making the usual inquiries after my health, and answering several questions on different subjects, which I put to him by means of my interpreter, he assured me that the story about the robbers was perfectly true—that seventy or eighty of them had come through the mountains from the district of Kholi-Palus on the Indus, about eight or ten days' march below Iskardo,—that they had been pillaging a village in his father's territories, and were driving away with them the inhabitants and their cattle also; and that his father had come in person, with a strong force, for the purpose of cutting them off at the head of a defile, through which they were expected to debouch.

"Accordingly, at an early hour the next morning, we all moved forward towards the place of the ambuscade. The whole country was, on account of its elevation, quite free from trees, but the ground was blind, rocky, and covered with coarse herbage, nearly up to the summit of the mountains, among which our path lay. After a few miles we came in sight of the Rajah's tent, on the opposite side of the mouth of the defile through which the marauders were expected to arrive, and near it were several hundred men, visible to us, but concealed from their approaching victims by a small eminence. The young Khan ordered a halt within one mile and a half of his father's tent, and we sat down for half an hour, quietly awaiting the preconcerted signal. He said that he had particular orders from his father to give me escort and protection ; and when I expressed a wish to proceed to the side of a hill opposite to the end of the defile, where I could without any danger to myself have seen the whole cortege of the robbers moving unconsciously along into the very jaws of the ambuscade, he said that I must not go, as they would probably see me, and all his father's plans would be spoiled.

"From the spot where we remained I could distinguish several parties lying in ambush in different parts of the mountains, but all was as silent as the place was desolate, although so many human beings were in sight. Suddenly, and I shall never forget the excitement of a scene so new and so savage, the band advanced rapidly into the open part of the defile, striking up one of its most wildest and loudest strains, and the mountains echoed again with the clangor of their huge trumpets, and the laugh-like cheers of the Baltis, as every man left his place of concealment and sprang forward upon the astonished marauders. Our party were instantly mounted, and we pushed forward to the top of the hill in advance of us ; but the work had been speedily finished, and was nearly over when we arrived. The bodies of five or six men who had attempted to escape towards us were lying on our right. They had been intercepted and killed, and stripped in an instant. At a short distance lay a wounded wretch, who had raised himself on his hand, and by his side was an old Tibetan soldier, coolly loading his matchlock, from which he gave him the *coup-de-grace.* Around another was a circle of the victors, from which one more ferocious than the rest would now and then step forward, to inflict a fresh wound with his sword. Others were busied in stripping the slain, and securing part of the spoil to themselves. Among the latter were my brave Cashmerian coolies, who, watching their opportunity, abandoned their loads in the melée, and contrived to seize upon several sheep, which they killed and buried, on the same principle that a dog buries a bone, to be dug up on their return.

"While I was surveying the extraordinary scene around me, my attention was attracted by a large crowd, and I was told that the Rajah was approaching. He and all around him dismounted as he drew near to me, and I, of course, followed the example. Of two who were taller than the rest I did not immediately know which was Ahmed Shah, but I afterwards found that the second was his brother, Gholám Shah. Ahmed Shah approached me bareheaded, and when near he frequently stopped and salaamed by bowing low, and touching the ground with the back of his hand, and then carrying it to his forehead. I advanced quickly, took his hand, and shook it *à l' Anglais*, bidding my interpreter inform him that it was the English custom to do so, with which piece of information he seemed much pleased. We then all sat down upon some tent rugs which had been brought for the occasion, and after mutual inquiries after each other's health, I congratulated him on the success of the expedition. He replied that these very marauders had pillaged part of his country two or three times before, and that he had determined to come in person and destroy them; that he had all his life prayed that he might set eyes upon a Frank before he died, and that now his wish was granted.

"I must have appeared an odd figure to him, being dressed in a white duck shooting-jacket and a broad-brimmed white cotton hat. I had come, he remarked, from a long distance to visit him, and had arrived at a very fortunate hour: he said that he would do all he could to make me welcome; and added, that what with my arrival and his having killed the thieves, he was really so happy that he knew not what to do. During this conversation the soldiers came in from different quarters, showing their wounds, some of them being very severe ones, and displaying the spoils, consisting of swords which the robbers had scarcely time to draw, and old matchlocks for which they had not been allowed the opportunity of striking a light.

"My friend, Nasim Khan, who had joined the ambuscades, came up without his cap, which he said he had lost in the conflict. Out of the whole number of the marauders, three or four only had contrived to make their escape; the rest were killed, or so severely wounded as to be supposed dead. About one hundred men, women and children, and a very large flock of sheep, were rescued from their hands, and some of them came up to thank the Rajah for what he had done for them. Meanwhile an unfortunate wretch, who had been shamming dead, or who had recovered a little from the faintness caused by his wound, was suddenly discovered in the distance, sitting upright on the mountain-side. Some of the bystanders instantly volunteered to go and dispatch him. I looked at the Rajah, and I suppose he understood as I wished, that I meant to ask for mercy, for he ordered them to fetch him, but to spare his life. He was brought in afterwards, a stout-looking fellow, with a dark swarthy skin (for he was nearly stripped) and a shaven head. He had a severe gash on the neck and another on the arm. I suppose they had told him that I had interceded for him, as he caught my eye instantly, and his wounds did not prevent him from raising his hands to his mouth, and making a sign for water,—which was also given to him immediately at my request, and he was afterwards dismissed with his liberty, but died, so I was informed, while on his way to report the fate of his comrades.

"Ahmed Shah said he wished to remain encamped where he was, for the night; but added that he would move elsewhere if I disliked the smell of the wild leeks, which were very numerous. I made no objection, and my tent was pitched at a little distance from his own, and I retired to rest, feeling thankful for the protection I had received from a danger which, according to all calculation of time and circumstances, must, had I been alone with my party, have certainly crossed my path. The next morning I observed the Rajah and several others standing round what, upon approaching, I found to be a heap of human heads, which had been collected and brought to him for inspection; and after breakfast, while my tent was being struck, I repaired to his, where I found him shamming ill, in order to see whether I was a doctor or not. This was nothing more than I expected, as Europeans are always supposed to possess, like Medea, the power of making gray hairs young again. I easily saw that there was nothing the matter with him; but as he seemed determined then and there to have some medicine, I accommodated him with some Morrison's pills. As he was soon very inquisitive on the subject of English brandy, for which, although a Mussulman, he had a great liking, I gave him a bottle, which he told me was sent off under a guard to Iskardo; and he afterwards, in great glee, told me how he had humbugged his brother-in-law, a rigid Mahometan, who upon inspecting a knife which I had given him, was most innocently anxious to know the use of the corkscrew.

"We soon afterwards started for Iskardo, and immediately commenced the ascent to the plains of Deotsuh. On the top were two small lakes, to the right and left of the path, but neither of them seemed to be very deep or clear. Couriers had been dispatched to Iskardo, with the news of the destruction of the thieves, and by this time the party, by constant accessions, had been increased to seven or eight hundred person. The elevated table-land of Deotsuh is about 30 miles long, by half that distance in breadth. The average height above the sea must be about 12,000 feet. A more dreary and desolate-looking tract the sun cannot shine upon. Its formation is usually of granite and gneiss, of which lofty barren hills and peaks are seen shining in different parts of the plain ; and an horizon of mountain summits, among which that of Diarmul is sometimes conspicuous in the distance, appears to hem it on every side.

"We wound in long array across the elevated plain. I was eager to arrive at Iskardo, and was always for moving forward, but the Rajah, whose yesterday's victory was a great feat, seemed determined to take it more coolly, and was perpetually calling for a fresh pipe, and stopping to enjoy it,— I, of course, being obliged, out of respect, to dismount and sit down with him. At length, after a march of sixteen miles, we arrived at our camp-ground, near a large but fordable stream. As night drew near, the air became extremely cold, and my Hindoo servants were in a state of despair. A quantity of dead dwarf juniper roots was collected by the Tibetans, and a large and cheery fire was soon kindled, which added much to their comfort. I contented myself with partaking of their supper, and while my bed was preparing, was keeping myself warm by walking to and fro with my hands in my pockets, having previously, as I thought, taken leave of the Rajah for the night, when he suddenly joined me and exclaimed, 'I'll walk with you.' Then sticking his hands into his sash, he forthwith began stalking up and down by my side, at a pace that his dignity had not often permitted before.

"The thermometer in my tent stood at forty-three degrees, and the ground, at seven in the morning, was covered with hoar-frost. Next morning the Rajah presented me with a pair of warm Tibetan stockings, and some moccasins made of the skin of the ibex. It is surprising how long a pair of them will wear, provided they do not get wet ; and on account of their roughness and pliability they are admirably adapted for walking over a steep and dangerous path.

"We proceeded on our march over the plain, and about mid-day Mohammed Ali Khan, a boy about twelve years old, the heir presumptive to the throne of Little Thibet, arrived from Iskardo. He had brought with him some small but very delicious melons, a most acceptable present, which, like all other orientals, they ate to the very rind. As we went on, the Rajah pointed to some mountains on the horizon, and said he hoped to pass over them before nightfall, because then we should be enabled to arrive at Iskardo on the morrow. Towards sunset we were at the foot of a steep ridge, and prepared for a further ascent of about 400 feet.

" The cortege commenced the ascent of the zig-zag ; the coolies toiled up the path, and were obliged to halt and take breath at every twenty paces ; then they advanced again, encouraging each other by loudly cheering, in a tone that might have been taken for the wild and discordant laughter of maniacs. I pressed forward with eagerness in advance of Ahmed Shah, riding as far as I could ; but finding I should attain the summit faster on foot, I left my horse with a groom, and soon stood at the upper edge of a glacis of snow, and thence—through a long sloping vista formed of barren peaks, of savage shapes and various colors, in which the milky whiteness of the gypsum rock was contrasted with the deeply red tint of those that contained iron—I, the first European who had ever beheld them, gazed downwards from a height of six or seven thousand feet upon the sandy plains and green orchards of the valley of the Indus at Iskardo, with a sensation of mingled pride and pleasure, of which no one but a traveller can form a just conception. The rock, of the same name, with the Rajah's stronghold at the east end of it, was a very conspicuous object. The stream from the valley of Shighur, which joins the Indus at its foot, was visible from the spot where I stood, while to the north, and wherever the eye could rove, arose, with surpassing grandeur, a vast assemblage of the enormous summits that compose the Tibetan Himalaya.

"The cold and lateness of the hour made it necessary to descend from the ridge, and we continued to move down a rugged and winding path till after nightfall, and then encamped under some juniper trees, about halfway down the defile. The next morning we passed through the gate of Burzeh, constructed by Ahmed Shah, and completely commanding the entrance to the vale. The defile here narrows to a breadth of only twenty-five feet. Precipitous rocks of gneiss and slate rise from each side of it, and between them is a strong wall of wood and stone, which is loop-holed for musketry, and a hole about three feet high, sufficient for the passage of the stream. Through this hole crept the Rajah, myself, his two sons and three or four others, and he seemed delighted when I remarked that a few men could defend it against an army.

"We did not reach the rock of Iskardo until the afternoon of the next day, and upon my arrival I found that a good house at its foot, in which some of the Rajah's family usually resided, had been emptied for my reception. I followed the Rajah up the steps to the upper room, where one of his attendants immediately presented me with a plate of small, thin, fancifully stamped pieces of gold, made from the gold-dust collected on the banks of the Indus, and another plateful of similar silver pieces, which I showered down from the balcony upon the crowd below. After these were exhausted, we threw down several bits of cloth for turbans, etc., and all laughed heartily at the furious scrambling and vociferations which took place even before the articles fell.

"The Indus was visible from my window, and I then turned to enjoy the view of it for the first time. It approached through a sandy plain, from the eastern end of the valley, and here, nine miles from the entrance, it washed the end of the rock within musket-shot of me, in a noble stream of more than 150 yards in width. The Rock is about two miles in length, and the peak over the east end rises some 800 feet above the river. The whole of this superb natural fortress, situated in the middle of the valley of Iskardo, which is nineteen miles long and seven wide, rises with mural sides from a buttress of sand, except at the western end, where it slopes steeply to the plain.

"The valley of the Indus, at Iskardo, is about 7,300 feet above the level of the sea. Enormous mountains, rising 8,000 feet or more above it, surround it on every side, bare, rugged and apparently inaccessible, with long, ascending defiles between them. The surface of the valley, but for the verdure supplied by partial irrigation, would be almost a sandy plain; but water may be found anywhere, I was informed, at the depth of ten yards. Almost all the owners of land are sepoys, who are bound by their tenure to perform any sort of service to which they may be called. The crops are of wheat, barley, turnips, a little rice, millet, buckwheat and cockscombs. The melons of Iskardo are plentiful, small and green, but of delicious flavor. The grapes are pretty good, apples excellent, pears indifferent; peaches and apricots are generally small. Good raisins are also made in the valley.

"I tasted a curious preparation called *sgurma*, and where there was so little variety for the palate, I did not despise it as a sweetmeat. It is made by putting two pounds of ripe wheat into a hair bag, which is then to be laid in a running stream for five or six days, or until the sprout is about an inch in length. Care is to be taken that the grains do not adhere, and for that purpose it should be gently stirred once a day. The grains are then dried and broken by pounding, and four pints of water are added to one of the mashed grain. It should remain all day in the water, which is to be strained off in the evening. The liquor is then boiled in a stone saucepan, which is first greased inside with butter: when boiling, a cupful of almond or apricot oil to about three quarts of the liquor, is to be poured in, and the whole stirred until it assumes the consistency of paste. I was surprised at the taste imparted by the sweet-wort, and could hardly believe that there was no sugar in the composition.

"The Rajah told me that the valley of Shighur is well worth visiting, and volunteered to accompany me, which proposal of course I did not refuse. We were ferried over the Indus, and afterwards marched across the sandy plain, parallel to the river, then turned to the left and wound among the bare and rocky hills which separate the valley of Shighur from that of Iskardo. The former valley lies nearly at right angles with the latter ; its length, by actual survey, is 24 miles, its greatest breadth between four and five. The Rajah and myself occupied three days in marching to the end of it.

"The complexions of the Little Tibetans are usually sallow, and their physiognomy shows an admixture of the Mongolian or Tartar, and the more noble features of the Indian or Persian races, which have originally met from the north and the south upon the banks of the Indus. But I noticed that their aspect was usually thin and care-worn, the result, no doubt, of the hard life and scanty fare of the mountaineer, the latter consisting chiefly of bread made from some of the grains already mentioned, and apricots dried in the sun, of which in the autumn, bushels may be seen upon every other roof. I do not think them long-lived, and Ahmed Shah seemed to think that eighty was an extraordinary age. They are certainly an interesting people. They appear to be contented, and fond of their native valleys, fearing nothing but the Sikhs and the small-pox, and are infinitely superior in a moral point of view, to the more sophisticated inhabitants of the Punjab and Affghanistan.

"The glory of the valley up which we travelled is the magnificent glacier at the end of it. Its lower extremity is a short distance from the village of Arindo, and the natives say that it is slowly but perceptibly advancing. It occupies the entire valley as far as the eye can reach; and a place that looks more like the extremity of the world does not exist. Vast mountains, alike bare, precipitous and rugged, appear to form a channel for it, and in the extreme distance their sides are colored with the red and white tints of iron and gypsum. The width of the lofty wall of ice, in which it terminates towards Arindo, is about a quarter of a mile; its height is nearly 100 feet. I have never seen any spectacle of the same nature so truly grand as the debouchure of the waters from beneath this glacier. The ice is clear and green as an emerald, the archway lofty, gloomy and Avernus-like. The stream that emerges from it is no incipient brook, but a large and ready-formed river, whose color is that of the soil which it has collected in its course, whose violence and velocity betoken a very long descent, and whose force is best explained by saying that it rolls along with it enormous masses of ice, which are whirled against the rocks in its bed with a concussion producing a sound resembling that of a distant cannon.

"Not far from the foot of the glacier is the opening of a defile, with a guard and watch-tower; and on the summit of the defile is another glacier, over which, with two or three days' scrambling, and being fastened together by ropes, there is a way to the valley of Nagyr, once tributary to Ahmed Shah, but now independent, and containing upwards of twenty castles. I was meditating an excursion over the Muzdagh (or Belor Dagh) to the district of Hunzeh, in order to pass thence to Pamir, and perhaps to Khokand ; but Ahmed Shah told me it was impossible, as he could not depend on the friendship of the people of Hunzeh."

CHAPTER VIII.

JOURNEY TO LADAK.

MR. VIGNE visited Iskardo twice, and during one of the visits (but which he does not state, nor in what year) he succeeded in ascending the Indus to Leh, the capital of Ladak, or Little Tibet. His narrative must be detached from the innumerable digressions in which he indulges, and set together in order, as in the foregoing chapters. The first day's march, after leaving Iskardo, was to the eastern end of the valley, which the Indus enters by a narrow and difficult pass.

"The next morning," he says, "we arrived at the place where the two branches of the Indus, one from Ladak, and the other, the Shayok, from Nubra and Karakoram, unite to form the main stream. The place of junction is distant 15 miles from the Rajah's castle. The western branch flows across an open space, its surface extending over a width 150 to 200 yards. The Ladak branch is narrower, flowing through a rocky defile, with a stream not exceeding 80 yards in width, but it is deeper, darker-colored, and is certainly the larger stream of the two. The natives of Baltistan call it the *tsu-fo*, or male river, while the other is called the *tsu-mo*, or female.

"I must first ascend the latter river, towards Khopalu. Barren and stupendous mountains of gneiss, frequently barred with broad streaks of quartz, sometimes plunge down from a vast height into the still pool or deep and roaring torrent, and sometimes recede from it, leaving a margin of sand, a few hundred yards in width. A village, built on a plateau over the delta of soil, at the confluence of one of the innumerable streams that pour their drop of water into the Indus, is generally in sight. The path is sometimes on a level with the river, sometimes rising above it, and carried along the side of a precipice by means of roughly-split spars, supported on wedges of wood driven tightly into the solid rock, and now and then continuing for miles, at an elevation that places the traveller within sight of snowy peaks, and almost in contact with the glacier.

"Khopalu (the place of the rock) is reached on the third day. The open district so named is a long sloping bank, two or three miles in extent, on the left side of the river, and exhibiting a green and shady confusion of stone walls, cottages and fruit trees. The most conspicuous object is the castle, built on the summit of a nearly isolated rock, which rises more than a thousand feet above the Indus. The view from its windows is very grand, and they overhang a height which it made me almost giddy to look down upon. Ahmed Shah took it from a refractory rajah, by cutting off the supply of water.

"At Khopalu I was visited by a native physician, who brought with him a book called the *manchuk*, composed of loose oblong leaves tied up between two boards, and written in Tibetan characters. He said he did not know its age, but informed me that it was written in Lassa, the capital of Great Tibet, and that it was the best book on medicine to be found between Lassa and Ladak; which was not, however, saying much for it. It was divided into four parts: 1,—a treatise on the pulse and veins; 2,—on plants; 3 and 4, on judging of disease by the inspection of the tongue, eyes, etc., of the patient. He appeared unwilling to part with it, saying that it was his bread, and I did not press him to do so. For fever he gave camphor, white sandal-wood, elephant's liver and saffron; for ague, cinnamon, pepper, pomegranate and quince seeds.

"We passed the castle of Chorbut, which is situated so as to command the entrance of the defile and pass of Hanu. Beyond the turn of the river, above a village called Pranuk, the path in its bed was not practicable in consequence of there being too much water. The footing on the granite rocks which arose from its brink became so alarmingly narrow and precarious, that, hearing that it became more and more difficult further on, I thought it best to alter my route, and visit Ladak before attempting to reach the sources of the Shayok river. At a place called Siksu we were entertained with a sword-dance. The performers, ten in number, moved around in a circle and back again, closing to a centre, and then retiring with a slow step, during which they merely held their naked swords perpendicularly in the right hand. As the music grew louder, their gestures became more animated ; they stamped and shouted again and again, writhing and twisting their bodies, and brandished their swords most furiously, the musicians exerting themselves to the utmost, and the bystanders cheering them from time to time, until they were obliged to cease from exhaustion. In the regions below Iskardo the dance is not usually performed until the parties have drunk deeply of wine, and they are then excited to such a pitch of frenzy that the effect is almost that of real madness, and it is a matter of some danger to approach them.

"The ascent to the summit of the Hanu pass was as dreary and desolate as possible, but not so difficult as many others. We crossed the snowy ridge at a very early hour in the morning, by which arrangement we obtained a secure footing for our horses. My thermometer gave me an elevation of about 15,500 feet; and I looked from it with amazement on a vast ocean of mountain summits, extending in every direction as far as the eye could reach. The descent was more troublesome, as the snow was softened, and we were constantly sinking in it up to the middle.

"We soon found ourselves among the villages of the Bhuts, or genuine Tibetans. Instead of the shorn head, the large, loosely-tied turban and drab-colored costumes of the Mahometans of Baltistan, I now saw for the first time the black felt cap, with a rounded top that flapped down to the wearer's cheek; the hair gathered and twisted into a regular pig-tail, and a long, dark, monk-like robe, reaching nearly to the heels. They smoked a tobacco-pipe of iron, precisely resembling the common clay pipe of England. The women, hideously dirty and not handsome, wear their hair also in a tail, but over it is fastened a leathern strap, two inches and a half in width, which descends from the top of the head to the heels, and on this are fastened large lumps of malachite, brought from the Chinese frontier.

"We were presented with incense-plates in which were small branches of dwarf juniper, frying in goats' grease. This species of juniper has been called *juniperus religiosa* by Dr. Royle, it being thus held in reverence by the natives of the Himalaya generally, because it grows at an extreme height, where their ideas have also given a local habitation to demons and spirits. Others made their salaam by raising the back of both hands to a height even with the forehead, and then repeatedly describing a circle in the air with them, dropping the fingers downward and turning the palms inward; by which it is meant to express a wish that all misfortunes may be averted from the person whom they are saluting, and be drawn upon themselves.

"The Hanu stream, along which we descended,

is an impetuous torrent, which in some places rolls along the large stones in its bed, with a noise resembling the report of a distant cannon, and afterwards leaps into the deep and more tranquil stream of the Indus, in a cascade of some magnitude and beauty. The whole party now sat down to rest themselves and hold a consultation, as we were approaching the frontiers of Ladak, which was in possession of the Sikhs. A few were gathered around the young Khan; the others sought repose and shade in different parts of the rock, and their wild and brigand-like figures, dispersed in groups, and reclining in various attitudes upon the gray stone, were quite in accordance with the savage and chaotic scenery around us, and fitting subjects for the pencil of a Salvator Rosa.

"Achmet Ali Khan gave me sundry hints, founded upon intelligence which he had received from spies at Leh, namely, that he and his people would not be allowed to accompany me thither; that all pains had been taken to make the place appear as poor and impoverished as possible in my eyes, and that I was to be supplied with the flour of barley, in order to make me believe there was no wheat in the place. To all this, however, I paid but little attention. Near this place, I came upon the first of those singular Buddhist buildings, called Moonis. They are of various shapes, but those in particular which I now saw, had at first the appearance of a long low shed, or outhouse, about twenty yards in length, five feet high, and its width may have been about twelve or fourteen. Upon closer inspection, it seemed to be a solid mass of earth and large pebbles; the roof, a little raised in the centre, was entirely covered, and as it were tiled, with flat stones of different dimensions, more or less than a foot in length, on every one of which was engraved the Buddhist invocation, *Om, Mani padma, Om.**

"At Skerwuchun I found the first large village, built after the fashion of Great Tibet. On the top of the hill where it first came in sight were some more Munis, of a different shape. The appearance of the village was alike singular and pretty, and reminded me of those formed with a child's toy. Instead of the mud and stone cottages of Little Tibet, I found small square and white buildings, neatly finished off with projecting eaves of wood. They contained, apparently, but one room and one window each, the framework painted red. Each of these, looking as if it formed part of one large house, was raised one above the other on the side of the amphitheatre, with apricots, mulberries and other fruit trees scattered among them. The Lamas and Gelums, or priests and priestesses, were seated at the windows, and on the flat roofs, which they left in order to have a nearer gaze at us, their dark red robes and monastic appearance adding

† *Mani padma* is one of the appellations of Buddha, and signifies the Mani, or holy person, who has the padma, or lotus, for his jewel. According to Professor Wilson, the best interpretation of the word *Om*, is: 'Let us meditate on the supreme splendor of that divine sun who may illuminate our understanding!'

considerably to the effect of the scene. They held in one hand the *skuru*, or praying cylinder, which they were incessantly twirling. The *skuru* is of wood, four or five inches long, and shaped like a drum ; a spindle of iron is passed through it, on which, in the interior of the cylinder, are wound written prayers and interjections. The lower end of the spindle forms a handle by which it is twirled, and on the upper point is fastened a bit of string, with a ball at the end of it. This flies round with great rapidity, and assists in making the whirring noise which comes from the cylinder when it is turned, and which would appear to be considered as an incessant utterance of the prayers contained within it.

"Upon our approach, the principal priests of the place came to salute us. They greeted Achmet Ali Khan as if he were come to deliver them from the yoke of the Sikhs, and the chief of them presented me with a small piece of white cloth, made of a kind of grass. Three-quarters of a mile before our arrival at another village, called Kulutzi, we found a wooden bridge thrown over the Indus, where it rushes through a rocky channel, only 25 yards in width. The next morning I was surprised by the intelligence that the bridge had been burned in the night, and my friends, the Baltis, laid it to the charge of some miscreants in the village, and said that it was done to give them and me a bad name. We were on the Sikh territory, and they knew, as they had told me, but I had not paid particular attention to it, that they would have to return by that route, without the presence of an Englishman to protect them ; and the Sikhs might easily have pushed a force across the river and cut off their retreat. In spite of their assertions, I had serious misgivings and suspicions that the bridge had been burned by the Baltis themselves, or by their connivance, that they might be unmolested on their return. Nevertheless, upon my return to Iskardo, one and all, in the presence of Ahmed Shah and myself, and with their hands upon the Koran, swore solemnly that they knew nothing of the matter.

"Gulab Sing, who, from the first commencement of my travels in the Alpine Punjab, had looked upon me with a suspicious eye, was exceedingly unwilling that I should visit Leh, because, for one reason, he knew that Runjeet Sing would be sure to ask me all about it, and the demand upon him for revenue might be thereby increased. He altogether concealed all intelligence of his conquest from Runjeet, in the first instance. It also became necessary, apparently, that his reception of me in Ladak should be such as would convince his newly conquered subjects that he had little respect for the name of an Englishman.

"Accordingly, as my Balti escort and myself were proceeding quietly on our march, a Sikh, accompanied by five men, with lighted matchlocks, suddenly presented himself, told me that I could go no farther, and coolly laid his hand on my bridle, but quickly withdrew it at my bidding. The Baltis gathered around me and would have overpowered the Sikhs in a moment, had I intimated a wish that they should do so; but it was not difficult to see that I had no right to persist in bringing a body of armed men, even in the guise of an escort, upon Gulab Sing's territories, without his permission. Annoying as it was, after having come thus far, I was obliged to take Achmet Ali aside, and represent to him the impossibility of his proceeding, against the positive refusal of the Sikhs, and that if I allowed them to force their way, it would afford Gulab Sing a just pretext for a counter invasion of Iskardo. In the mean time the Sikhs promised to take care of me, and the affair ended by our all sitting down upon the ground and talking, until my tent was pitched and my dinner was prepared. I took leave of Achmet Ali and my Balti friends the next morning, and then proceeded towards Leh in company with my new acquaintances.

"The village of Kemis, through which we had previously passed, is situated on an elevated plain, and I noticed several little water-wheels, so constructed as to turn a fly-wheel shaped like a windmill, and made apparently for the mere purpose of amusement. On the mountain-side facing the village stood a solitary dwelling, discernible only as a small speck among the rocks. It is the residence of an ascetic lama, who never leaves the spot, being supplied with provisions by the peasants from the neighboring villages, who receive in return the benefit of his blessings and prayers. Before arriving at Ladak the country becomes more open, and the path descends to the green margin of the river, on which goats, sheep and cattle were feeding. The water of the Indus was clear, and the stream about 40 yards wide.

"Pituk is a large and very picturesque village, built on the side of a steep hill; its numerous rows of *munis*, and the red priests and priestesses moving among them, gave it a most singular and lively appearance. It stands at the corner of a large sandy plain, and immediately after passing it I found myself within sight of the town of Leh (Ladak is properly the name of the country), and at the same time could discern for a great distance the course of the Indus, as it meandered towards me, through its very grand and open valley, from the north-east, and the enormous mountains in the direction of the Spiti valley, some of which (but these were not in sight) are supposed, by those who have seen them from the passes behind Simla, to attain an elevation of upwards of 30,000 feet, or double the height of Mont Blanc. Several villages were scattered along the banks of the river, and the whole scene was exceedingly enlivening.

"Leh stands on the north bank, on the eastern side of the upper extremity of a plain, three miles in length, covered with sand and loose stones, and sloping gently down to the bank of the Indus. A small stream, which fertilizes a nook in the mountains behind the town, finds its way through the plain, where it is so full as to be neither expended in irrigation nor lost in sand. On the opposite side of the river is a very long sloping plain, of still larger dimensions, generally barren; but the upper part of it, called Tok, was green and well sprinkled with white villages. Behind it arose a chain of very high mountains. Another chain of mountains, more than 16,000 feet in height, rise beyond Leh, and divide the valley of the Shayok from that of the Indus, the nearest distance between them being about twenty miles in a direct line.

"The town of Leh is about 11,500 feet above the sea; it is situated at the foot of a spur from the lofty ridge, and contains four or five hundred houses, with flat roofs and neatly-finished windows. On the south side of it is a small verdant space, partly edged with poplars, such as in England would be called 'the green.' The best houses and caravanserais are built around it. The interior of the town seemed to be only a confusion of dark valleys, sometimes covered over, or rather running under the houses themselves. The Rajah's residence, behind it, commands a view of the whole town, with the plains and river. It is a singular but not inelegant structure, painted white, and its numerous stories and windows reminded me of an old continental chateau. The walls slope inwards, so that the base occupies a larger space than is covered by the roof. On the summit of the rocky hill, at the foot of which it is built, is the residence of a lama.

"In the neighborhood of Leh, the mountains are everywhere as barren as possible; but where there is a stream, willows, poplars and aspens, and here and there a bunch of fir-trees, do their utmost, and not unsuccessfully, to make the scenery green and pleasant to the eye. The Rajah has another house, in a garden near the town, at the termination of a glen which follows up the banks of the little stream that supplies Ladak, for a distance of two miles.

"The commencement of the high plains of Central Asia is but a few days' march from Leh. The only inhabitants are wandering shepherds, who range with their flocks and their families over an almost boundless extent. Those of Pamir, or *Bam-i-Dunia* (the Roof of the World), to the westward, are 16,000 feet high. The peaks that rise above them are generally covered with snow, and the cold is so intense that not only the goats but other animals, such as the yak, the ibex and the dog, as I have already remarked, are provided by nature with a covering of *poshm*, or shawl wool, next the skin.

"When I arrived at Leh, I pitched my tent near the poplars by the green, and I soon found that it was the intention of Gulab Sing's agents to prevent me from proceeding further. Nobody but my own servants were allowed to approach me. An old Patau, who came to pay his respects was ordered to quit my tent, and was, I believe, actually beaten for what he had done; and what was worse, two Lamas, who came directly to call upon me, and to whom I began to put questions concerning their religion, were peremptorily ordered to leave. I was also prevented from purchasing provisions, or making preparations, necessary for the prosecution of my journey. Even if I walked into the town the bazars were cleared and the people hid themselves, terrified at the approach of the ruffians who, by thus following me, were virtually interfering with my projects and rendering me powerless.

"I several times saw the temporary Rajah ot Leh, a minion of Gulab Sing, but the Sikhs would never allow him to stop and speak with me. One day I met him suddenly on horseback, and was struck with the appearance of the principal Lama of Ladak, who was in the cavalcade ; his red dress and broad-brimmed hat made me fancy for an instant that I beheld a cardinal. I turned my horse to ride with the Rajah, but the Sikh officer, Juan Sing, instantly came up and motioned him to proceed.

"I at last determined to see him, so one morning suddenly ordered my horse and galloped off to the Rajah's residence, attended by my secretary and a groom. The attendants endeavored to prevent my going up-stairs, but used no force. I ascended towards the Rajah's audience-room, having first frightened two Sikhs down-stairs, by half drawing my sword upon them. Then, attended by my faithful Tibetan secretary, I walked without ceremony into the Rajah's chamber. He was seated alone, on a carpet at the further end of it, near the window. His dress differed but little, except that it was more ornamented, from the usual dress of the Tibetans, and a canopy of rich Chinese figured silk was suspended over his head. His attendants and others in the apartment stood around at a respectful distance, and wished me to do the same, but it was no time to be ceremonious. I walked up to the Rajah, made my salaam, and then sat down close by him, and warmly demanded assistance in the name of the Maharajah, Runjeet Sing, whose guest, and under whose protection, I considered myself.

"Juan Sing, hearing that I had gone to see the Rajah, soon afterwards made his appearance, breathless with haste; and the Rajah, who was decidedly alarmed, told me at last that he was willing to give me the assistance I wanted, but that he was prevented by the fear of Gulab Sing. And having got this answer, I quitted the room. The next morning the Rajah sent me a dress of honor, but of no value, merely as a matter of form, and which I therefore accepted. I afterwards found that there did not seem to be any longer an objection to my visiting Nubra and the Shayok valley, provided I did not go further, and I availed myself of the opportunity of employing the remainder of my time so profitably.

"The way by which I travelled first took an easterly direction, over the sands, to the village of Ayu, and then turned to the north, ascending by a long, rocky and very fatiguing zig-zaz to the summit of the pass. The thermometer gave me an elevation of nearly 16,000 feet, the formation being a dark-colored trap. I there suddenly came in view of the mountain masses that arose on the other side of the Shayok, and the whole horizon was serrated by snowy peaks in every direction.

Among those to the north, the range of the Mus-dagh arose in conspicuous and most majestic grandeur.

"A long and cheerless descent brought us to the village of Jugur, our resting-place for the night. The next morning we descended upon Morkum, on the banks of the river. The stream was low, and its average breadth was about forty yards, when it was confined within its proper channel. Above the village the valley assumes the appearance of a defile, and two days' march up its side brings the traveller to the village of Shayok, from which the river takes its name. Beyond this there is not, I believe, any fixed human habitation for the remainder of the way to Yarkand, the whole distance to which from Ladak occupies a little more than a month.

"The road to Yarkand ascends the bed of the river, which is constantly crossed and recrossed by wading ; and the mountains or pass of Karakoram are in this manner reached, about the ninth or tenth day from Ladak. The aspect of the lateral valley of Nubra, which enters that of Shayok on the north, is altogether very pretty and enlivening, and I was surprised at the number and appearance of the houses scattered on different parts of it, but not now occupied, as formerly, by persons of some property. A castle stands on a rocky eminence of about 150 feet high, with a village at its foot. The villages are numerous and picturesquely built, after the Ladak fashion, and there is no lack of apricot or mulberry trees around them.

"I returned from Nubra to Leh by another pass, to the south of that by which I went thither. It was of about the same height, but more covered with snow. Upon my arrival at Leh, I found it as desolate as I had left it; but those of my servants who had remained there told me that in my absence the town had presented quite a different appearance; that the bazars were well filled, and no one had been afraid of showing himself; travellers and merchants had come in from the northward, and a flock of the large sheep, already mentioned, had arrived with their burdens of *poshm*, or shawl-wool. On my way back, I noticed by the path-side a small building of loose stones, covered with the horns of the ibex, and different species of wild goats, while the centre was a horrible but grotesque countenance, carved in wood, intended to represent an evil spirit. The pile, in fact, was erected for the purpose of propitiating some imaginary element of evil.

"I soon afterwards set out on my return to Iskardo, where old Ahmed Shah received me with the same kind hospitality that he had ever shown, but could not repress a smile, in which I joined him, at my having run up and down so many miles of the Indus, to so little purpose.

"On my way back to the Punjab, Gulab Sing took occasion to send and inform me that, if I wished, he would order Juan Sing's nose to be cut off, and forwarded to me by way of punishing him for his insolence. He afterwards sent one of his principal secretaries with a large bag of rupees, and a valuable dress, as an earnest of his wish that I would come to be his guest at Jamu, or would give him an interview on the road. I refused, however; and when I got to Lahore, I made a regular complaint to Runjeet Sing, at an interview which he gave me in his private audience-room."

Mr. Vigne made another visit to Iskardo, during his stay in India, and endeavored, but without success, to reach the little Alpine state of Gilgit, lying to the north-west, between the Indus and the source of the Oxus. A second attempt to ascend the Shayok branch of the Indus to its source in the lofty Karakoram range, was also unsuccessful. His explorations, however, established a broad base of knowledge of the Upper Indus and the Tibetan Himalayas, from which all expeditions towards Central Asia have since been undertaken. He returned to England in 1839, after an absence of seven years.

CHAPTER IX.

MR. SHAW'S PREPARATIONS TO EXPLORE CENTRAL ASIA.

FOR several years after the murder of Adolf Schlagintweit became known, there was no further attempt made to follow in his footsteps. Little by little, however, the sum of information concerning the region was increased, by intercourse with those of its natives who visited Ladak, by the Hindoos sent thither by the English surveying officers, and by brief excursions along and over the frontiers of the dangerous territory. In 1858, a Russian officer, Capt. Valikhanoff, who was the son of a Kirghiz chief, disguised himself as a wandering trader of the tribe, succeeded in crossing the range of the Thian-Shan, and penetrated to Kashghar, when he was compelled to return. On the southern, or Tibetan side, Mr. Johnson, an officer of the English survey, crossed the range ot Kuen-Lün, and safely reached the city of Khoten, where he was received in a very friendly manner by the native chief.

In the mean time, important political changes had taken place. The Tartar chief, Wallé Khan, by whose order Schlagintweit was executed, did not succeed in gaining possession of the cities of Yarkand and Kashgar, which were still held by their Chinese garrisons, but his invasion had the effect of stirring up all the elements of revolution among a people so mixed in blood. In the spring of 1863, the Toongânees, who are said to have sprung from the intermarriage of Tartars and Chinese, using the language of the latter while they are Mussulmen in religion, rose against the Chinese officers in Yarkand and Khoten, and, after a severe struggle, gained possession of both places. In Kashghar, the Chinese, anticipating a similar revolt, invited the Toongânees to a feast and then massacred them all in cold blood.

EASTERN CAMEL.

Through these events the whole country was aroused. Immediately the Kirghiz Tartars descended from all the neighboring mountain regions, drawn together by the desire of plunder, and attacked Kashghar. The Chinese and their Turcoman partisans defended the city, until they were reduced to the greatest straits. "First they ate their horses, then the dogs and cats, then their leather boots and straps, the saddles of their horses and the strings of their bows. At last they would collect together in parties of five or six, who would go prowling about with ravenous eyes until they saw some one alone, some unfortunate comrade who still retained the flesh on his bones. They would drag him aside and kill him, afterwards dividing the flesh between them, and each carrying off a piece hidden under his robe." Thirty or forty men died of hunger every day. At last, when no defenders were left on the walls or at the gateways, the Kirghiz made good their entrance.

Their victory was marked by indescribable barbarities. The whole city was given up to plunder, and numbers of men, women and children were murdered. In the midst of these horrors, a new force appeared upon the scene. The news that Wallé Khan had subjugated all the open country, had crossed the western mountains ; and a member of the royal Tartar family which reigned in Central Asia more than a hundred years ago, Bozoorg Khan, accompanied by Mohammad Yakoob, an energetic general, a native of the Khanate of Khokand, gathered together eighty followers, and set out to reconquer his lost inheritance. The people of Kashghar welcomed him with professions of allegiance, and his little band of adventurers soon became so strong that they routed the plundering Kirghiz, seized and executed many of the chiefs, and established themselves in the city. This took place in January, 1864.

The Chinese still held the strong fortress of Yangee-Shahr, situated about five miles to the south of Kashghar. Bozoorg Khan, reinforced by five hundred men from Khokand, commenced a siege, which lasted fourteen months before the supplies of the garrison were exhausted. From the accounts given by the people, he was an indolent man, whose only interest was in the ceremonies belonging to his new royal state. The leading spirit of the movement was Mohammad Yakoob, who was formerly known to the Russians as a bold and desperate fighter, and bore on his body five marks left by their musket balls. Tired of the slow siege operations, Mohammad Yakoob took a small body of soldiers and marched against Yarkand, which had been for a year in the possession of the Toonganees. A battle was fought under the walls of the city, but he was defeated and obliged to retreat. The Toonganees and their allies followed. Having rapidly reinforced his army, he lay in wait in the jungle, near a town called Kizil, and completely routed the enemy, after which he was obliged to return to Kashghar to suppress some dissensions which had broken out among the besiegers.

Early in 1865, the Ambân, or Chinese Governor of the fortress, called a council of his chief officers, and proposed making terms with Mohammad Yakoob. The officers assented, and began apportioning among themselves the respective shares they should furnish as a present to the conqueror. Meanwhile, the Ambân, who had collected his whole family—his daughters behind his seat, and his sons serving tea to the guests, who were seated on chairs around the room—listened attentively for signs of the capture of the place. Presently he heard the shouts of *Allahoo-akhbar!* by which the Mussulmen announced their entry into the fortress. Thereupon he took his long pipe from his mouth, and shook the burning ashes out on a certain spot of the floor where a train of gunpowder communicated with a barrel which he had previously prepared under the floor of the room. While the unconscious officers were still consulting about a surrender, the house was blown up and all perished in the ruins.

Having now the use of his whole army, Mohammad Yakoob took a city called Maralbashee, by which he cut off the communication between the allies of the Toonganees at Yarkand and their homes. He then advanced against Yarkand, which, after a siege of a month, was forced to surrender. These successes so increased Mohammad Yakoob's popularity with the soldiers, and his influence over the people, that he felt himself able to assume the sovereignty. Quietly ignoring Bozoorg Khan, the heir to the ancient throne, who had given himself up to idleness and debauchery, he sent his envoys to the neighboring nations, and took into his own hands the government of the kingdom. The Ameer of Bokhara responded by addressing him as *Atalik-Ghazee* (Tutor of the Champions), by which title he still reigns.

What part Wallé Khan, the first invader and conqueror of Central Asia, took in this last, complete subjugation of the whole country, is not stated. He appears to have been among the princes of royal blood, who opposed Mohammad Yakoob's assumption of the sovereignty, for he was soon seized and executed by the latter's orders. Bozoorg Khan was held in a kind of honorable restraint, until 1868, when he was set at liberty on condition of making a pilgrimage to Mecca. On returning therefrom, he betook himself to his old home among the mountains of Khokand.

After having spent two years in consolidating his power, Mohammad Yakoob set about extending his conquests. His first march was against Khoten, and it was darkly signalized by an act of treachery towards the chief of that province and all his principal men, who were invited to visit the conqueror and then basely assassinated. The city of Khoten resisted, and was only taken after 3000 men had been slaughtered. During the same year, 1867, he subjugated the eastern countries of Ak-su, Koo-chee and other regions inhabited by a mixed Tartar population, who had long been under Chinese rule. The extent of his sway to the eastward cannot be accurately ascertained, but it apparently embraces nearly all the territory to the west of the desert of Lob, lying between latitude thirty-five and forty-five degrees, and seventy-five to eighty-five degrees east longitude.

The news that the Russians were constructing a fortress in a pass near the head-waters of the Syr-daria, or Jaxartes, a week's journey westward from Kashghar, compelled Mohammad Yakoob to return from his eastern conquests. In the autumn of 1868 he received a visit from Captain Reinthal, a Russian officer, and soon afterwards sent an envoy of his own to St. Petersburg. At the same time he set about fortifying the passes in the high range of the Thian-Shan, to the north of Kashghar. In the winter of 1869, he also took possession of the high valley or table-land of Sirikol, part of that region called Pamir (or Pamere), where the Oxus finds its source.

The success of Mohammad Yakoob was the means by which Central Asia was opened to European explorers. The dangers which surrounded this region were not the terrific mountain passes, far higher than those of the Andes—not the character of the inhabitants, many of whom are of Aryan blood, and nearly all of whom are cheerful, social, and hospitable—but the jealousy and suspicion of all previous rulers, whether Tartar or Chinese. The first traveller who was so fortunate as to take advantage of the new state of things, was Mr. Robert Shaw, at present British Commissioner in Ladâk, or Little Tibet. In twelve years after Schlangtweit's fate seemed to illustrate the impossibility of such an undertaking, he reached Yarkand and Kashghar, and returned in safety.

For several years Mr. Shaw had been stationed

in the Kangra Valley, among the Himalayas. Repeated shooting excursions, extended as far as Cashmere, had rendered him familiar with Asiatic travel, and his familiarity with the southern side of that gigantic mountain-wall which defends India on the north, led him to desire an acquaintance with the half-known or unknown regions beyond it. Natives from Ladak frequently made their appearance in the Kangra Valley. "Black tents of peculiar make appear for a few days at a time in the winter on open spaces by the roadsides, and shelter dingy families of narrow-eyed Tibetans—petty traders, who come down with their wares. They are not prepossessing in appearance, with their high cheek-bones, their dirt, and their long pig-tails. But they are the most good-tempered of mortals, and they always greet you with a grin.

"Moreover, every year the few English sportsmen who penetrate into the wilder parts of Ladak bring down reports of the wonderful animals to be found there, and of the curious customs of the Booddhist inhabitants. Wild sheep as large as ponies, wild cattle with bushy tails like horses and long hair on their flanks reaching nearly to the ground, besides antelopes and gazelles, are to be obtained by those who toil sufficiently; while, for non-sportsmen, the curious monasteries perched on almost inaccessible rocks, with their Romish ceremonial, their prayer-wheels, their gigantic images, and ancient manuscripts, form the chief attraction.

"But while Ladâk was thus tolerably well known, though situate at the distance of nearly a month's march across the mountains, the region beyond it seemed to combine all the attractions of mystery and of remoteness. Some few native traders had been known to penetrate to the distant marts of Yârkand, and even Kâshghar, and they brought back frightful tales of toil endured and ot perils escaped. Men's lives were there said to be of no more account than sheep's, and few traders ever dared to repeat the venture. Rumors of rebellion in those regions also reached India. The subject Moghuls, a Mussulman race, were said to have risen and massacred their Chinese masters, and to have established the independence of the 'Land of the Six Cities,' as they called the country which is shown in our maps as Chinese Tartary."

Attracted towards this region in 1867, Mr. Shaw extended his usual yearly excursion as far as Ladâk. His companion and himself were anxious to meet those caravans from Central Asia which annually came to Western Tibet. Their plan was to make acquaintance with the merchants, join then if possible, and push on at least to Khoten, which Mr. Johnson had reached two years before. These hopes, however, were frustrated by the news of the conquest of Khoten, and the murder of its former chief, by Mohammad Yakoob. Although the intelligence was received by the travellers before crossing the Himalaya range, they determined to go on to Ladâk. Mr. Shaw gives a most vivid and picturesque description of the scenery, and the sights which the traveller encounters on the way:

"After leaving the narrow fir-crowned gorges, the precipitous cliffs and the glacier-passes of the real Himalaya, we entered upon the vast tableland of Tibet in the district called Roopshoo; which, however, reminds one at first sight of the British soldier's remark about Abyssinia: 'Well, if it is a table, it is a table with all the legs uppermost.'

"Lying at an elevation equal to that of Mont Blanc, this plateau consists of broad valleys without water, which seem a few hundred yards wide, and are really plains of many miles in extent. On either side arise rolling mountains of all shades of red, yellow, and black; the rock occasionally cropping out near the summit to break the uniformity of the long shingly slopes of *débris*. Everything is bare gravel, both mountains and plains. Not a glimpse of verdure is to be seen, save in some slight depression where the eye at a distance catches a faint yellow gleam along the ground, which a nearer approach shows to be the effect of some scattered blades of a harsh and prickly grass, piercing up through the gravel like so many discolored porcupine quills. When you begin to despair of finding those great traveller's requisites, water and wood, your guide will lead you into a recess of the hills, where a small stream derived from some distant snow-bed far up the hill-sides, has given rise, before disappearing under the gravel, to a thicket of brushwood two or three feet high, and where groups of shallow pits, surrounded by loose stone walls, each with its rough fire-place in the middle, point out where the wandering tribes of Tibetans occasionally pitch their tents. If you are wise, you will take advantage of these sheltering side-walls, low and creviced though they be, for suddenly, in the afternoon, there will arise a terrific blast of deadly cold wind, which will numb all the life in your body under a dozen covers, if it strike you. The Tibetan traveller cares for no roof overhead if he can shelter himself from the wind behind a three foot high wall. Hence the numerous little stone enclosures clustered together like cells of a honeycomb at every halting-place, with one side always raised against the prevailing wind. While thus sheltering himself from the cold of the afternoon, the traveller will scarcely believe he is in the same country where in the morning he was guarding against sunstroke, and nearly blinded by the insufferable glare.

"It is a terribly unsatisfactory country to travel in. On those endless plains you never seem to arrive anywhere. For hours you march towards the same point of the compass, seeing ever the same objects in front of you. If you discover another party of travellers coming towards you in the distance, you may travel for half a day before you meet them. The air is so clear that there is no prospective ; everything appears in one plane, and that close to the eyes. When, after threading these interminable valley-plains, you descend again towards the inhabited country of Ladâk, the first bits of village cultivation seen on an opposite hill-side have a most singular effect. 'Cela vous saute aux yeux.' They seem to come right out of the surrounding landscape of desert, and to meet you with almost painful distinctness. Imagine patches out of the best cultivated parts of England, dropped here and there into a parched and howling waste of mountains, such as one might imagine the Atlas to be, or such as Aden is; and this under an Italian sky, with an atmosphere which acts like a telescope, bringing the most minute and distant objects into notice. No gradations of verdure; each bit of cultivation is as distinctly defined from the surrounding desert hill-side as if it had been actually cut out by measurement from another country and dropped there.

"Approaching the village, you pass a long, low, broad wall, covered with flat stones, inscribed with sacred sentences in two different styles of the Tibetan character. This is a 'Mané,' and not a village is without several of them. At each end there is probably a 'Chorten,' in form a large square pedestal, surmounted by a huge inverted tea-pot, all whitewashed; while crowning all is a small wooden globe or crescent supported on a sort of obelisk. These erections, varying from ten to twenty feet in height, are supposed to contain the remains of sainted Lamas, whose bodies have there been buried in a standing position. Little pigeon-holes at the sides are filled with numerous small medallions, looking like lava ornaments. They are moulded into wonderful figures of hundred-handed deities, venerated by this denomination of Boodhists, and are composed of clay, mixed with the ashes of other dead Lamas, who are thus, in a material sense, transformed at death into the image of their gods.

"On reaching one of these structures, the devout Tibetan invariably passes it on his right; hence the road here always bifurcates to allow of this being done both by goers and by comers. The scattered houses of the village are flat-roofed, two-storied, built of huge sun-dried bricks, with walls sloping considerably inwards, and finished off with brilliant white and red stucco over the doors and windows. On the roofs are generally small piles of horns (either of wild animals or of domestic sheep and goats) stuck all over with small flags and rags of colored cotton. Fierce-looking black 'yaks' (the cattle of Tibet) with their bushy tails, and long hair hanging below their knees, and giving them a petticoated appearance, graze about the fields or grunt discontentedly as they are led in by the nose to carry the traveller's baggage. They are generally conducted by the women, who wear red and blue petticoats with the stripes disposed up and down, cloth boots gartered up to the knee, tight-fitting jackets covered with a sheepskin cape (hair inwards), sometimes lined with a scarlet cloth, bare heads with curious cloth lappets protecting both ears from the bitter wind, and, above all, a 'perâk,' their most precious ornament, consisting of a broad strip of leather hanging down the back from the top of the head, and sown all

TIBETAN PEASANT.

over with rows of large false turquoises gradually dwindling away to single stones near the tip. The men, beardless all, wear similar cloth boots, thick woollen frocks girt round the waist and just reaching below the top of the leggings, and on their pig-tailed head a kind of black Phrygian cap, like an English drayman's, of which the hanging end serves a variety of purposes, being brought down either to shade the eyes from the sun or to shelter either ear from the cold, chilly blasts of the afternoon.

"Amongst the group collected to stare at the traveller there is generally a Lama, dressed in a red robe which allows one arm and shoulder to be bare, as is also the head. In his hand he carries a prayer-cylinder, which he whirls round on its wooden handle by an almost imperceptible motion of the hand, aided by a string and small weight attached to it, and assisting the rotation. Perched on some neighboring pinnacle, or jammed against the vertical face of some rock, is the Lama's monastery. Such is a Tibetan village, without a tree except a few stunted willows along the life-giving water-courses ; while all above, to the very edge, is a howling wilderness of gravel, with no signs of man's existence.

"In the broad valley of the Upper Indus, which constitutes Ladâk, the villages in places extend continuously for several miles. The crops are here wonderfully luxuriant, and the climate is milder, the elevation being only 11,000 feet. The town of Leh itself is nestled under the hills, at a distance from the river of some four miles up a long gentle gravelly slope.

"Arriving here, I was preparing to study the Tibetan manners and customs more attentively, but the first walk through the town at once dispelled all the rather contemptuous interest which I had began to take in the people of the place, by introducing a greater interest in lieu thereof. For stalking about the streets, or seated in silent rows along the bazaar, were to be seen men of a different type from those around. Their large white turbans, their beards, their long and ample outer robes, reaching nearly to the ground, and open in front, showing a shorter under-coat girt at the waist, their heavy riding boots of black leather, all gave them an imposing air ; while their dignified manners, so respectful to others, and yet so free from Indian cringing or Tibetan buffoonery, made them seem like men among monkeys compared with the people around them.

"Perhaps it was partly the thought of their mysterious home which imparted to these Toorkee merchants such a halo of interest. Visitants from a world of hitherto forbidden access to all others, these very men must have witnessed the tremendous vengeance which, like a second Sicilian Vespers, had recently consigned 50,000 invaders to a violent death. They had probably themselves taken part in the massacre of the Chinese idolaters. Their eyes must be quite accustomed to the wholesale executions which were said to be of daily occurrence in those distracted regions. Their ancestors, right back to the time of Tamerlane and Chenghiz Khan, must have taken part in those convulsions which, originating in Central Asia, have been felt even in the distant West.

"When we began to make their acquaintance, their disposition seemed hardly to correspond with the terrific character which was ascribed to their compatriots. They came and sat with us in our tents, and talked in a friendly way with us through an interpreter, sipping our tea the while with great gusto, despite the horror-stricken looks of our Indian Mussulmans who are so far Hindooized as to consider such an act a breach of caste. Our guests were essentially 'good-fellows,' able to enjoy a joke and give one in return, talking freely, and yet never stepping beyond the proper limit. They seemed to respect both themselves and those they conversed with, and when they rose, they took their leave with the deferential bows of a courtier. In color they were scarcely darker than Europeans, with red lips and ruddy faces. On our first arrival a man approached me dressed in a felt wide-awake, a long flowered dressing-gown and high riding-boots. His beard and moustache were light brown, his face quite fair, and he stared me in the face like an Englishman. I was on the point of addressing him as one, when he turned aside and sat down by my Mussulman servants. He was a Yarkandee 'Hajjee' or pilgrim!"

It was fortunate for Mr. Shaw that just at this time the Indian Government enforced a considerable reduction of the duties on the trade between

Cashmere, Ladâk and Central Asia. The natives of Yarkand, who were then in Leh, came to him to express their gratitude for the measure, and it was evident that the good reports sent home would enable him to undertake the journey under very favorable auspices. He stayed a month at Leh, studying the character of the people, and collecting information. Leaving late in October, he was barely able, by forced marches, to cross the pass into India, before it was closed for the season by the snow. Having finally reached his home in the Kangra Valley, he at once began to prepare for an expedition the following year. His companion was not able to accompany him, so he determined to go alone, as an English merchant, with a stock of goods suited to the markets of Yârkand and Kashghar.

In order to avoid suspicion, Mr. Shaw decided to make no measurements, take no observations, and to rely only on a small prismatic compass, which might be considered as a trinket by the natives. As an assistant and confidential agent, he engaged a Mussulman named Diwân Baksh, who had been in his service as a writer. The latter understood Persian and Arabic, was familiar with the etiquette of the native courts, and the fact that he had a family in the Kangra Valley seemed to be a sufficient guarantee for his fidelity.

CHAPTER X.

JOURNEY TO THE KARAKASH RIVER.

ON the 6th of May, 1868, Mr. Shaw started on his second journey to Ladâk. His progress at first was very slow. His assumed character of merchant obliged him to take a large quantity of goods, the transport of which became a serious matter. He was obliged to go ahead and provide change of mules or porters, at the end of every seven or eight days' march. On reaching the valley of Kooloo, a native doctor, maintained there by the Government, came to report that an orphan boy of Yârkand, the only survivor of a family which had gone on a pilgrimage to Mecca two or three years before, had been left in his hands. He was a rosy, fat-cheeked youth, apparently quite self-possessed and happy, with high cheek-bones and narrow eyes, very Mongolian in type, dressed in a curious combination of the garments of Mecca, India and Toorkistan. He wore a red skull-cap from the first place, a white cotton frock from the second, with a stout pair of Yârkand riding-boots reaching to the knee. When Mr. Shaw asked him whether he would accompany him back to his old home, he at once answered "Yes." He was immediately attached to the expedition, in the belief that his restoration to his family would be a good introduction to the officials of Yârkand.

The Bara Lacha pass of the Himâlayas, by which Ladâk is entered, could not be crossed until the 2nd of July, on account of its great elevation and the quantity of snow. Mr. Shaw thus describes the region :

"The Bara Lâcha is the boundary between two separate regions distinguished by their physical characters. That which we have already passed through may be called the true Himâlayan region. Here the gigantic ranges are covered with perpetual snow, furrowed by glaciers, and they rise from amidst dense forests which clothe their flanks up to a certain elevation. They are separated by deep gorges, whose sides are precipices, and through which large rivers flow. In fact, the scenery is Alpine. Once across the Bara Lâcha Pass, however (or any other pass on the same range), you enter a region where all gorges or valleys appear to have been filled up by an encroaching sea of gravel, which has risen to within a few hundred feet of the summits of the ranges. The space between the mountains no longer plunges down into a seemingly bottomless ravine, whose sides narrow down till they barely leave room for the stream. Instead of that it is occupied by a broad high-level plain, out of which the summit ranges merely rise like undulations. We notice the prevalence of the *horizontal*, after the *vertical* lines to which the Himâlaya has accustomed us. It is like leaving a *Gothic cathedral*, and approaching the *Parthenon*. At the same time, a kind of drought seems to have fallen over the face of the country. There are no vast fields of snow to supply streams of water, and no frequent showers to maintain verdure. Such must be the aspect of a landscape in the moon.

"It seems as if we had here a rough block, from which Nature intended hereafter to carve out the usual features of a mountain country by some change of climate, which should bring snow, ice and water to sweep out the masses of earth or gravel by which the mountain ranges are now glued together. The almost entire absence of rainfall suggests a speculation as to whether its presence might not (after geologic ages) bring the country into resemblance to its neighbor region, where copious rain and deep-cut ravines exist together.

"Henceforward, however, we must bear in mind that we are in the barren or Tibetan region, where green spots are about as rare as islands in the ocean, and universal gravel is the rule."

Before proceeding to Leh, the capital, Mr. Shaw determined to make a trip to the eastward of Ladak, skirting the borders of Chinese Tibit, in order to avoid the town by crossing the Indus higher up its course, and strike into a new route which was supposed to lead more directly into Eastern Toorkestan. He left the main route to Leh at a point called Rookshin, and travelled eastward for twelve days over the high table-land of Roopshoo, the average elevation of which is 15,000 feet above the sea, while the scattered peaks frequently rise to the height of 20,000. The road then gradually descended towards the valley of the Indus, after crossing which and another barren range of mountains, Mr. Shaw reached the Pangong Lake, on the Chinese frontier. Writing from his camp on its shores, on the 20th of July, he gives the following picture of the scenery:

"It is altogether about eighty miles long, but only four or five miles wide. The color of its water, the shape of its mountains, the climate (at this moment), everything almost, reminds me of the Lake of Geneva. But there is one great exception to be made: there is not one blade of green! For the distant mountain view this does not make much difference. The purples and blues remain the same. But, for the nearer view the alteration is most striking. Instead of the green vineyards and trees of Lausanne and Vevay you have a great sloping plain of gravelly white sand, with less grass than on a well-trodden gravel walk. This slopes down on the left from a little snowy range (little only because it rises from such a prodigious altitude) whose glaciers come down to within a few hundred feet of this plain. Some of them are bright and sugary like the Glacier des Bossons (a rare sight in the Himâlaya). One of them runs down between its dark *moraine* sides, like an old gentleman's white shirt-frill. Three times to-day we have seen grass, and our camp is actually at a village, where a glacier stream is made with great trouble to fertilize a few acres of ground. The lake being brackish, although beautifully clear and deep blue, does not produce any grass on its banks.

"Four or five days ago we crossed the Upper Indus (north-eastward). With great difficulty, I saved all my things from a wetting; for the men were up to their necks in water crossing, and the current strong. I lashed my loads on the top of two parallel tent-poles, which four men carried on their shoulders; four other men assisted these at each crossing, and so in the course of four or five hours we managed the job. I had to wade and swim across, sending my clothes on the top of the loads. The stream was only fifty yards across,—rather a contrast with the same river as it passes through the Punjab and Sinde, where during the floods it is ten miles wide! Have you noticed what a curious course it has? It rises in the mysterious and sacred lake of Mansorawâr, near the source of the great Brahmapootra. It runs north-west for many hundred miles before its course becomes known. It continues in the same direction through Ladâk and Baltistan, after which it again enters a mysterious and unexplored country, where it entirely changes its direction, emerging at Attock, with a south-westerly course through the Punjab and Sinde. It is very curious knowing little bits of a river, while the rest is altogether unknown."

A week later, Mr. Shaw met Dr. Cayley, then British Resident at Leh, who had been exploring the region eastward, as far as the Kuen-Lün range. On returning with him to Leh, which place they reached in the beginning of August, Mr. Shaw found there a Yârkand envoy who was on his way homeward from a mission to Cashmere. Here was an opportunity too auspicious to be neglected. "I mentioned to him," says Mr. Shaw, "that I intended to go as far as the Karakash River, where Dr. Cayley had just been. He said, 'If you come as far as that, you must come on to Yârkand; for how could I report to my King that I had left an Englishman so near his country?' I said that I heard a great report of the justice and greatness of his King, so that I was devoured by a desire to go and witness his virtues for myself, and that I should be very happy to join him (the envoy) in his journey, if he were willing. He said, 'Certainly he would take me.' Afterwards, I had another private talk with him. I said that perhaps my best plan would be to ask permission of his King first, and, for that purpose, to send my agent with him. He replied, 'Khoob ast' ('It is good'); and promised that an answer should reach me at Leh in forty days. After giving him and his suite some tea to drink, I again said, 'Then I will consider it settled that my servant goes with you, if that be your pleasure.' He turned round, and clapped my man on the back in a hearty way, saying, 'Of course, it is my pleasure—he is my brother.' Since then he has desired my man, Diwân Bakhsh, to be in readiness to accompany him; so I trust that is settled. I intend to send with him some presents for the King and other chiefs there, in order to procure permission for myself to follow. The envoy, I hear, has just sent off a letter to his master, saying that an Englishman (myself) whom he had met at Lahore when he went down to visit the Lord-Sahib (the Governor of the Punjab) had now come to Ladâk, and had asked to be allowed to go with him to Yârkand; but that he had refused permission until his Highness's pleasure was known!"

The Yârkand envoy left Leh on the 28th of August. Mr. Shaw's agent, Diwân Baksh, accompanied him, bearing a letter and presents for Mohammad Yakoob, the new ruler of Central Asia. It now only remained to make the necessary preparations for the journey, and then follow, in the expectation of receiving permission to proceed, on reaching the Yârkand frontier. The chief difficulty was to procure means of transport for the goods and supplies. The carrying trade between Ladâk and Yârkand is in the hands of a set of half-breeds, called argoons, who own some miserable, half-starved ponies, for which they demand exorbitant hire. The fact that Mr. Shaw, as a stranger, might be unfavorably received in Yârkand, enabled these men to practise all sorts of imposition upon him. Those who had good horses, after making him agree to pay an enormous price for them, would finally start away without a word of explanation, with some other employer; while those who had skeletons of horses, or no horses at all, eagerly entered into agreements which they were utterly unable to fulfil. The Yârkand merchants always make the journey with their own horses, and Mr. Shaw's better plan would have been to buy, had it been possible at that time to obtain good animals.

"All these troubles," he says, "I will leave to the imagination, merely saying that I did not start from Leh until the 20th of September, being compelled to trust the greater part of the goods to the tender mercies of an Argoon named 'Momin' (the faithful one), who promised to start after me in eight or ten days when his horses should be ready. The native Governor of Ladâk promised to give the man guides to take him by the new route which I was going to try. The Governor also gave me an order on several villages near the Pangong Lake for ponies, which, according to the custom of the country, the villagers are bound to hire out to travellers at fixed rates. This determination I had come to when I found I could not get enough horses from the Argoons to carry both the goods and also my own camp and baggage. I thought I could shift for myself, and secure ponies from the villagers better than the servant in charge of the goods could do.

"Just before starting a companion offered himself for the journey. Mr. Thorp, who had formerly been in the 98th Regiment, and had recently been travelling about in Tibet, hearing that I was starting for Yârkand, volunteered to go with me. For the moment I accepted the offer, but afterwards, on consulting with friends who had the best means of judging, I was advised that it would be over rash to take a companion. I had spoken to the envoy only about myself; I had written to the King only in my own name; and now, if a second Englishman were to appear with me on the frontier, the suspicion of these Asiatics would be deeply aroused. Mr. Thorp, with great good-nature, gave in to these reasons, and consented to abandon his intention of accompanying me—preferring to do that rather than risk the failure o my expedition.

"At this time I also heard a report that another Englishman, of the name of Hayward, was on his way up with the intention of attempting to reach Yârkand. I wrote him a letter on the chance of its catching him in Cashmere, urging the same reasons against his coming which had already prevailed with Mr. Thorp."

The progress of the expedition was at first very slow. On account of the difficulties of obtaining serviceable ponies from the country people, Mr. Shaw was six days in reaching Chagra, at the head of the Pangong Lake. He was obliged to use yaks as beasts of burden; since in addition to the stock of goods, it was necessary to carry flour and parched barley for the men, and barley for the horses, for two months in advance, and to take along a small flock of sheep. A seal was placed upon the forelocks of all the ponies, to prevent their being exchanged for worse animals. The grain and flour were also sealed up in sacks, and arrangements were made for serving out on each successive Sunday the provision for the ensuing week. The sacks were to be afterwards carefully re-sealed with Mr. Shaw's own signet-ring. This was necessary in order to prevent pilfering and waste, which might prove fatal in such a desert as he was entering upon.

While halting at Chagra, and making final preparations, a message came from the agent, Diwân Baksh, instructing Mr. Shaw that he ought to be at Shahidoolla, on the Yârkand frontier, in one month from the time of writing. "This (Chagra) is the place," Mr. Shaw writes, where I had met Dr. Cayley on his return from exploring the new route onwards, while I had traversed that part of it which goes direct to British India without passing through Ladâk. My journey hence to Ladâk, and back again, had been a mere surplusage, caused by the necessity of making the arrangements detailed above. So from this point we resume the new direct route from India to Yârkand, which it is hoped will come into use more and more, to the exclusion of the old and more difficult route through Lâdak, and over the Karakoram Pass, which merchants had hitherto been compelled to use by the Cashmere officials.

"Leaving Chagra, the last Tibetan encampment, on the 29th September, we crossed the high but very gradual and easy pass of Masimik on the 30th, and entered Chang-chenmo.* This district consists of open downs and plains at an elevation of

* Chang-chenmo means "Great-Northern (River.)"

about 14,000 or 15,000 feet. The small stream which drains it runs eventually westward into the great Shayok River, which is one of the sources of the Indus. At the head of the Shayok River, and separated from us by enormous mountains, is the Karakoram Pass (the old route into Yârkand). From the Karakoram Pass the Shayok runs nearly directly south towards Ladâk, but, meeting a great range of mountains (one of the sides of the Ladâk Valley), turns off abruptly westward, and runs for a dozen marches parallel to the Indus, and only separated from it by this great range, which it finally bursts through, joining the main Indus in Baltistân.

"Having thus traced down the Chang-chenmo River into the Shayok, and the Shayok into the Indus, we will resume our march, which takes us up the Chang-chenmo instead of down it. In this valley I stayed till the 16th of October; waiting for the faithless Argoon with my remaining things from Ladâk, and also giving time to my Moonshee, Diwân Bakhsh, to accomplish his negotiation at Yârkand. I employed my time in shooting wild yak (a magnificent sort of wild cattle, twice the size of the tame ones used in Tibet), and also in exploring the heads of the various valleys to discover the easiest way northward.

"The character of the Chang-chenmo Valley is a wide, smooth, shingly bed, amidst which the stream meanders from side to side. It is bordered by small cliffs of clay or conglomerate, sometimes several of them in tiers one above the other, divided by wide terraces, especially at the embouchures of side streams. Above these terraces rise the barren mountain sides. The soil is absolutely bare."

While waiting for the goods and ponies from Leh, on the high plains of Chang-chenmo, Mr. Shaw first received a letter from the other traveller, Hayward, saying that he was sent by the Geographical Society, and must continue his journey ; and, immediately afterwards, came the announcement that Hayward had actually arrived, and was encamped near him. On the 14th of October the two met. "We dined together," says Shaw, "and talked over plans. He said that the Geographical Society had commissioned him to explore the route through Chitrâl (far away to the west on the borders of Kâbul), and to try and reach the Pamir Steppes. The frontier war which had just broken out led him to try the more easterly route through Ladâk, hoping to get permission at Yârkand to visit the Pamir Steppes. He proposed going in the character of an Afghan, having brought a complete Afghan dress, and having discarded most of the marks of European nationality, such as tents, &c. After some consultation, and seeing that I was going in the character of an Englishman, he determined to do so also. Indeed, it would require a most perfect acquaintance both with the Afghan language, and also with the Mohammedan religious ceremonial (an acquaintance only to be obtained by years of expatriation), to pass muster as an Afghan in a bigoted Mussulman country, which swarms with Afghan merchants and soldiers.

"The question then remained whether we should go together or not. On consideration it seemed better that I should appear on the frontier first and alone, in accordance with the announcement which I had sent on before. For if, after asking permission for one Englishman to enter, two were suddenly to appear together, suspicions would be aroused, and they would probably turn both of us back. It was determined, therefore, that I should go on before, trusting to the effect of my presents and letter for admission, while Hayward should follow shortly after in the hope that they would not turn him back after admitting me. If I saw an opportunity, I was to do what I could to obtain admission for him. This seemed the best solution of the difficulty caused by the unfortunate coincidence of our two attempts.

"Meanwhile, Hayward determined to explore the head of the Chang-chenmo Valley for a possibly better route in that direction."

On the 16th, Hayward started on his way, and Shaw on his, following the track of the Yarkand envoy up a long ravine to the eastward. After some miles he came to a cliff rising thirty feet perpendicularly from the bed of the stream. Here Adolf Schlagintweit, on his way to Yarkand in 1857, had built a very steep and sloping path, but there was great difficulty in getting the ponies to the top. The same day the expedition met some of the Envoy's men, returning with the horses he had hired. They gave Shaw a letter, *without date*, from his agent, saying that he would find somebody to receive him at Shahidoolla in a month *from date!*

The next day, following the dry bed of the stream, they reached the summit of the Pass. The view to the south, very broad and stormy, embraced ranges of mountains, streaked with glaciers: to the north stretched a flat table-land, scarcely lower than the Pass itself, which was about 19,000 feet above the sea. "Tashee (one of the attendants) and I walked on to keep ourselves warm, but, halting at sunset, had to sit and freeze for several hours before the things came up. The best way of keeping warm on such an occasion is to squat down, kneeling against a bank, resting your head on the bank, and nearly between your knees. Then tuck your overcoat in all around you, over head and all; and if you are lucky, and there is not too much wind, you will make a little atmosphere of your own inside the covering which will be snug in comparison with the outside air. Your feet suffer chiefly, but you learn to tie yourself into a kind of knot, bringing as many surfaces of your body together as possible. I have passed whole nights in this kneeling position and slept well; whereas I should not have got a wink had I been stretched at full length with such a scanty covering as a great coat. At last the camp arrived. We had brought a little fuel with us, and melted some ice for water. No grass at all for the cattle.

"The next day I breakfasted as usual while camp

was breaking up. We travelled through the high downs till we reached a little plain, bounded on the further side by a sandy ridge, and then crossed this plain northwards. My Mussulman table-servant, Kabeer, was here quite done up with the rarity of the air at this great elevation, so I gave him my pony to ride. We ascended the sandy slope at the end (almost 100 feet high), and then saw another immense plain at our feet, about 400 feet lower than our own level. This has been christened by the Tibetans who have crossed it, 'Lingzee-tang.' To the east and west of it snowy mountains loomed in the distance, peering up over the edge of the plain like ships at sea that are hull-down. In front of us to the north, it was bounded far away by a long sandy ridge with the tops of smaller hills showing over it. Descending into this plain, we encamped about five miles out on it, under the lee of a small clayey rise. The soil is all clay, covered with flinty stones and rough agates. Not a vestige of grass; but a little fuel in the shape of the *lavender-plant*, as it may be called. This consists of a little bunch of shoots, three or four inches high, looking like lavender. These little bunches are scattered about seven or eight yards apart, or more. They have a woody root, much more substantial than might be imagined from their insignificant appearance above ground; and these roots are a perfect God-send to the traveller. His men go out with little picks and dig them up, but it takes several hours, even where they are most plentiful, before a man can collect enough to light a fire with. The shoots are sometimes eaten by famishing horses, and to a certain extent stay their hunger where there is no grass, as here. So late in the season there was no water anywhere on this plain, but we found a few patches of snow, and melted enough to cook with and drink. There was not, however, fuel enough to melt any for the horses to drink, and they had for many days to content themselves with munching snow to allay their thirst.

"The 20th brought a lovely morning to cross the plain. We marched straight for the opening between two hills which I called the 'dome' and the 'chorten' (a common Tibetan monument), from their shapes. Kabeer, as yesterday, was constantly lagging behind and lying down. I stopped the caravan for him, and made him keep up. He said, as an excuse, that neither his father nor his grandfather had been in such a country. There was really no reason to lag, within a mile of the start, as the walking was good and there was no cold to speak of. Of course the great elevation has its effect. But my Guddee servants (the Guddees are a hardy and primitive race of hill men, living on the Kangra Mountains, who make capital and faithful servants), were swearing at the flatness of the plain and wishing for mountains again. Lots of mirage, but no real signs of water. After several hours across the plain we came to the rising ground about 100 feet high. Another flat on the top, then a descent into the mouths or upper ends of a lot of rocky-sided valleys. Took one leading to the right of the 'dome,' and camped about a mile down it near a rock. Fearfully cold wind : almost impossible to pitch the tents : a real hurricane, blowing the concentrated essence of east winds. Managed to get something to eat and get to bed. *Third* night of no grass for the cattle. We give the ponies barley, but the yaks refuse it."

The next day the expedition reached Lak-zung, or the Eagle's Nest, a name given to the valley leading down northward from the lofty plateau they had just crossed. Although the elevation was still 16,000 feet above the sea, there was a little grass to be had for the famished animals. On the top of a lofty granite rock near the camping-place, there was an ancient eagle's nest, below which the ground was covered with the horns and bones of antelopes, killed by past generations of eagles to feed their young. Mr. Shaw saw a male Tibetan antelope, with lyre-shaped horns, but his hands were so numb that he was unable to pull the trigger. At this place he was detained four days, in order to rest and recruit the animals. The cold was intense and the winds were so fierce and keen that even the natives suffered from their exposure. It was impossible to write, as the ink instantly froze in the pen.

On the 26th the expedition started again, and after a long day's march, over a plain slightly descending to the northward, reached a small lake of ice, at a place called Tarldatt. Here Shaw was delayed another day, on account of his Hindoo servant, Kabeer, having lagged behind with some of the animals. Both yaks and ponies now began to show signs of giving out, and the marches became very short and wearisome to all. Beyond Tarldatt extended the same desolate region, but with patches of grass in the hollows. The uplands were beds of salt or soda. "Above is a very thin cake of earth, below which the foot sinks into the finest loose powdered soda, pure white, four or five inches deep. Below this is a sheet of impure common salt and saltpetre, which you can hear crack like thin ice under fresh snow, as you walk. In many places the coat of earth is absent, and the soda is hard and irregular. It was horrible walking for five hours over it; although we saw our halting-place from the first, we never seemed to approach it."

Finally, on the 30th of October, the soda plain gave place to a narrow valley, bounded by a broken granite ridge on its north-eastern side. Beyond this ridge was the valley of the Karakash, one of the six rivers of Central Asia. It flows past the walls of Khoten, and finally loses itself in the sands of the great Desert of Lob. Over the hills beyond the river rose the high, snowy peaks of the range now called the Kuen-Lün by European geographers, which was first crossed by the brothers Hermann and Robert Schlagintweit.

By this time several of the yaks had been left behind, but most fortunately, two which had been abandoned by the Yarkând envoy's party, and had entirely recruited themselves on the meadows of the Karakash, were caught and made to do service.

The cattle all drank of the river, breaking the slushy ice with their feet. This was their first drink of water in fifteen days: since leaving the Chang-chenmoo they had quenched their thirst with snow.

"Beyond the point we had now reached, none of my men had gone. We were thus quite ignorant where we should find grass or wood, or how long to make our marches. It often depends on the distance of the next grazing ground whether you will encamp after a certain number of hours' marching, or continue. This is especially the case with exhausted cattle, for if the next place is near, it will not hurt them to go on, but if far, you would for their sake rest contented with your progress for that day. But we now had to do without such facilities. I had to feel the way by riding on ahead of the caravan, and towards evening surveying the route before us from some high point. The Karakash here has a broad valley quite flat and half a mile wide. The dry and shingly bed of what is sometimes a stream occupies the centre, with low terraces on either side, the barren mountains rising north and south of the valley, which itself runs westward. Anxiously I looked forward as each new vista opened out; every side-valley I examined with care. Imagine my horror, as the afternoon advanced, to find that this sterile soil did not supply even the *lavender-plant* for fuel, which had not hitherto failed us. Grass I entirely despaired of finding, and the bed of the stream was dry! The three great requisites for a traveller's camping-ground were all absent—fuel, grass, and water! Evening was beginning to close when I reached a high bed of shingle and *débris* which issued from a ravine on the north, and closed the view down the main valley. I mounted this to get a view, and at the lower end of a small plain I distinguished a dark strip of ground. Hope began to revive, but I could hardly believe that I saw bushes! However, my glass showed them distinctly, and, what was more, there was a glimmer of white ice visible amongst them. I pushed on, and after a seemingly interminable stretch of level in the valley I reached the first bushes that I had seen for a month. There was a horrible wind blowing up the valley, but I picked out a sheltered spot under a bank, collected a lot of dry branches for a fire (how often had I shivered and longed for this moment in the cold plains above!) and sat down to wait. After waiting an hour, I began to fear that the caravan might pass me in the dark, so I commenced shouting. No reply. At last my pony showed signs of hearing something on the opposite side. I rode across, and presently was answered. They had actually passed me. Now, however, it was all right. I took them to my sheltered nook, and presently we had such a glorious blaze as gladdened our hearts. We found that the ice I had seen was on the banks of a stream of water,* which came in through a narrow

* Mr. Hayward afterwards struck the head of this stream about eighty miles up, and followed it down to this spot. He proved it to be the real head of the Karakash River, and that it offers a better route than that which I had taken across the high plains.—*Shaw*.

gorge from the left or south side of the valley, and filled the hitherto dry bed of the main valley. I had thoughts of exploring up this gorge the next day, as its stream seemed more important than that which I had come down. But it was necessary for the cattle's sake to push on to some grass."

The next day the temperature rose to 40°, and the Karakash flowed freely between borders of ice. The blood of man and beast, which had almost congealed in the icy winds of the terrible heights, began to thaw again ; brushwood for fuel continued abundant, and grass increased until it became a thick turf. For five or six days more they followed the valley, until a break in the mountain-range to the northward (a spur of the Kuen-Lün) announced the point where the Karakash turns eastward and descends to the warm plains of Khoten. Every day some of the yaks left by the Envoy's party were picked up, until there were nine fresh animals to replace those which had fallen by the way. The physical difficulties in the way of the expedition were now over, but the more serious moral obstacles were yet to be overcome.

CHAPTER XI.

DETENTION AT THE FRONTIER.

SHAW'S account of his arrival at the frontier of the Yarkând country, and his reception there, is so animated and picturesque that it must be given in his own words, written on the spot:

"I am now writing in my tent, which is pitched on the flat roof of a little fort on the Karakash River. It consists of a lot of little rooms, surrounding a court-yard, into which they open. A little parapet of sun-dried bricks with loopholes for muskets runs round the outer edge of this flat roof, while at the corners little round towers, also loopholed, command the four sides. This primitive fort stands in the centre of a little shingly plain. The Karakash, a small trout-stream, runs past a few hundred yards off, fringed with low bushes, while all around rise the barren rocky mountains. Inside is a more cheerful scene. A group of Moghul* soldiers are sitting round a fire at one end of the court-yard, which is not above fifteen yards long. Their long matchlock guns hang

* Moghul is the name given in India to natives of Central Asia. I learnt afterwards to call them, as they called themselves, "Toork."

KIRGHIZ MOTHER.

from the wall behind them, twelve in number; three or four high-peaked saddles are ranged above them. The dress of the Moghuls consists of a long robe fastened round the waist, with very wide trowsers below. The officers' robes are made of a stuff half silk, half cotton, with large patterns in very bright colors. Some of the men wear dull red Yârkandee cloth, some of them English printed calico, and some white felt ; there is no uniformity. Some tuck the long robe into the wide trowsers, some wear a second robe, open in front and loose at the waist, over all. The chiefs have on their heads a conical cap, with a turban tied round it. The men mostly have lambskin caps. One of the two officers is now fitting a fresh match into his gun; the rest are looking on, or cooking their food in one of the rooms. Meanwhile they talk a language harsh and guttural, in which the consonants are constantly clashing. My 'Bhôts' from Ladâk sit reverentially in the distance, rubbing the skins of the sheep we have killed by the way. The Moghuls treat them kindly, but as if they were animals of some sort, monkeys for instance. They call them *Tibetee*, a name which I have hitherto heard used only by the Europeans. My Indian servants keep out of the way ; they don't know what to make of our hosts, and are more than half afraid of them. As for me, they and I are the greatest of friends. In a short time, I shall be going down to entertain the officers at my four o'clock tea. We sit over my fire, and drink an endless succession of cups of tea together, eating my biscuits, and trying to converse. Now, as three days ago, my knowledge of Toorkee was confined to the word 'yok,' *no*, which I had picked up in Atkinson's book, and as they know no Persian, and, of course, no Hindostanee, we have to make up by smiles and signs for our lack of common words. The rifles, the watch, the compass, the revolver, are, unfortunately, exhausted subjects now, so we come to actual conversation. I have picked up a lot of Toorkee (there is no master of languages like the absence of interpreters), and we talk about peace and war, geography and history; what could the most skilful linguists do more? I will tell you presently what news I have gathered from them. At first their great delight was to get me to fire my breech-loader. They used to put a mark about thirty paces off, and were greatly astonished at my always hitting it. They are just like public schoolboys, of boisterous spirits, but perfectly well bred. They will clap me on the back, and call me a good fellow when I send for more sugar for their tea; but when I pass their fire, they will all rise and bow with their hand on their heart; this is their mode of salaaming. The man who clapped me on the back surprised me the next minute by stroking his beard with both hands, and exclaiming, 'Ameen, Allaho-Akber' (Amen, God is great). All the assembly chimed in with Allaho-Akber, solemnly stroking their beards. This was 'grace after meat.'

"As day dawns, I hear one of them intoning the 'Arise and pray, arise and pray, prayer is better than sleep.' Yesterday two of the soldiers had their hands tied in front of them, their clothes were stripped from their shoulders, and they were ferociously lashed by one of the officers with his whip, till they were covered with blood. My servants, who saw this, asked the reason ; they were told it was because the men did not get up early to say their prayers. The same evening one of these two men was singing Toorkee songs, to which accompaniment two others were dancing before the fire. I joined the party, and was fed with Yârkand walnuts by one of the officers. The two dancers wound in and out, keeping time with a beat of the feet and a *chassé*, and slowly waving their arms. When tired, they bowed to the assembly and sat down.

"Meanwhile, you don't know whether I have been taken prisoner in a foray by Yakoob Beg's soldiers, or how I came to find myself shut up in a fort with a dozen of them ; so I must begin again from where I left off.

"After a wearisome march of six days, altogether, down the same valley, without any incidents worth notice, on the morning of the sixth day, shortly after leaving our camp (which was in a fine meadow of really luxuriant grass, produced by the numerous arms into which the stream branched), we came upon a spot where a large flock of sheep had evidently been penned. This sign of the former presence of men put us all on the *qui vive*, as we were utterly ignorant what reception we might meet with should we come across any of the wandering tribes of shepherds that frequent these mountains. All we knew was that certain nomads, calling themselves Kirghiz, had formerly rendered the more westerly road to Yârkand unsafe by their depredations (the name ot Kirghiz Jungle is still retained by the spot which they haunted), and that tribes of the same name occasionally brought their sheep up the valley of the Karakash. However, the sheepfold was ot last year, and did not denote any recent visit. But later in the day, as I rode on before the caravan, the fresh print of a man's foot struck my eye. It was on a soft piece of earth, after which the path was hard and stony. I was thus unable at once to verify my impression, and thought I must have been deceived. A little further on, however, the footmark was again visible by the side of a horse's track. I could not help laughing as I thought ot Robinson Crusoe and *his* footprint. Mine, however, was not such a portentous sign, although it was sufficient to inspire caution; for there was every possibility that, if the Kirghiz were in force, they might attempt to plunder us, and on none of my servants could I depend in a scrimmage, even to load for me; at the least, our journey might be interrupted. Therefore, when we came to the end of the open plain in which we were travelling, and the valley narrowed at a projecting point, I halted the caravan, and went on myself on foot to spy. Scrambling over the hill, I soon came to a ridge which commanded a view down the valley. Carefully, as when stalking game, I raised my head, and a minute's inspection through my glass showed me a grassy plain, sprinkled with bushes, and in the middle a Kirghiz 'yourt.' There was no mistaking it after reading Atkinson's books. A circular structure, with a low dome-shaped roof, covered with a dirty-white material, evidently felt. Around it were tethered four or five horses and yaks, while the glass showed a man in a long tunic and high boots, busied in attendance on the cattle. From the centre of the roof a light cloud of smoke was escaping.

"I can't describe to you my sensations at beholding this novel scene. I felt that I had now indeed begun my travels. Now, at length, my dreams of Toorks and Kirghiz were realized, and I was coming into contact with tribes and nations hitherto entirely cut off from intercourse with Europeans. I drew carefully back and rejoined my caravan. After a short consultation, we determined to go and encamp alongside of the yourt; as we must pass the Kirghiz, and our halting short of them, though so near, would be ascribed to fear if they discovered our camp. Loading all the rifles, four in number, we set out again. I was amused to see my Hindostanee table-servant Kabeer, who had hitherto caused endless trouble by lagging behind, now, with scared face, keep himself close to my horse's tail, as I rode on in advance of the caravan. The Kirghiz was so busy at his occupation that he did not see me till I was within twenty yards of his yourt. At the sound of my voice, he turned round, and, apparently without astonishment, came forward smilingly to meet me. A second man now came out of the yourt. We could only at first say 'salâm,' and smile at one another ; but he told me that he was a Kirghiz, and we thought we understood from him that there were some soldiers of the King waiting for me at Shahidoolla. This would account for his non-surprise at what must have been our strange appearance to him. Both the Kirghiz were quite young fellows, apparently brothers, with fine rosy complexions, about as dark as a bronzed Englishman. A woman presently appeared, but kept in the background. She was rather pretty, and wore a strip of white cotton-cloth wound round her head, quite evenly, to a considerable thickness, like a roll of white tape. A long streamer of the same cloth, ornamented with a colored pattern, hung down her back. Her dress was a long tunic, girt round the waist like the men's, and reaching nearly to the ankles, which displayed a pair of high red leather boots. The men's tunics or robes were shorter, and their head-dress a fur cap with ear-lappets.

"Here I encamped ; the Kirghiz good-humoredly assisting in the erection of the tent, lighting a fire for me, &c. Presently arrived a large flock of sheep, with another Kirghiz, in a long sheep and ibex skin robe. My Guddee servants, themselves shepherds by birth, estimated the flock at over a thousand. The sheep resemble those of parts of Afghanistan, having large flat tails. When the lambs had been brought out, and given to their mothers, the three Kirghiz retired into the yourt.

KIRGHIZ MAN.

Thence they emerged again, and came up to me bringing a present of a sheep and a huge skinful of butter. These were most thankfully accepted, and the sheep immediately killed ; the butter was excellent. I gave them, in return, some English powder, with a looking-glass for the young lady, at which they were delighted.

"The next morning, very early, I sent off two of my Ladâk men down the valley to Shahidoolla, which the Kirghiz said was near. Shahidoolla is the place where I had appointed that a messenger should meet me with a letter from Diwân Bakhsh (the Mussulman whom I had sent on before me to ask permission of the King for me to enter his country). There is no village ; it is merely a camping-ground on the regular old route between Ladâk and Yârkand, and the first place where I should strike that route. Four years ago, while the troubles were still going on in Toorkistân, the Maharaja of Cashmere sent a few soldiers and workmen across the Karakoram range (his real boundary), and built a small fort at Shahidoolla. This fort his troops occupied during two summers; but last year, when matters became settled, and the whole country united under the King of Yârkand, these troops were withdrawn.

"However, leaving such matters, I will continue my story. While I was at breakfast, arrived two Moghul soldiers from Shahidoolla. We could not converse, but I looked at their guns, and gave them some tea ; after this they departed. In the afternoon, three other Moghul horsemen arrived, dressed in finer clothes, consisting of long robes of bright colors, one above the other, wide trowsers, and turbans tied over pointed silk caps. I made them sit down, and gave them tea (an unfailing part ot the ceremony). The Kirghiz (with whom our acquaintance was but a few hours older) acted as interpreters, by signs and by means of a few words of Toorkee which I had picked up from them. They made me exhibit all my curiosities, the breech-loading rifles, the revolver, the spy-glass, the watch, &c., &c. When these prodigies had been duly wondered at, they explained to me that one of the three was going to ride off immediately to Yârkand to announce my arrival to the King, and that I must give him a token of some kind, or a letter. I accordingly wrote a short note to his majesty in *English* (distrusting my Persian writing), and, having put it in a pink envelope, sealed with my ring (bearing my full name in Persian characters), delivered it to the messenger. Immediately all three mounted, and started off at a gallop, bearing my best wishes for their speedy journey.

"This was Sunday, the 8th November. Next day I halted again, to allow the yaks to catch us up. These animals, carrying our supply of flour, &c., were, as usual, a day or two behindhand, and the week's allowance of food was now due to the whole party. In the afternoon, the yaks having arrived, the flour was distributed; and on Tuesday morning we marched down to Shahidoolla. Here we were received by two of our friends of Sunday, who were in command of a detachment of about a dozen soldiers. We were most civilly treated, the best rooms in the fort given up to us (you must remember the fort much resembles an English pigstye, and not picture to yourself apartments of Oriental luxury). I was told that they had been stationed here by the King nearly a month ago, to await my arrival, with orders to treat me as an honored guest, and see that I wanted for nothing. Before proceeding further, however, I must await the orders of the King in answer to the news of my actual arrival. The messenger, they said, would reach Yârkand on relays of horses in three days, and return in the same time, so that I should be detained about a week. I resigned myself to this fate, and during the next day or two tried to improve the occasion by learning a lot of Toorkee words. It was really rather amusing to work out the meaning of words, and build quite a vocabulary out of a most slender beginning. Men and officers all joined in explaining their meaning, and guessing at mine; they showed considerable cleverness in this, and I progressed rapidly.

"By Thursday, however, I begun to get very tired of my detention, and proposed a wild-yak hunt. I understood that these animals were to be found within a day's march of Shahidoolla. Allowing a day for hunting, we should be back just in time for the return of the messenger. Next morning the two officers and three or four men and I started to ride up one of the side valleys. We ate our mid-day meal together (consisting of Yârkandee biscuits), and were so fortunate as to espy a herd of sixteen wild cattle shortly after noon. Leaving our horses at the proposed camping-ground, we started to stalk our game. But a horseman was seen galloping towards us; the glass showed that he was a Moghul, and as he approached, he shouted to us to come back. When he reached us, he announced that some great man from Yârkand had arrived to fetch me; that he had turned back the cattle, carrying my tent, &c., and we must return at once.

"Delighted at the news, I mounted, and away we galloped down the valley, reaching Shahidoolla in less than half the time we had taken coming. At the gate a soldier in fine clothes was mounting guard (a thing they had not done before, nor, in fact, did they do it afterwards). When I entered the court-yard, a dignified Moghul, in a long silken robe, and wearing a silver-mounted sabre, was sitting in solitary grandeur on a carpet before the fire. He did not rise at my approach, but motioned to me to sit down by his side. This I did, and tried to address him in Persian. He shook his head, and after this seemed to pay no further attention to me, talking loudly with the others, who were now allowed to sit down on the other side of the fire. I was rather nettled at this treatment, and presently got up and walked to the other end of the court-yard, where I had another fire lit. As I rose, the great man got up, and made signs to me that he was going to say his prayers (by putting his hands behind his ears, which is a gesture frequently repeated during their devotions). Sure enough, he said them three times within the next hour. I suppose during the journey he had been unable to perform his full number daily.

"My first friends saw that I was displeased, and, after a whispered consultation, one of them came and sat down by my fire to explain matters. This officer, he said, was a very great man, who always sat before the King. He had been sent to meet us in the capacity of Mihmandâr (or welcomer of guests), to show me honor, and supply all my wants. Presently we discovered that an old man who had come with the Mihmandâr from Sanjoo (a frontier town), had some knowledge of Tibetan. Conversation immediately became easy, for I had with me a Tibetan interpreter named Tashee, a most useful fellow. The great man sent to say that he wished to pay me a visit in private, if I would spread a carpet in my room. The carpet was accordingly spread and a candle lit, and in came the Mihmandâr. At this visit, and at a still more formal one which he paid me the next morning after breakfast, he loaded me with civilities of an Eastern sort, presenting me with about a dozen trays of fruits of different kinds (pomegranates, dried raisins, 'Pistachio' nuts, &c.), together with a loaf of Russian sugar, while a couple of sheep, after much pushing and shoving, were made to show their faces at the door. Many complimentary speeches followed in the name of his King. I was to have no trouble or care; whatever I wished for, I had only to mention; he would procure anything

I desired. All his men and horses were at my disposal. I replied that my chief feeling was gratitude at the condescension of the King in sending such a very great man to meet me; and my chief care was at the inconvenience which he was suffering in coming to such a desolate spot. Compliments, I believe, can never be too fulsome for Orientals; they require them strong and highly flavored.

"Then followed a series of questions as to my profession, whether I was a soldier or a merchant, the number of horseloads of goods that were following me, when they would arrive, how many loads I had with me, what they could consist of, as they were not merchandise, &c., &c. Every now and then the series of questions was broken to assure me that, in any case, I need be under no apprehensions, for the King's orders were to welcome me, whoever I might be. I thought to myself, you must be very guileless yourselves to imagine that I could be caught in such a trap. If I were assuming a false character, it is not likely that such assurances, coupled with such anxious questioning, would induce me to reveal myself without disguise. As, however, I had nothing to conceal, my only fear was lest my servants, with Indian abhorrence of truth, should tell unnecessary lies in my absence; for I felt sure they would be carefully cross-examined. When, therefore, the great man had taken his leave (this time he politely motioned to me not to rise from my seat), I called them all together, and pointed out to them that we were all in the same boat, to sink or to swim, and that our success and safety depended greatly on our present conduct. I therefore cautioned them against talking more than they could help about our own affairs; but what they did say must be the exact truth. Thus only could we be sure of all telling the same story when separately questioned, and of not being caught giving different versions. Of my Guddees I have not much fear, but the others are by birth and education liars. When doubtful of the intentions of a questioner, or afraid of vague ill-consequences, they naturally seek for safety in untruth, as a wild beast does in darkness. It is a simple and artless precaution, singularly inappropriate in our present circumstances. The Moghuls are devoured with suspicion. The unheard-of event of an Englishman arriving on their borders seems to have put them out of all their calculations. Not a day passes but one or more horsemen arrive and depart with orders or messages. Never has this road been so much trodden, never has Shahidoolla witnessed such animation.

"And this reminds me of my chief source of anxiety, the incubus that constantly weighs upon me. If their suspicions and fears are thus excited by the arrival of *one* Englishman who had announced his visit and explained his intentions long before, what will they not imagine when he is suddenly joined by a fellow-countryman without ostensible object, though really bent upon surveying their country? Yet this I am daily expecting.

"I have been very much delayed on the road by the badness of my cattle, and I am now being detained day after day at Shahidoolla. Hayward must have been delayed also, or he would have arrived before this. His sudden appearance would have the worst effect on the minds of the Moghuls, and I should come in for my share of extra suspicion as having arranged the meeting. As one of my Guddees says, their first thought will be, 'How many more Feringhees (Franks) are concealed in these valleys?' The simultaneous approach of two Englishmen to Yârkand (never before visited by an Englishman) will at once be magnified into the advance of the pioneers of an invading force.

"Revolving this in my mind, and taking counsel with my Guddee servants, I came to the conclusion that the Moghuls should be told that another Englishman was near. Thus they would not be able to reproach me with practising concealment; for they would certainly find out from his interpreter that we had met before. I therefore called in Tashee, explained the matter to him, and told him to find an opportunity during conversation with the old man of Sanjoo of mentioning that we had met an Englishman shooting wild yak at a distance of twenty days back from Shahidoolla. This did not please my interpreter at all; he could not persuade himself that the safest way out of a difficulty could be to tell the truth. My authority, if not my arguments, prevailed however, and he was soon reconciled to his task by the congenial labor of contriving a good opening for his tale. I let him do this as he liked, and he succeeded admirably. Talking of shooting, and enumerating the game I had shot, he said that Englishmen were mad after sport; that one of them had come ever so many days beyond Ladâk to shoot. As I expected, they jumped at the news. Tashee was asked whether the Sahib was coming any further, but professed utter ignorance as to his intentions.

"The subject was not referred to by the Mihmandâr when I paid him a visit in the afternoon; but two horsemen were sent off to bring news of the Englishman, if he were to be found, and to hurry on my caravan, should they meet with it. I think they are rather anxious to test my veracity in the matter of the caravan, though they profess to be only anxious lest their King should blame them for not bringing the whole of my property with me.

"I have succeeded in breaking the ice of my Mihmandâr's haughtiness. We were sitting on the roof, surveying the mountains through my glass (the old man of Sanjoo asked me gravely whether it would show him his two sons, who are probably some ten days' march distant, on their return from Ladâk). I unscrewed one of the lenses, and as there was a bright sun, I quickly set fire to a piece of tinder. This was quite a prodigy. Amid many ejaculations of 'Tobah! tobah!' (Repentance! repentance!) the Mihmandâr was taught to do the same himself. Immediately he loudly shouted for the whole garrison to come and see ; they crowded up the ladder. His next attempt was, unfortunately, a failure ; but he soon succeeded in burning a big hole in his robe. This was charming. I was immediately challenged to a shooting match. We fired a lot of shots at a mark 200 yards off, which I and my Guddee servants alone succeeded in hitting. He fired several rounds from my rifle ; his own matchlock twice refused to go off until he had removed it from his shoulder.

"This morning he has amused himself cutting the mustachios of half the men in the place with my scissors. All orthodox Mussulmans only let the moustache grow at the two corners of the mouth, removing the hair between ; they also shave the whole head. My Hindostanee servant, who has most heretically allowed his hair to grow long, as all Indian Mussulmans do, had his upper lip trimmed by the Mihmandâr himself, who then sent him out with a sepoy, to remove his too luxuriant locks. I found him sitting with a rueful face under the wall of the fort, while a Moghul standing over him triumphantly wielded the shears. Great was the laughter and applause, in which I cordially joined, for the neatness of my servant's appearance was decidedly improved."

On the 17th of November, the messenger who had been sent on to Yârkand to announce Shaw's arrival at Shahidoolla, returned. He was accompanied by one of the caravan-men, named Jooma, who had been sent with Diwân Bàksh, Shaw's agent, to prepare for his coming. As this man

Jooma spoke Hindostanee, Shaw learned immediately that the pink English letter he had sent to the King, on reaching the frontier, had been forwarded from Yârkand to His Majesty, who was then in the mountains, four days' march beyond Kashghar. The messenger who carried the letter had not waited for a reply, but had immediately returned from Yârkand, bringing large supplies of flour, barley and other articles. The answer of the King would be forwarded by a messenger travelling day and night, as soon as it reached Yârkand, and might be expected at Shahidoolla in two or three days more. Shaw also received a long letter from his agent, and a short note from the Envoy whom the former accompanied, but, as they were written in a close Persian running-hand, he was unable to read them. Nevertheless, his mind was easy; for there was no private signal of danger, which he had instructed his agent to give, by cutting off one of the corners of the letter.

The man Jooma reported that he had overheard a conversation of some of the native officials at Yârkand, in which they agreed that Shaw would probably be allowed to visit the King, Mohammad Yakoob, but that he would be made to wait at the frontier some time before receiving permission to proceed. Shaw thereupon decided to wait two or three days longer, and then, if no permission came, to send off another messenger to the King. The approach of Hayward, which was already reported to the native authorities, gave him great uneasiness, as the appearance of another Englishman at this critical stage of the negotiations might easily arouse their suspicions. On the 18th, Shaw writes:

"Towards evening the Mihmandâr came and sat down by my fire. After other conversation, I introduced the subject of my business with the King; for, on reflection, it struck me that, if I waited till orders came for me to stay at Shahidoolla before I announced this, it would be thought that my object was thereby to escape from detention on the frontier. As soon as the Mihmandâr understood what I said, he at once promised to send off a man in the morning, who should go direct to the King with the news. I trust that I have been wise in taking this step.

"I had further conversations with Jooma. To-day, at his suggestion, I have assumed the full Moghul dress—high black riding-boots, an inner tunic of cotton-silk (given me by the Afghan tea-merchants at Ladâk), a long scarf round the waist; over this I wear a light brown cloth robe, open and loose, while one of the red Cashmere shawls comes in splendidly for a turban. I flatter myself that I look like a dignified Toork; my appearance produces an evident effect on the Mihmandâr; he is several pegs humbler in manner to-day.

"Jooma says the King is in the habit of going about quite alone, *à la* Haroon-ar-Rasheed. He has several times been taken up as a vagabond by his own police. On these occasions, he tries the probity of his capturer by offering a bribe for release. Those who accept the bribe are seized and brought before him next morning, when the least punishment they suffer is a severe scourging. On the contrary, those who have resisted the temptation are honored and promoted."

The very next day news came that Hayward's approach had been announced, and that he had declared himself to be engaged in Shaw's service. The Mihmandâr, whose suspicions were immediately aroused, was about to send off an officer to recall the messenger whom he had dispatched the day before; but the man Jooma declared that Shaw had nothing whatever to do with the other Englishman, beyond meeting him on a shooting excursion. Afterwards the Mihmandâr went to Shaw's tent, whereupon the latter made the same statement to him, and he appeared to be satisfied. The same afternoon eight horse-loads of provisions arrived from Yârkand, with fifteen sheep.

Two days after this Hayward arrived, and the Mihmandâr, whose business was to visit and question him, came to Shaw to procure an interpreter. Shaw gave him the man Jooma, upon whose tact and fidelity he believed he could rely, and the result proved the wisdom of his choice. Hayward began by stating that he was Shaw's partner, which Jooma refused to repeat to the Mihmandâr, but made his own statement, in accordance with Shaw's instructions. The same evening the latter sent a note to Hayward privately, through Jooma, explaining his situation, and urging him to give up the design of going on to Yârkand. The predicament was very embarrassing; but Shaw clearly had the start of Hayward, in all the arrangements which he had made in advance, and could not allow his dearly-bought chances to be imperilled.

On the 21st, good news arrived. The last messenger sent towards Yârkand returned, bringing a letter from the King, which he met at the foot of the Sanjoo Pass. It directed the Mihmandâr to pay every attention to Shaw, as he valued his head, until the arrival of the brother of the Governor of Yârkand, who was coming to escort the traveller into the country. Shaw writes, on the 22nd:

"Our delight is unbounded at the prospect of getting away from here. All the horses were brought up and shod, and four were sent to the Kirghiz camp to bring provisions for the great man and his party. Late in the afternoon, the Mihmandâr and Jooma went over to see Hayward. On their return, the greater part of my guard left the fort and established themselves near his tent. I do not know what this means, as I cannot get hold of Jooma, who is also over there.

"An answer came privately from Hayward, explaining that he must at any rate *try* to get in this way. He wants very much to see me. I wrote back to advise him not to try and see me, but if there were any necessity actually, then to speak to my Mihmandâr, and say he wants to give me a message for the King.

"Before my letter reached Hayward, he did what I recommended in it, not having received my further caution not to do so unless absolutely necessary. The Mihmandâr came to me in the morning, and said, 'The other Sahib wants to speak to you ; what are your orders ?' I answered that there was no advantage in our meeting, and that I had rather not ; what was his advice ? He replied, 'I am here to obey your orders, not to hamper you in any way.' I then said, 'But give me your advice as a friend.' He said, 'Well, then, I think you are quite right.' Finally, I said, 'Ask the Sahib what he wants to talk to me about ; if it is of real importance, I will meet him for five minutes in your presence.' All this I did, so as to give Hayward a chance of taking my advice, and not insisting on seeing me ; while, if he thinks it quite necessary, he can give the reason which I suggested in my letter."

By the 24th of November, Shaw began to be exceedingly weary of waiting. In his journal of that day he says : "I called in the Mihmandâr, and said I could not stand it any longer, but should go off shooting, or else march down to the nearest Kirghiz encampment. He tried to pacify me, and finally agreed that, if no news of the Governor's brother arrived during the next two days, we would begin marching northwards on the third. He came back again shortly, with a peace-offering of fruit. While we were discussing it, an arrival was announced. He rushed out, and presently came back again crying, 'Moobârak ! Moobârak !' 'Good news has come ! You are to start to-morrow to meet the great Mihmandâr, who has brought his camp as far as the Sanjoo Pass !'* Immediately

* The letter which Jooma brought from my secretary is dated 9th November. The first news of my approach had reached Yârkand

all was bustle and preparation. All the servants are as pleased as myself, at leaving this dull spot, and starting again for the goal of our journey."

---

two days before, and my first Mihmandâr was sent off at once. Jooma started on the 9th. Thus news of my approach reached Yârkand on the 7th. If it was not a mere foundationless report, they must have had spies out as far as the head of the Karakash, or further; for I myself did not reach the Kirghiz camp till the 7th, the very day that news of me reached Yârkand.

"I afterwards ascertained the following facts. When the first hint of my intention of coming reached Yârkand, a party of soldiers was sent to Shahidoolla to stop me. When I got nearer, the Mihmandâr was sent for the same purpose, although he amused me with promises of being allowed to proceed. Thirdly, Jooma was sent with a lot of provisions and the secretary's letter (in which, as it appeared afterwards, I was told to go back to Ladâk). Jooma was to conduct me back, and the provisions were sent, lest I should make the want of them an excuse for not returning. It was hoped that I should be tired of waiting, and go back of my own accord. Hence Jooma's hints that I might perhaps be kept at Shahidoolla for two or three months.

"Lastly, when my secretary had produced my letter and presents, the Yoozbashee was sent to meet me; but he delayed so long that it was evident they would have been very glad had I taken their first hint and gone back.

"From this I conclude that, had an Englishman presented himself on their border without explanation and without previous arrangement, he would have been simply turned back; as, in fact, I was at the first."

INTERIOR OF A TURKOMAN TENT.

CHAPTER XII.

THE MARCH TO YARKAND.

THE permission to advance having arrived, and so much more promptly than might have been anticipated, Shaw set out from Shahidoolla in high spirits. "On the 25th of November," he says, "we made a long march down the Karakash. We saw the entrance of two valleys leading to passes over into Toorkistân, the second being that of Kiliân, which is the summer route of the merchants. At the mouth of this side-valley was a ruined fort, perched on an isolated rock rising out of the valley. Round it were traces of old cultivation. I learned that a robber chief named Ali Nazzar had some forty years ago established himself here. He kept his wife with a few attendants in a hut built against the rock some distance away up a valley, and guarded by a ferocious mastiff of the Tartar breed. The Chinese emissaries from Yârkand managed to poison this mastiff, and then seized Ali Nazzar when he was alone with his wife and unprotected. He was thus got rid of, when all attempts to take his fort had failed.

"A third valley or rather gorge, in the north

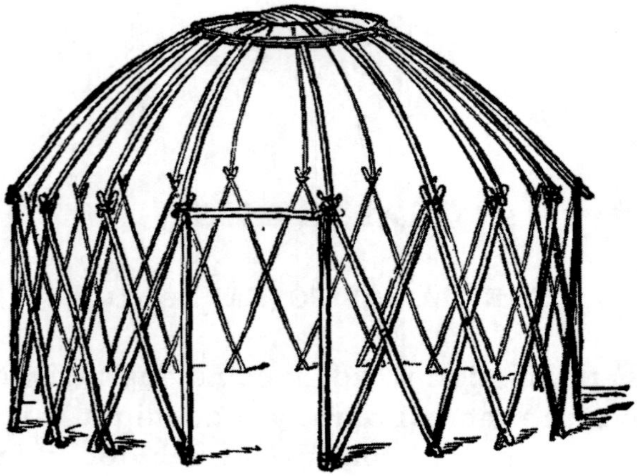

FRAMEWORK OF TENT.

side, was, late in the afternoon, pointed out to me as leading to the Sanjoo Pass. On reaching it, we immediately discovered a group of Kirghiz 'akooees,' or felt tents, snugly pitched in a sheltered nook. In the main valley, a few hundred yards lower down, were several fields of stubble, the barley having lately been reaped. This was a charming sight to eyes accustomed to deserts for so long a time. I was led into one of the 'akooees,' and seated in front of the central fire. Presently, two Kirghiz women came in and began preparing tea for us, which I and my Mihmandâr drank out of wooden bowls, adding some Yârkandee biscuits out of his saddle-bags. Meanwhile a larger 'akooee' was being prepared for me, into which I was ushered. Now, for the first time, I had leisure to examine the structure of these singular tents. You remember those toys made by a kind of trelliswork, which lengthen when open and shorten up when shut. A line of these (with *meshes* nearly a foot wide) are half-opened, and set up on edge in a circle. They compose the side walls of the tent, some four feet high. To the upper edge of these, and at intervals of a foot, a set of curved rods are tied. These have a bend some two feet from the lower end, so that they all eonverge inward, towards the centre, forming the skeleton of a low dome. But they do not meet, for their inner ends are fixed into holes in a large hoop (some three feet across), thus leaving a large opening in the middle of the roof. The hoop is supported by these rods at a height of ten or twelve feet from the ground. A lot of large sheets of felt, cut so as to fit over the different parts of the framework, and sewn round the edges with a cord, are tightly stretched over the whole, and fastened with ropes, leaving only the opening in the middle of the roof for the smoke to escape. The framework of a door is placed in an opening of the side-walls, and a felt curtain hangs before it.

"You cannot conceive a more comfortable dwelling. The satisfaction of seeing the smoke go straight up and away, is inexpressible, after the horrors of a fire in front of one's tent, which, pitch it how you will, is always full of smoke. The Kirghiz have all the comforts of a house in these moveable dwellings. The furniture forms a yak-load, while the 'akooee' itself is carried by two more. Felt carpeting covers the ground, while around are piled bedding for the inmates, wooden

TENT, AS COMPLETED.

vessels of all sorts, large copper caldrons, sacks of flour, saddles, and saddle-cloths. From the framework hang large bags of embroidered leather, in which are placed the smaller household goods, also matchlocks and swords. At night, when the fire goes out, a sheet of felt is drawn over the opening in the roof, and the snugness is inconceivable; while nothing could exceed its cleanliness and neatness.*

"Such was the dwelling in which I was now established. Under a cloth I discovered several joints of meat, with a look of strange flesh about them. On inquiry, I found they were *horseflesh*, thus giving me, at my first approach, a sample of

* Marco Polo (Yule's 'Marco Polo,' i. 220) says, "The Tartars' huts or tents are formed of rods covered with felt, and, being exactly round and nicely put together, they can gather them into one bundle and make them up as packages, which they carry along with them in their migrations."

the habits of the country. Seated on the felt carpet, I enjoyed a comfortable dinner, and went to bed, for the first time, in a Kirghiz 'akooee.'

"The next morning, our road lay up a narrow winding gorge, northwards, with tremendous vertical cliffs on either hand. Dead horses were passed at every few hundred yards, marking the difficulties of the route. We took up our abode in a kind of cave, so as to save the delay of striking the tents in the morning. On the following day, we started for the pass into Toorkistân. The gorge gradually became steeper and steeper, and dead horses more frequent. The stream was hard frozen into a torrent of white ice. The distant mountains began to show behind us, peeping over the shoulders of the nearer ones. Finally, our gorge vanished, and we were scrambling up the open shingly side of the mountain, towards the ridge. Up to this point I had ridden, out of deference to the feelings of my Mihmandâr, who was himself mounted on a yak. But here I could stand it no longer, and dismounted to walk. As I feared, my Mihmandâr, after vainly trying to persuade me to mount his yak, himself got off and attempted walking. A hundred yards were enough for him, and, then, when I pressed him to ride, he was glad enough to do so. Politeness yielded to fatigue.

"Before long, I and my two Guddee servants were far in advance of the rest of the party, although walking slowly. In the morning, my Ladâk interpreter, Tashee, had warned the other servants that they would never get to the top of the pass, and that they would now see what mountains were like. Like all ignorant races, the Tibetans seem to think that in no other country is the equal to be found to their own. But it was amusing to think of their instructing a couple of born mountaineers as to the nature of passes! The end was that Tashee was soon left laboring up the ascent, while we three arrived at the top of my *eleventh* pass since leaving India. The pass is very little lower than the rest of the narrow ridge which tops the range. The first sight, on cresting the 'col,' was a chaos of lower mountains, while far away to the north the eye at last rested on what it sought, a level horizon indistinctly bounding what looked like a distant sea. This was the plain of Eastern Toorkistân, and that blue haze concealed cities and provinces, which, first of all my countrymen, I was about to visit. A step further showed a steep descent down a snow-slope, into a large basin surrounded by glaciers on three sides. This basin was occupied by undulating downs, covered with grass (a most welcome sight), and occupied by herds of yaks.

"We here rested, lit a fire, and boiled water to ascertain the height of the pass. A lot of yaks were crossing the ridge under the charge of several Kirghiz, who had been sent for to help my luggage across. We waited three-quarters of an hour, but as the Mihmandâr did not appear, I began to descend. The path was a zigzag, through the snow, which had been trodden into most slippery ice. My pony, having arrived, was taken down by two men, one of whom supported him by the tail, while the other led him. More than one horse had recently lost his footing here, and rolled down the slope, and we saw the crows having a feast off the carcases on the snow at the bottom. After a few hundred feet, the snow ceased, but the descent continued steep for a couple of miles of zigzags. Then we were landed on the uppermost grassy downs, where presently we found a party of Moghuls waiting to welcome me. Each of them came forward and took my hand between both of his, with which he afterwards slowly stroked his beard. They assisted me to dismount, and conducted me to where several sheets of felt were spread on the ground. While tea was being made, they advanced in procession; the first man spread a cloth on the ground before me, and each of the others deposited his tray of fruit on it. Our eyes were gladdened by the sight of rosy apples and pears, besides other fruit which we had seen before. Our hosts then informed us that they were the servants of the Yoozbashee* (the Vizier's brother), sent to welcome me at the foot of the pass, and that their master's camp was in the valley not far down, to which they were instructed to bring us on at once. At this stage of the proceedings, the Mihmandâr arrived from the pass; two sepoys were sent off on yaks to announce our approach, and I had my breakfast, rather a late one. Soon

* Derived from "yooz," *a hundred*, and "bashee," *an officer* (Toorkee), and therefore meaning a "centurion."

after, we also started, escorted by the 'Akskal,'* or elder of the Kirghiz. A pretty rapid descent through the grassy downs brought us into the head of a gorge, down which we continued our route. It was getting late, and there was no sign of the Yoozbashee's camp; so, as our things were far behind, a halt was called. We lit a fire, and waited for two or three hours before the tents arrived and were put up. The gorge was barren and sandy, with a small ice-bound stream fringed with bushes.

"On Saturday the 28th, after breakfasting, we continued our march, fording the stream several times. All the servants were provided with horses or yaks to ride, and when we passed several of my Ladâkees on foot, my Mihmandâr made some of the Kirghiz followers dismount and give their yaks to my men. About five miles after starting, as we mounted the steep bank of the stream which we had just crossed, a group of horsemen met us on the top. The foremost advanced, and took my hand in both of his, holding it while he asked me several questions in a cordial tone of voice, which I needed no interpreter to tell me were inquiries after my welfare. He then turned his horse, and motioning politely to me to ride by his side, we continued our journey. One of his followers started off at a wild gallop in front of us, discharging his matchlock, and afterwards whirling it round his head with a loud whoop. This I found was a salute intended to do me honor.

* Derived from "ak," *white*, and "skal," *a beard* (Toorkee).

"I had now leisure to examine the appearance of the Yoozbashee. He was a young man of apparently little more than thirty years, with a bright intelligent face and energetic manners. His head-dress was a green turban. A sober-colored outer robe covered the richer clothes beneath, and was fastened round the waist by two separate blue belts ornamented with numerous silver clasps and bars. To these belts were attached a silver-hilted sabre much curved, and a series of nondescript articles, including pouches of embroidered leather, a priming-flask of peculiar shape, &c. The ends of a pair of very wide trowsers of soft yellow leather covered with embroidery were just visible below his robe, and his feet were enclosed in boots, or rather high moccasins, of the same, with a row of silver nail-heads round the soles. He rode a small but handsome gray with an almost Arab look about the head, but a heavier neck, and his seat on horseback was perfection.

"We rode about a mile, and then reached a little flat covered with small trees. Here was an encampment of Kirghiz, together with the followers of the Yoozbashee and their horses. I was taken into a Kirghiz akooee that had been prepared for me, and led to the place of honor, viz., a carpet spread over the sheets of felt directly opposite the door; this carpet I was left to occupy alone in my glory, while the Yoozbashee seated himself on the side carpet to my right, with my former Mihmandâr below him; two of his principal attendants were seated near the door, outside which the remainder, armed with match-locks, were drawn up as a guard of honor. Now I must explain to you the Toorkish manner of sitting on state occasions; it is a mode of torture unknown to Western nations. Natives of India, as a rule, squat down with their feet still on the ground, and their knees just below their chins. Others cross their legs in front of them, and sit like a tailor. But in Toorkistân the ceremonious manner is to kneel down with your robes well tucked in, and then sit back on to your heels. When your toes are by these means nearly dislocated, you have the option of turning them inwards, and sitting on the inside flat of the feet. By this means the dislocation is transferred from your toes to your ankles and knees.

"The sword is a further source of difficulty. If, when first kneeling down, you forget to keep the point in front of you, so as to lay it across your knees, you can never bring it round afterwards, and it remains fixed behind you, hitching up the left side of your belt in the most uncomfortable manner, and forming a stumbling-block to all the attendants who bring tea, &c. I must tell you that swords are here worn in a frog, like a French policeman's, and not loosely attached by straps, like those of English officers. After thus seating yourself, you spread out both arms, and then bring your hands to your face, solemnly stroking your beard (if you have one), and saying, 'Allahoakber' —'God is great.'

"Thus seated, a conversation was carried on

through Jooma as interpreter. The Yoozbashee asked whether I had suffered any discomfort by the way, and apologized for my detention at Shahidoolla, saying it was caused by the arrival of the other Englishman regarding whom they were obliged to get the King's orders. He asked me who he was, and what he wanted. In reply I repeated the old story of our meeting while on a shooting excursion, of his desiring to accompany me to Yârkand, and of my refusal without the King's orders. The Yoozbashee then took his leave, after giving me a short note from his Majesty, giving me a military salute which I fancy they must have taken from the Russians, as it is in continental style. Immediately afterwards the procession appeared, headed by my former Mihmandâr, whom I now learned to call the Panjabashee (which is his real title, meaning 'captain of fifty'). They laid before me a cloth, and covered it with trays of fruit of all sorts, eggs, sugar, bread, &c. This I found was a regular institution ; it is called a 'dastar-khân,' and during the remainder of my journey the ceremony took place every morning and evening on the part of the Yoozbashee ; beside which, dastar-khâns were presented by other officials. I generally ate one or two of the fruit, and offered some to the person who was in charge ; for the giver did not himself accompany it as a rule, but sent his highest subordinate. Presently a sheep was brought to the door, and a cold fowl on a dish. From that day to this a fresh sheep has appeared daily at my door, and though all my servants are feasted on mutton, and I constantly give away whole sheep, yet my flock keeps on increasing.

"Up to this time my Ladâkee yak-drivers had been brought along with us. Their yaks and ponies had been left beyond the pass, and they had themselves petitioned to be discharged there. I was ready to do so, but the Panjâbashee had considered it necessary to bring them with us, nominally in order that they might not be dismissed without presents, but in reality I imagine it was feared they might carry away letters from me. Heaven knows I had but little news to give! No reports had I to make of the nakedness of the land. No expeditionary force was waiting at Ladâk for my instructions as to the route. But the ignorance of this people, accustomed to the isolation of centuries, conjures up dangers out of the least scrap of Feringhee writing.

"Arrived at the Yoozbashee's camp, the Ladâkees made another desperate effort to obtain release. They importuned with such success that at last it was decided they might go. In all this I took care not to mix myself up, for had I shown the least anxiety to procure their discharge, an ulterior object would have been at once imagined. However, the Panjâbashee was sent to tell me that the Ladâkees were to be sent back. They were to be given yaks to ride as far as Karakash, with provisions of every kind sufficient for their return journey. This was of course intended as a compliment to me, for the Ladâkees themselves confessed that, had they been alone they would only have received kicks and cuffs instead of presents, as reprobate heathens.

"Later in the afternoon I paid a visit of ceremony to the Yoozbashee in his own akooee, attended by my two Guddee servants (arrayed in the gorgeous cotton silk khilats sent by the Moonshee from Yârkand), and preceded by the Panjâbashee. I went to his door. He put me on the carpet of honor, and ordered in a dastar-khân and tea. He had now taken off his outer robe, and was dressed in a Yârkand silk 'khilat,' loose and shining; beneath it a 'kamsole,' or inner robe of English printed muslin fastened by a scarf round the waist. On his head, instead of a turban, was a tall cap of dark green velvet turned up with a fur lining. I am always looking out for something Scythian in Toorkistân; for it is pretty well agreed, I believe, that the Asiatic Scythians at any rate were the progenitors of the modern Tartars, under which very vague title the Toorkees are certainly included. Sir H. Rawlinson indeed thinks that the ancient Sakae or 'Amyrgian Scythians' of Herodotus inhabited Yârkand and Kâshghar. Now their characteristic dress was a tall pointed cap and trowsers. Here I saw them before me on the first Toork of rank that I had met! The head-dress is probably peculiar to Central Asia. Opposite the Yoozbashee were seated his moollah or scribe, who knows one or two words of Persian, and reads and writes all letters for his master. Also the 'Alam' of Sanjoo, who is the chief minister of religion, and as such wears a peculiar round cap with fur border, over which is neatly tied a large white turban of peculiar shape. The Yoozbashee assured me of his King's good will towards me, and that the purpose of his mission was to see that I received every attention and honor by the way. When I left the tent a silk robe was put over my shoulders, the Yoozbashee begging me to excuse the poverty of the gift on account of our being out in the jungle, and saying that he ought to have presented me with a horse and trappings, &c. I replied that the pleasure of meeting him was quite sufficient without any presents, and then I was shown to my tent by the Panjâbashee.

"Shortly afterwards he returned my visit; on which occasion I presented him with a yellow silk Cashmere turban, which was tied on his head in place of the Scythian cap. Then he rose, and performed the usual 'Allahò-akber' (stroking his beard), which ceremony I find comes in everywhere. If you receive a present, or enter a house, or finish a meal, it is always '*Allâ-â-â-ho-akber!*' The Moghuls pronounce the *â* very broad in this as in all other words, sounding it like our *aw*.

"After breakfast the next morning, the men of Lâdak having been sent off, we started on our ride down the mountain gorge, a horseman galloping off frantically in front of us to fire the usual running salute. Constantly fording the stream through sheets of ice, and raising clouds of dust as we rode along the barren sides, we got through two days' march. I was disappointed in my expectation of finding the hillsides clothed with forests or verdure as we reached a lower level. A few small deciduous trees, and a little grass on the banks of the stream, was all that broke the barrenness of the sandy valley. The mountain-sides were covered with a coat of light soil, through which the rocks cropped out. On such precipitous faces a few heavy showers of rain would have washed it all away ; it would thus appear that heavy rain is unknown here, or even much snow.

" The interpreter was in constant requisition, as the Yoozbashee was very friendly and communicative. Among other questions, he asked how it was that Shaw Sahib was not *black*, as he lived in Hindostan ? I explained that the real home of the English was in a cold climate, and that I was now delighted at reaching a country where the people resembled my own countrymen in color, after the dark faces of India ; for he and his party had about the complexion of a well-bronzed Englishman, and were no darker than myself, in fact, at that moment. He showed me the pistol he wore in his waist, a rough old cavalry pistol of English make, evidently much prized, for which he carried a few musket-caps in a box. I then showed him my breech-loading revolver. He was wild with delight and astonishment, and insisted on firing off all six chambers, loaded with ball, into the air !

" At our night's encampment, I showed him my breech-loading rifle (Dougal). This, too, had to be fired, and he pointed out a large stone some way up a ravine opposite. His two shots went astray. Then I fired. The first missed, but gave me the distance, and with the second barrel I was lucky enough to hit. He asked, 'How many yards is it?' I replied about 250; but he exclaimed, 'No, it is far nearer a thousand!' He seemed much struck with the powers of the rifle, and went away in a silent mood. In the morning before I was dressed, he was practising at the same stone with his own matchlock, but, my servants said, did not go near it.

"Toward afternoon of the second day, the valley began to widen, and the hilly sides to become lower. Numberless red-legged partridges were calling all around. I was made to load my gun, but told to come along on horseback. Instead of allowing me to walk up to the birds, no sooner was a covey seen than our whole cavalcade scattered wildly in chase. Some of the party even crossed the stream after them, yelling with excitement. I and my Guddee servants roared with laughter at seeing these people galloping after the partridges, as if they wished to put salt on their tails instead of shooting them, or letting me do so. I watched my opportunity, and, when they were out of the way, I dismounted and went after a covey which I heard in another direction. Returning with a bird I had shot, I was met by the Yoozbashee holding five live ones in his hand, and shouting for Shaw Sahib to come and look. I was astounded, but soon discovered that this apparently childish amusement of galloping after partridges was really a most effectual way of catching them. Several were afterwards caught in my sight. The birds fly from one side of the valley to the other. If put up again immediately, they soon get tired, and after two or three flights begin running on the ground. Then the men gallop up, and strike at them with their whips. It is a most exciting amusement over rough country. I had heard of quails being caught in this way when tired by a long flight during their annual migrations, but did not imagine a partridge could be taken so.

"When the partridges ceased, my companions began skylarking among themselves, displaying the most perfect horsemanship in so doing. The two clerical gentlemen chiefly distinguished themselves, viz., Moollah Shereef, and the Alam of Sanjoo, who pulled off his outer robe for greater freedom. They caught one another round the waist, each trying to dislodge the other from his saddle, and wrestled on horseback ; meanwhile their horses were leaping ditches and banks, and going headlong over the roughest ground. Finally, each remained in possession of his adversary's turban. The Yoozbashee encouraged them in all their antics, occasionally starting forward at full gallop with a shout and a laugh, to the great discomposure of my Guddee servants' seats, and of my turban (which I had not yet learned to tie firmly). While amusing ourselves thus, we reached the first cultivation. The valley was no different from before, but we crossed several fields of fallow ground, and several dry irrigation channels ; while on the other side of the stream there was a clump of leafless trees, and two or three mud-built houses with flat roofs. Presently a flock of sheep appeared, and then a lot of donkeys grazing. I hailed all these signs of inhabited lands with delight, to the great amusement of the Yoozbashee, who, however, seemed quite to understand what the pleasure must be of leaving behind us the deserts where we had been so long. He called my attention to each fresh object that presented itself, saying with a smile: 'Here, Shaw Sahib, here is a tree, and there is a heap of straw earthed over to keep for the cattle; and look, there are cocks and hens, and a peasant's house!'

"The hills had by this time sunk into long low ridges a few hundred feet high, still chiefly sand slopes with a few rocks cropping out. The name of the first cultivated ground was Kéwas, but the houses were few and much scattered. In fact I could distinguish no separation of villages, although different names were given me by the way. From the first hamlet, a succession of habitations appeared; at first very far apart, and then getting more and more numerous as we proceeded. At last we halted at a little farm-house. The Yoozbashee dismounted, and led me into a little courtyard surrounded by mud walls, and thence into a room opening into it. It was empty, the people being employed somewhere near, but we took possession. After sitting down with me, and saying 'Allaho-akber,' he hurried off with a smile and a wave of the hand, to find lodgings for himself. The other principal room of the house, on the other side, was taken for this purpose, while the remainder of our followers pitched tents outside. My cooking-fire was lit in the court-yard. I was very curious to examine the first Toorkistânee house. The walls were all of mud, a couple of feet thick. A straight thick log of poplar supported the roof of the room, passing from wall to wall, while small sticks were laid across from each side, resting on this beam in the middle. A good coating of dry mud on the top of this formed the roof, through which a small opening was left near the door to give light. After entering, a step led up to the floor of the room, which was covered with felt carpeting. There were shelves for cups and dishes all round the room, and a large wooden bedstead at one side, with a great quantity of good bedding. The fireplace projected from the wall, forming a kind of arch about four feet high; behind which the chimney went up through the wall. About a foot above the hearth were recesses on both sides to hold the cooking-pots over the fire. Several vessels for water were standing in the corner, being large double calabashes, the larger half below and the smaller above, joined by a neck round which a rope is tied. There was another similar room in the house; also several store-rooms, and a large cattle-house. Outside the court-yard was a small shed for the fowls.

"A cat appeared and made great friends with me, taking me quite under its protection, purring and sitting down by my side opposite the fire. I accepted this as a happy omen on first entering a strange land. I really felt the company of this friendly cat quite a comfort; it seemed at once to make one at home. We afterwards found that cats were a favored race in Toorkistân, not the scared, half-starved things that disappear round corners in Indian houses; but sleek, well-fed creatures which know how to purr, and scorn to steal. While I write, there are four of them lying in all positions on the rug in front of my fire!

"The owner of the house, and his family, had a glorious feast, for I gave them the greater part of my dastar-khân, consisting of a dozen or more large *sheets* of bread (I measured some two feet in diameter! they are delicious, being made of Yârkand flour; as light as French rolls, though made without leaven), and of fruit of all sorts. In the morning we rode about three miles, the cultivation being continuous, and the houses more and more numerous, while the hedgerows were planted with poplars, apple and pear trees, all leafless now. We now saw, on ahead, a small body of horsemen drawn up by the side of the way, and their leader dressed in black, and sitting on a splendid black horse. The Yoozbashee told me this was the 'Beg' or Governor of Sanjoo come out to meet me, and conduct me in, and asked whether I would get off, or salute him on horseback. I said, 'I will go entirely by your advice in these matters; for you know the respective ranks of the different officers whom I shall meet, and to whom the various marks of respect are due.' He said, 'Then

TURKOMAN FUNERAL.

do as I do.' When within twenty yards, he pulled up, and dismounted, the Beg riding forward and doing the same. They ran forward to meet one another, and embraced, each putting his chin on the other's right shoulder, and his arms round his body. Then the Beg turned to me, the Yoozbashee introducing me by name, and we clasped both hands, finishing by stroking the beard, and saying 'Allaho-Akber.' After remounting, the Yoozbashee told me that his friend the Beg had just lost a wife, which was the reason of his being all in black upon a black horse. I told him this was also the color we used in mourning.

"By this time we reached a fine clump of tall poplars, with a little square, and a mosque (which was merely a room open at the front, where a row of wooden pillars took the place of a wall). A street opened into the little square, but consisted merely of two opposite mud walls, with a door in them every thirty yards. Entering one of these doors on the right, we passed through one clean-looking court-yard into a second ; then up four or five steps across a wide verandah into a room, well carpeted, and with a bright fire. Here, after complimentary speeches and inquiries, the Beg and the Yoozbashee left me.

"The other end of the verandah was divided off from mine by matting hung up, and was occupied by my kitchen apparatus. The floor of the verandah was two or three feet above the ground, but through it a passage at the ground-level led into the interior of the house, where the women lived. Mine was the guest-room. A door led out of the court-yard into an orchard behind the house, planted with apple, pear, and walnut trees, and where a crop of Indian corn had been grown last season. Beyond were other fields and orchards divided by mud walls and hedges, with groups of houses scattered over the whole. In fact, Sanjoo is more a thickly populated *district* than a town or village. It has a central bazaar, where a market is held every Monday (the day before we arrived there was one), and here and there the houses are so numerous and close as to form short streets, but there is not a continuous town. All this I observed in a ramble which I presently took at the suggestion of my entertainers. The people here, as elsewhere in Eastern Toorkistân, seem very well-to-do. No rags or appearance of poverty anywhere. Every member of the crowd that gathered round our party as we arrived and started was dressed in several good thick robes reaching below the knee, with high leather boots, and a cap turned up all round, showing a handsome fur lining. The women did not appear much, but I saw one or two in long robes, not fastened in at the waist and reaching to the ankle, boots like the men, and a similar fur cap on the top of a white handkerchief which covered the ears and back of the head and neck. I noticed that they examined *me* quite freely, looking over the tops of their gates, but the moment the Yoozbashee appeared, they immediately hid. I find that, as a rule, in this country the women go about openly unveiled, but whenever a religious magistrate is seen coming, they either run away or draw down an openwork veil over their faces.

"The Yoozbashee showed me the horses which he had left at Sanjoo. Toorkee horses are taken immense care of and well groomed, but their treatment differs from ours in some particulars. The saddles are never taken off night or day, but covered over with horse-clothing, which extends to the neck and head. They are walked about for a great part of the time that they are not on the road, sometimes for four or five hours after coming in. Even the common horses are tied up, and not allowed to feed indiscriminately. They get plenty of corn (barley or Indian corn), and but little grass. This makes them very fit for long journeys. The saddles are of painted and polished wood, with a very high peak in front, and are well raised from the back-bone. Their trappings are very rich, with embroidered cloths and silver mountings. The Yoozbashee said, 'You must take your choice of one out of these three horses of mine, with all his belongings.' I pretended to be shocked at the idea, and said 'No.' He laughed, and we parted. This offer he repeated once more before we reached Yârkand, but I again politely refused ; and learned afterwards that I had done quite right, as it would not have been the thing for me to accept a present from any one but the Vizier or the King.

"It would only tire the reader if I were to trace the remainder of my journey, step by step, as I have done hitherto. I need only describe the general features of the country, and our manner of travelling. As for the former, on leaving the fertile valley of Sanjoo, we ascended the sandy cliff to our north, several hundred feet, and then came into an immense undulating plain of sand, scantily spotted with small and scraggy bushes. This plain sloped down from the foot of the mountains to our left (south), and we could see in the distance to our right that it was cut up into ravines at its descent into the level plains. For four days we rode westward along this desert, which was broken in four places at unequal distances by streams coming down from the mountains, and fertilizing the land on either side of them. These fertile strips, sunk below the surface of the neighboring desert, form oases covered with villages and highly cultivated. Thus we always had a village to rest in at night, though our day's journey was entirely over barren sand.

"All this time the line of the mountains, which from Sanjoo were very conspicuous southward, diverged more and more from our route, till on the fourth day they were barely visible. On the fifth day we turned right away from them northward, passing through some broken ground where our desert sloped into the level plain. This was also bare sand, communicating, I was told, with the great 'Tâkla-Makân,' the central desert of Asia, which, under the name of Gobi, stretches eastward into China. But presently we reached fields and houses near the town of Kargalik, and from that place to Yârkand we passed through a well-cultivated country full of villages, and without a trace of sandy or waste land. At intervals, tall poles with sign-boards marked the distances along the road, the measurement being by the 'tâsh,' equalling nearly five of our miles, I reckoned.

"It was market-day as we passed out of Kargalik, and for three or four miles there was an unceasing stream of people, young and old, men and women, pouring in from the villages (the majority on horseback) either to buy or to sell for their weekly necessities. Some carried fowls or baskets full of eggs, some had sheep and cattle, others droves of donkeys laden with cotton or other produce of their fields for sale. I saw several handsome horses being led in to find purchasers. In fact, but for the dress of the people you might have thought it was market-day at some country town in England; the rosy-faced farmers' wives bringing in their children for a treat, while the men were transacting all the business of the country side. The villages even, with their surrounding orchards and crowds of noisy fowls, reminded me of home, but lacked the high gables and numerous doors and windows of the English farmhouse. Instead of this, blank walls surrounding courtyards, and low buildings with no visible roof, put one in mind of a man both bald and blind. There are no hedges, but the number of trees both round the houses and along the watercourses prevent the country from having the bare appearance of some of the French provinces.

"Numberless little hamlets of two or three

houses in a group are scattered over the whole face of it, and bear witness to the long existence of a settled government, and security to the inhabitants, so different from the Punjab, where former misrule and anarchy have accustomed the people to crowd all their houses together for safety, till a village resembles a huge ant-hill with many exits. Irrigation seems to be carried to a great extent; in fact all cultivation depends on it, as there is little rain.* The watercourses run in all directions, being carried over and under one another at the road, and by small aqueducts over marshes and hollows. The falls and sluices are utilized in driving stamping-mills for husking the rice, and in the manufacture of gunpowder, pounding the saltpetre, &c. These are driven by a wheel with a single cog, a pair of pestles rising and falling alternately, like long slender hammers. Besides Kargalik, we passed through two other towns, one smaller and one larger than it. They are much like Indian towns, except that the streets of the bazâr are covered over for the sake of shade—a precaution not much wanted at this time of year, when all the pools and tanks are hard frozen. The great difference from the appearance of Indian towns is in the greater look of well-being in the inhabitants. Their clothes are all so

* In the travels of Hwui Seng, the Chinese pilgrim, A.D. 519, it is written:—"The people of this region use the water of the rivers for irrigating their fields; and when they were told that in the middle country (China) the fields were watered by the rain, they laughed and said, 'How could Heaven provide enough for all?'"

good and substantial, and they are indebted to the tailor for the whole of their garments, ignoring that untidy Indian custom of throwing loose sheets over their bodies! There is an absence of the *coolie* class too, with its blank stare of utter stupidity; here every one looks respectable, brisk, and intelligent. The townspeople all gather in rows on either hand, and bow low to the King's guest with both hands crossed on their breasts. This is their mode of salutation. Women bow with their arms hanging down instead. The 'as-salâm aleikoom' is for my conductor, the Yooz-bashee, a *true believer*, who replies with a constantly repeated 'o aleikoom as-salâm.'

"At Kargalik one of the features of the place was rather startling, viz., a *gallows* standing by the side of the principal street at the entrance of the town. It was unoccupied at the time, but seemed well-worn.

"At one of these places I was shown a newly-caught black eagle of the sort called 'Birkoot,' which are trained to catch antelope and deer as falcons do birds. The unfortunate creature was hooded, and wrapped up, wings, talons and all, in a sheep-skin, and this bundle was suspended (head downwards) from the man's saddle during the march. They consider this treatment has a tendency to tame the bird!*

---

* Marco Polo (Yule's "Marco Polo," i. 343, and note at p. 355) says, "His majesty has eagles also which are trained to stoop at wolves, and such is their size and strength that none, however large, can escape from their talons."

"I now saw for the first time the two-humped or Bactrian camel used as a beast of burden. We passed several strings of them. They are darker in color, stouter in make, and are clothed with a thicker coat than the common camel of India, which has only one hump. Another mode of conveyance too betokened considerable advance in civilization; this was the 'arabah,' or cart.* It is a covered van or tilt-cart mounted on two very high wheels (just like English wheels with many spokes), and drawn by three horses, one in the shafts, and two leaders drawing abreast with traces. They are driven from the cart with reins and a long whip. It is altogether a far superior turn-out to the common cart of India, where two bullocks, straggling right and left at the point of a long triangular tray, mounted on solid wooden *disks* for wheels, have their tails twisted by the half-naked coolie who squats between them with his knees in his face.

"I cannot say much for the road, although it would be ungrateful in me to speak ill of it, for it had been smoothed and mended expressly for me all the way, and the small streams and water-courses were all carefully bridged as far as there was time. This was an honor that I hardly expected. I learned afterwards that they had asked my agent, Diwân Baksh, about the custom in India, and what was done there when any illus-

* Marco Polo (Chap. xlvii. Bk. I., Bohn's Ed.) says, "They (the Tartars) have a superior kind of vehicle on two wheels, covered likewise with black felt, and so effectually as to protect those within it from wet, during a whole day of rain."

trious stranger came. He told them the usual preparations that were made, such as mending roads, etc., and they took the hint so thoroughly as even to prepare spare beams at all the bridges, in case the press of horses accompanying me should break through. I confess I was made rather uneasy by these unexpected preparations, coming upon the top of the other honors which they poured upon me. It struck me that my agent might not have been sufficiently careful in his expressions, and the Vizier might imagine that I came on a mission from our Government.

"But I have not yet given an account of the manner of our journeying, and of the treatment bestowed on me. They gave me a capital horse to ride, as they did also to all my servants. A couple of troopers were put in charge of my baggage, which followed us well. The Yoozbashee had about a dozen attendants with him; besides which two or three of his men were always on the road either to or from Yârkand, carrying reports of our progress, and rejoining our party in an incredibly short time, dressed in new robes, and bringing complimentary messages from the Shaghâwal to the Mihmân (myself). What they can have found to report, I cannot imagine; but it was evident they still had great misgivings about the coming of an Englishman, though they outwardly veiled them under the show of the greatest politeness. As for the Yoozbashee, he was the most cordial and agreeable of companions. As full of fun as a schoolboy home for the holidays, he kept the whole party alive and merry. At one moment he was talking to me in a kind of *lingua franca* chiefly Toorkee, with a few words of Persian, to which I responded with the languages in the inverse ratio. Our alternate mistakes were of course a great fund of amusement, in which the whole party joined. When, as sometimes happened, we managed to understand one another, he would poke me in the ribs, or pretend to pull me off the horse, laughing heartily. When I mentioned to him anything that struck his fancy, for instance any of the arts and contrivances of civilization, he would hold up his finger at me, shaking his head with a smile, and saying, 'Ah, Shaw Sahib,' in a voice that implied, 'You "Frangs" are certainly leagued with "Shaitân."'

"The next minute he would begin an Andijânee song, flourishing his whip about, and suddenly bringing it down on the shoulders of some unconscious attendant. One day, sitting with me at our abode for the night, he saw my warm gloves, and put them on. A confidential servant was passing the door; he called him in, and, pretending he had something to whisper to him, brought him close up. Then he gave him five or six hearty cuffs on the face with my gloves, as gravely as possible. The man looked quite scared, and I thought he must have committed some fault, when suddenly the Yoozbashee burst out laughing, and showed him his two hands with the gloves on. The man took the joke, and, following the Scripture precept, presented his other cheek to the smiter, who immediately took advantage of the offer. Once we had stopped at a road-side mosque for the purpose of saying afternoon prayers. He and his party having finished, came running out like a lot of boys when school is over. Three women, who were coming along the road, seeing the crowd, turned aside into a field. Upon which my friend stood still, and cried, 'Khanem, khanem,' which means, 'lady.' At last they were obliged to answer, when the Yoozbashee, with the greatest mock politeness, began a long speech to them about the happiness of meeting them, his having come expressly for the purpose, and brought the Mihmân with him, and regretting he had not time for any further conversation. The women, meanwhile, half-amused and half-shy at so many people, stood with their heads turned away. My friend finished with a low and ceremonious bow, and a solemn salaam, and then turned to see whether I was amused at the joke, joining himself in the laughter.

"At every village we were welcomed by officers of the district to which it belonged, and conducted to rooms prepared for us, as at Sanjoo. About three miles from Kargalik, the Beg of that town met us, and, after dismounting and saluting him, I was led to a carpet spread under some trees, and seated in the place of honor, while all our attendants sat down on other carpets at a distance. Dastar-khâns were then brought, consisting of basins of soup, pilao in huge bowls, big sheets of bread, and numberless dishes of fruit. After we had all eaten in our several places, the Yoozbashee requested me to sit still while the whole party spread their outer coats in front of me, and recited their afternoon prayers. We afterwards resumed our journey through horrible clouds of dust caused by our augmented cavalcade. By my side rode a Bokhâra hajjee, who with a companion had ridden out to meet us about half a day's march. He had travelled through India, Arabia, and even Room (Turkey).

"I gathered from this man, who is a merchant, that a considerable trade could be carried on between India and Toorkistân. He says that 10,000 camel-loads of tea (or nearly five million pounds) enter Bokhâra annually, but considers this very short commons, the breach with China having closed their principal source of supply. Yârkand would take immense quantities of tea as well as of English piece-goods, and would repay us in gold, and silk, and horses, all of which abound.

"Crossing an arm of the great Takla-Makân Desert, we saw two 'keek,' a small antelope which frequents it. They have peculiar lyre-shaped horns of which I brought home a specimen. The Yoozbashee says they go in large herds, as do also *wild camels* (?) in the great desert eastward. This desert is connected with wonderful superstitions. They say there once dwelt a heathen nation there, to whom went Jalla-ooddeen preaching Islâm. They agreed to become Mussulmans if the saint could turn all their dwellings into gold. A few prayers, and the thing was done. But now these infidels turned round on him and said, 'Old man, we have all we want; why should we be Mussulmans?' The holy man turned away, but, as he left them, the sand rose and overwhelmed them and their possessions. Many a search has been made for these treasures, but some magic delusion always destroys those who wander in this desert. I told the Yoozbashee the story which Herodotus relates of the gold-digging ants in this very place.

"At each town the Governor or Beg rode out with his retinue three or four miles to meet me, bringing a 'dastar-khân,' or dinner, which was prepared for the whole party (nearly twenty in number). Bowls of soup, huge platters of pilao, roast-fowls by the dozen, fruit, bread, &c., were put before us, and afterwards I was escorted into the town, riding between the Beg and the Yoozbashee. The chief merchants met us outside the gates, while the people of the town were ranged in rows along the streets.

"After conducting me to my lodging for the night in the Governor's house, and sitting a short time with me, the Beg would take his leave, but would come again in the morning to escort me out of the town. After parting with him at the gates, and riding a couple of hours, we always found another 'dastar-khân' awaiting us under some grove of trees, sent out by the Beg of the town we had just left. Even the heads of little unwalled towns, which we did not stop at, would bring out dastar-khâns' and entreat us to honor them by at least drinking a cup of tea. I began to get quite frightened at the name of dastar-khân.

The quantities of superfluous food and unnecessary tea which I consumed during the journey were enormous.

"As we approached Yârkand, the honorary messengers were despatched more frequently than ever, returning in their new robes. We crossed a considerable river, which I was told is navigated by boats in the summer months when its bed is full. Now it is divided into five streams, all of them fordable. The Yoozbashee had told me that I should be met outside the city of Yârkand by some person of consequence, the brother or son of the Shaghâwal (Vizier, or Governor), to whom it would be proper for me to present a 'jâma,' or robe. He asked me whether I was provided with such a present, and told me that I might command him for anything I required, were it 1000 tillahs (about £600). At the same time he wrote in to the Shaghâwal to hint to him that my caravan being delayed, I had not by me the proper robe to present to a man of high rank, and should therefore feel uncomfortable if one came to meet me, and that a smaller man had better be sent. Accordingly, I was met three miles from Yârkand by another Yoozbashee in gorgeous clothing, with about thirty horsemen, who were drawn up in line to receive me. We dismounted, and embraced in Eastern fashion (I had practised this on the Beg of Poskyam, and signally failed from raising the wrong arm). He astonished me by the vigorous clasp he gave me, and completely stopped my breath as I was preparing to accompany the

INTERIOR OF A YÂRKAND HOUSE.

embrace with a series of polite questions as to his health. I then presented him with a new robe (lent me by *my* Yoozbashee for the purpose), which one of my servants put over his shoulders. After this we all remounted, and continued our journey. Shortly afterwards a long low line appeared in front of us, in which I recognized the object of my long journeyings: it was the wall of Yârkand. As we approached through a perfectly flat country, one object was conspicuous, rising above the wall directly in front of us. It was a tall square scaffolding, like that of a tower that is building, with an upper and a lower platform at the top. Seeing my look of inquiry, Moollah Shereef whispered to me in Persian that it was the execution-stage! This is the first thing a stranger sees of the city of Yârkand.

"After passing through a small bazâr outside, we entered through a gate in the mud wall, which is between twenty and thirty feet high, as well as I could judge, tapering towards the top, which is ten or twelve feet wide. A short distance down the first street we passed under the stage which I had seen. It rises from the roof of a strong building, which I fancy is the Yârkandee condemned cell. Our route did not take us through the best parts of the city, but the streets we saw were full of traffic and lined with shops of all kinds. Most of the shop-keepers were women, and in several places I saw a regular cradle with a baby in it being rocked by the mother's foot. This is a decided improvement on the habit of the Simla hill-men, who hang their young children under a spout of water to put them to sleep. Presently we passed a second high wall, which I took for another town-wall, but found it was merely the boundary of one of the colleges. The streets are ten or twelve feet wide, and some of the houses have an upper story.

"After twenty minutes' ride through a labyrinth of winding streets, we passed out through another gate, and crossed an empty piece of ground, some 400 yards across, which divided the old from the new city. A few tumble-down houses marked the site of a bazâr which, under the Chinese *régime*, united the two towns. The 'Yang-Shahr' (New Town),* which we were approaching, had been built as a place of habitation and refuge by the foreign rulers of the country. Whenever any tumult or rising took place, the Chinese troops seem to have retired inside and patiently waited till matters blew over, when they would issue out and resume their former position in the country. The walls are of the same material as those of the old city, but surrounded by a deep ditch, and sur-

---

* There is a "Yang-Shahr" or cantonment at each of the cities of East Toorkistan. This word must not be confounded with "Yang-Hissâr," which is the name of a town, itself provided with a "Yang-Shahr."

Marco Polo says (see Yule's 'Marco Polo,' i. 300,) "Whilst on the subject of the armies of the Grand Khan, it may be proper here to observe . . . . that it became necessary to keep armies in such of the provinces as contained large cities and an extensive population, which [*armies*] are stationed at the distance of four or five miles from those cities, and can enter them at their pleasure."

mounted at intervals by curious pagoda-like buildings, relics of Chinese occupation. The gateway was in similar style; while round about it were congregated great numbers of Toorkee soldiers in red tunics and trowsers. Inside many more were lounging about in picturesque attitudes, singing and dancing with such a studied air of ease, such a careful assumption of *nonchalance*, that I immediately discovered the purpose of the assemblage. Nor did they seem sufficiently at home in their uniforms for me to believe that they were in the habit of wearing them. Two or three were practising the goose-step, and I am to this moment undecided whether they were meant to represent recruits at drill or sentries walking up and down at their post. A short way down the street we came upon an artillery barrack with a row of small guns and howitzers in front. The artillerymen were dressed in blue, and my eye immediately rested on a group better dressed than the others, apparently officers. There was no mistaking them for anything but natives of India, possibly old mutineers.

"A few hundred yards further on the street led into an open space, beyond which was another wall and a gate. Before reaching this we pulled up and dismounted, and I was led into a house on the left by the two Yoozbashees. Passing through three courtyards, we reached a kind of pavilion at the end of the third. The flat roof projecting in front formed a broad verandah supported on high pillars; in the middle, a recess carried back to the further wall held a kind of raised divan, matted and carpeted for visitors to sit on ; on either side of the recess doors opened into comfortable rooms, furnished with Bokhara carpets and with bright fires burning. The Yoozbashee informed me that this house was mine, and that, after resting a little, I should be taken to see the Shaghâwal or Governor."

THE SHAGHÂWAL OF YÂRKAND.

CHAPTER XIII.

RESIDENCE IN YARKAND.

SHAW was left alone for a short time, after being installed in his residence, and then the Yoozbashee who had accompanied him from the Sanjoo Pass, appeared to conduct him to the Shaghâwal, or Governor. This officer, he had discovered, is not only the Governor of Yârkand, but also the second man in the kingdom, corresponding to the Grand Vizier in Turkey. During the absence of the Atalik-Ghazee, or King, in Kashghar, he occupied the palace at Yârkand.

"Passing through the great gate which I had before seen," says Shaw, "and which was full of soldiers (no sham appearance of *néglígé* here), we reached a second similarly guarded portal, which gave access to the interior of the palace. One large court-yard was crossed. Its four sides were lined with officials sitting solemnly with eyes fixed on the ground, and each bearing a white wand in his hand. The silence prevailing amid such numbers of men made an impression quite in keeping with the scene, the palace of an Oriental despot. Before the door of a second court-yard, a large screen concealed everything until we entered. Here the solitude of the inner penetralia was as effective as the silent crowd without. An usher with a white wand preceded us, and half-way up the court stopped me to point through a distant door, where he whispered to me the Shaghâwal was visible. I saluted him as required by bowing, and then was conducted up some steps to the door of the room. Here every one left me, and the usher motioned to me to enter alone. A small elderly man in sober-colored clothes was sitting on a cushion by the fire. He rose, and hurried forward, to meet me near the door, where he embraced me after the Eastern fashion, and then led me by the hand to another cushion near the fire opposite his own, all the while welcoming me most cordially and inquring whether I had received every comfort and attention by the way. After sitting down, I rose again as I had been instructed, and uttered the Allaho-akber! with the sweep of the arms. Then sitting down again, Toorkee fashion, I received and replied to many complimentary speeches from the Shaghâwal.

"He expressed his pleasure at the arrival of an Englishman, saying that they know the friendship of our nation for the Sultan of Room, who was the chief of the Mussulman religion, and thus regarded us as already their friends also. But the arrival of an English Sahib, who has undertaken all the trouble and difficulty of so long a journey for the purpose of visiting his King, was a further bond of friendship. Friendship, he said, makes everything to prosper; but by enmities countries become waste. I replied, suitably I hope, saying that I trusted my visit might be the means of establishing a friendly intercourse between the two countries, as we on our part entertained the most amicable feelings towards the Toorks. I added that, when my Sovereign heard of the kind treatment extended to one of her subjects in Toorkistân, she would be extremely pleased. After this the Shaghâwal said he must apologize for my detention at Shahidoolla and for the incompleteness of the reception I had met with; which were owing to my not having announced my coming beforehand. I stared in astonishment at this, and said, 'Did not my servant, the Moonshee, deliver the letter and messages to the King with which he was charged?' The Shaghâwal answered, 'No.' I replied, 'Then I must have seemed to you guilty of great want of respect to the King, in not applying beforehand for his permission to come. But in truth that was the very object with which I sent my Moonshee on before me. I request that you will send for him, and ask him for the casket in which he brought my letter for the King. I much regret the apparent want of respect on my part.' He answered, 'No, no; there is no want of respect; I was only sorry that you should have been detained at Shahidoolla, and that we had not longer notice, so as to prepare for you a more honorable reception. As for the Moonshee, he is your servant, and will be called whenever you send for him.'

"During this conversation a 'dastar-khân' had been spread, and tea given to me by an attendant. After a little further talk in rather lame Persian on my part, I rose to go.

"The Shaghâwal put his hand on me to detain me, and in a few seconds an attendant brought in a rich silk robe, which was put over my shoulders as I took my leave. The Shaghâwal also rose, and conducted me out by another door through a long room which I heard afterwards was used as a mosque for the royal household. At the further end of this he parted from me with a bow. My people here rejoined me. In solemn procession I was ushered back to my house, where all my baggage had by this time arrived. At the outer gate of the palace we met a person of some distinction on horseback. He immediately dismounted, and advanced to embrace me. The Yoozbashee muttered some words of introduction, and I threw myself into his arms with all the fervor of a long friendship. To this moment I have not the slightest idea as to who he was.

"Behind me followed a procession of the Shaghâwal's servants bearing the 'dastar-khân' which had been put before me. This appears to be the custom.

"On reaching home, I immediately sent for my Moonshee. He presently appeared, dressed in gorgeous robes, the gift of the Shaghâwal, and I told him to send for the casket with the letter at once. I had enclosed my letter to the King which he had brought in a handsome little box of the enamelled gold which is known as Goojerât work. This speedily arrived, and I put it into the hands of the Yoozbashee without opening it, requesting him to give it to the Shaghâwal. This I did that they might read the letter themselves, and see that I had spoken truth when I said I had sent beforehand to ask permission of the King to come. About an hour afterwards the Yoozbashee returned, bringing the letter and casket back with a message from the Shaghâwal, saying that I should keep them to give to the King myself when I saw him. However, they had evidently read the letter, which was all I wanted.

"My Moonshee now related to me all the circumstances of his journey and stay at Yârkand. I was immensely vexed at his not having delivered my letter, nor apparently mentioned its purport. His explanation was such as to silence me for the time, but I still suspend my judgment regarding it. Mahammad Nazzar, the returning Envoy to whose care I had entrusted my Moonshee, had, it appears, turned out a regular scoundrel. He treated Diwân Bakhsh very badly on the journey, and after their arrival spread reports about his being a spy, while he did not even mention that I was on my way hither. Yet he had been full of promises of assistance to me before he left Ladâk, when I gave him several handsome presents to secure his good-will. My Moonshee was, however, very well treated by the Shaghâwal, who sent to meet him on the road, and caused 'dastar-khâns' and all the usual honors to be provided for him, and Mahammad Nazzar had fallen into disgrace for his conduct in this and other respects. On arriving at Yârkand, Diwân Bakhsh was confined to one house, he and his servants, although otherwise provided with all they wanted, and presented with honorary allowances every day. Seeing this, and fearing that men would be sent to turn me back on the road if he mentioned my approach, he remained silent until he calculated that I must have reached Shahidoolla. Then he announced the purpose of his visit.

"Even put in this way, I cannot consider this conduct judicious. It avoided one evil, but produced another. The long concealment must have seemed most suspicious to them.

"I now began establishing myself in my house. The first court-yard contains stables, with room for ten or twelve horses (the mangers very high even for a large animal). Here live my pony and my flock of sheep. Opposite were two or three rooms, which were made over to a Panjâbashee (captain of fifty) and his lieutenant, who are appointed to remain in attendance on me. Here, also, all visitors are entertained while their arrival is announced to me. There is also a raised and roofed floor for receiving visitors in the summer. The next court-yard contains a chamber, which I converted into a bathing-room for myself, and next to it is the kitchen, with rooms for the servants and for their stock of fowls. Two slaves of the Shaghâwal's own household arrived to assist in the kitchen. At the end of the third court-yard is the kind of pavilion in which I myself live. Behind this is a small garden with a summer-house looking into it, or rather a room with an open front. Over the wall of the garden, about 200 yards from the house, the view is shut in by the battlemented wall of the Yang-Shahr, with little houses on it at intervals of sixty yards or so. A little to the left it is surmounted by a regular Chinese structure of two stories, supported on wooden pillars with the characteristic pagoda roof cocked up at the corners.

"My sitting-room is most comfortable, with a well carpeted floor, a spacious fire-place, just like a European one, and which I have never yet known to smoke. The walls are white, and the ceiling carefully papered. It has an opening for light, covered with the likeness of a cucumber frame (with thin paper instead of glass). There are also two windows opening down to the ground with double 'battants.' The outer ones are composed of trelliswork, covered with transparent paper; the inner ones form shutters to be closed at night. All the woodwork is painted green, and the whole house inside and out had been thoroughly refitted, whitewashed, papered, &c., for my accommodation. It had previously belonged to the former Governor of Yârkand, who has only just been released from prison. Next door is the Shaghâwal's own house (he only occupies the palace during the King's absence as his vicegerent). Everything is clean, neat, and comfortable.

"Before I sat down to dinner, arrived the Yoozbashee again, with a crowd of servants, bringing furniture. First, a table (only two feet high), painted in bright colors with patterns. Then two high straight-backed arm-chairs, of which the seats were on a level with the table! Next two bedsteads, with large thin mattresses lined with silk. These were for sitting on in the day as well as for sleeping on. Every one of these pieces of furniture had been made expressly for me, as none of them are known in Yârkand. The Toorks always sit on carpets, and sleep on wooden shelves or on mattresses on the floor. The Shaghâwal had asked the Hindostanees in his service what were the requirements of Englishmen, and these pieces of furniture were made from their descriptions. The comparative height of the table and chairs is unfortunate, but luckily my American folding camp-chair is exactly the right height for the table. The tall chairs I reserve for occasions of ceremony, seating my visitor in one and myself in the other. When these things had been displayed, the Yoozbashee produced a skull-cap such as they all wear under their turban, a tall velvet cap turned up with fur (like his own that I described to you), an embroidered silk purse or pouch of peculiar shape to wear at the girdle, a pair of high boots, and, finally a long robe of crimson silk thickly wadded, which he said the Shaghâwal had sent for me, as the weather was getting cold. There was a considerateness in all this that made me feel quite friendly towards the old Shaghâwal for the trouble he had taken to find out the things that would be agreeable to me."

On the 10th of December, Shaw had another

talk with the Shaghâwal, which we quote as an excellent specimen of Oriental conversation :

"He said, 'The reason why we have not sent any envoy to the English is that we are ashamed to meet them, on account of the murder of the Englishman (Schlagintweit) some years ago. It is true the present rulers had nothing to do with that murder, which was committed by a madman, who was then in authority ; but, as he was a Toorkistânee, we feared the guilt might be imputed to the present rulers.'

"I answered that we knew the circumstances of the murder, and that the country was then under a different rule, and therefore we did not impute guilt to those who could have had no share in it. I further explained that Schlagintweit was not an Englishman, but that, nevertheless, we had been much grieved at hearing of his murder, because he had gone from India to the place of his death, and had thus been a guest of ours. I added that it would be considered a great favor and kindness if any articles that had belonged to him could be found and given to me for his friends.

"The Shaghâwal said, 'The time elapsed is so great that there is no chance of this, and in a matter of shame like this, we hope to have the whole matter forgotten.'

"I said, 'That is best ; let us on both sides wipe away all recollections of it ; we, on our side, entertaining no ill-will to you for the deeds of another ; and you, on your part, meeting us without shame.'

"He laughed, and said, 'Good; the matter is wiped away from between us.'

"I said to him, 'God has so created our two countries that we seem intended for mutual friendship. He has placed between us such a mountain barrier that neither can entertain any jealousy or fear of being attacked by the other, while the wants of each country are supplied by the other, and thus the strongest incentive is offered to commerce.'

"He cordially agreed, and said that, when hearts are joined, no mountains can divide; but when hearts are not in unison, mountains arise even in the plains.

"I said, 'Although I have not been sent here by our rulers, yet their mind, and the mind of my countrymen, is known to me; and I hoped to let the King know their friendly intentions and wishes. My reception as a private Englishman will highly gratify my Sovereign, as showing the honor in which our country is held.'

"He said, 'If you had come in the name of the Lord Sahib,* or bringing a letter from him, any attentions we might show you would be thought to be given to him, and with some object in view. But now it is plain to all men that we bestow honor on you for your own sake, and out of pure friendship to your nation. As you are friends and allies of the Sultan-i-Room (who is the chief of our religion), we already felt great friendship for

* The Viceroy of India.

the English; and thus, when a friend came and *shook our door*, we at once said, "Come in." As for the attentions paid you, they are nothing, and we are only ashamed we could not do more for you.'

"I said that I was hoping for a speedy interview with the King, and hoped to be the means of establishing great friendship between the two countries.

"He said, 'If you want to go on quickly to Kâshghar, I will write and get the King's orders; but it is not my part as host to say to my guest, "Move on." However, if it is your own wish, it shall be done. As host, I say to you, "Stay and rest from the fatigues of your journey."'

"I said, 'I don't feel in any way tired, thanks to the comfort in which I have been brought along, and I am ready at any moment, by day or night, to start on a visit to the King. I shall feel no fatigue in anything which conduces to bring me before him.'

"He said, 'Good; I will get his orders for your journey.'"

The same day the Yoozbashee left Yârkand, and Shaw accidentally discovered, from one of the other officials, that he had gone to Kâshghar, to see the King. This was a promising sign, and Shaw would have been contented to wait, but for his irksome confinement to the house and courtyard. When he made application to be allowed to ride out into the country, the polite answer was: "It is the custom in this country that no guest goes anywhere out of doors before seeing the King." He went once upon the roof of the house, but this was immediately reported, and he prudently refrained from going again. His servants, however, were allowed to go into the bazâr, and purchase the necessary supplies.

"On the 15th one of the officers came with an English letter from Hayward to the King, and a request that Shaw would translate it. He accordingly put it into Persian, and made his agent write it out fairly. The latter stated that Hayward had come 8,000 miles for the purpose of trading, and requested permission to enter the country for that purpose. Reports were also brought to Shaw that Hayward was on his way from Shahidoolla to Yârkand, and he was closely questioned in regard to the latter's character and purposes. His persistent denial of any knowledge of, or connection with him, seemed finally to make an impression upon the authorities.

On the 20th, Shaw writes: "This morning the Yoozbashee came to say that the Governor was ready to receive me, and whispered to my servant Jooma: 'The gifts may be brought now.' Nothing was ready, as I had had no notice. However I got together in a great hurry a rifle, revolver, pink silk turban, some cloth, and one hundred and twenty pounds of tea, and off we went to the palace. In presenting my gifts to the Shaghâwal, I said I hoped he would accept them, though they were not such as I should have wished to give him, had my caravan arrived. He seemed very much pleased, and said that I should not have given them, but that, as I had done so, he accepted them with great pleasure.

"He then said he had written to the King to announce my desire to go to him, and that he expected the answer in a day or two, when I should go to Kâshghar and tell the King all I wished to say.

"I said, 'I know the feelings and wishes of our nation with regard to you, although I am a merchant, and not sent by the Lord Sahib, who could not send an envoy until one should come from you.'

"He answered, 'We have not sent one because we were ashamed of the murder of Schlagintweit; but the Lord Sahib was not ashamed of anything; why did he not send an envoy first?'

"I laughed, and said, 'Well, now that I have explained matters, I hope there will be a constant interchange of envoys, and of all good offices between us and you.'

"He replied, 'As for seeing the King, I trust the orders will come in a few days. Formerly, the King used to transact all business at Yârkand; but now that he has transferred his seat of government to Kâshghar, I believe he will send for me to be there with him also. I have detained Shaw Sahib at Yârkand, that I might make his acquaintance and friendship; for if he had gone on directly to Kâshghar, he would have forgotten me quickly.'

"I answered, 'There is no fear of that, after

your kindness to me ; and I am delighted to hear of your coming to Kâshghar, as I shall have a friend there to assist me by his advice.'

"He said, 'I fear my going will be rather delayed, whereas yours will probably be in a few days.'"

As Christmas approached, Shaw ordered his servants to buy a joint of beef in the bazâr. Thereupon he received a long and ceremonious message from the Governor, to the effect that he must ask the latter for all he wanted, and get nothing out of the city,—that he had heard of the approaching festival, and would supply everything himself. Accordingly, on Christmas Day, twelve men appeared, bringing an enormous 'dastar-khân,' two silk robes, and a cap. The agent also brought twenty different kinds of bread made in Yârkand. In the evening Shaw sent the Governor a gold pencil-case for himself and a gold-enamelled revolver for the King, and received in return a handsome garnet ring.

On the 29th, Shaw gave a dinner or rather breakfast party in state—for it was the fast-month of Ramazan, during which no good Mussulman touches food until after sunset. The guests, who were the Yoozbashee and three or four other officers, arrived about five o'clock. "Before breaking the fast, it is necessary to go through a form of prayers. Accordingly a large sheet was spread on the carpets (my table had been taken out of the room), and the Yoozbashee began the call to prayers, motioning to my Moonshee to take the front place as 'Imâm,' or leader of the devotions. This is a piece of politeness, implying the superiority ot the person so put forward. The others, standing behind, take their time from him. Diwân Bakhsh accordingly faced towards the Kiblah and went through the usual Mussulman prayers. At intervals the leader utters aloud the word *Allah*, at which all prostrate themselves with their foreheads to the ground. Sometimes he repeats some verses of the Koran in a low voice, but the greater part of the time there is silence, each man saying his prayers within himself, kneeling down and rising up again according to the motions of the leader. Meanwhile, I was sitting in my chair by the fire, and each guest, as he finished his prayers, came and sat down by me.

"When all were ready, some white table-cloths were spread on the ground in front of us, and I left my chair and seated myself, Toorkee fashion, near the fire. Next to me sat the Yoozbashee, then my Moonshee, Diwân Bakhsh, then my former Mihmandâr of Shahidoolla, who has just arrived here with Hayward. Then four more Panjâbashees, who attend on me, so forming two sides of a square. Before anything else, the fast was ceremoniously broken by eating a piece of bread dipped in salt. I gave them a kind of mixed dinner; mainly English dishes, but lots of their own to fall back upon in case of necessity. I luckily had a few tins of English soup left, after which came pigeon-pie, roast-fowls, legs of mutton, &c., and then apple-tart with cream, and plum-pudding. But they evidently relished most a huge pilao of rice, boiled mutton, and sliced carrots, which seems to be their usual dinner. Finally, a dessert of grapes, melons, apples, pears, pomegranates, &c. At this the Yoozbashee exclaimed to the servants, 'Halloh, you should have brought this in first!' I could not get him to use a knife and fork, but he consented to take a spoon for the apple-tart. We finished up with tea and coffee. The latter they did not know, and would not drink."

On the last day of the year 1868, Shaw received a dinner of a different kind from any that had been sent before. First came an immense vessel of real Irish stew, very savory and good; the principal vegetable it contained was a large kind of "gram," like yellow peas. The other dish was a large sweet omelette, with molasses, and both were enough to have fed twenty men. Afterwards came a smaller bowl of whipped cream and eggs.

"No sooner," he writes, "had I finished dinner than in came the band. The chief musician had a kind of harpsichord [dulcimer?], like a miniature piano without any keys, played with a pointed instrument in the right hand, while the left hand follows its motions, stopping the vibration of the wires. Next to him sat a man with a long-necked guitar, called a 'citar,' played with a bow like a violoncello. It has nine strings, but only one is played upon, the rest being depressed below its level, and helping to swell the tone of the instrument. The third musician blew upon a sort of slender fife, while the other three had tamborines,

MUSICIANS OF YÂRKAND.

and also accompanied the music with their voices. It struck me that their playing was much superior to that of India and even of Cashmeer. There was a precision about it, an exactitude of time and tune, which showed great proficiency. You will say I am no good judge in matters of music, and I confess that my opinion regarding a new opera would not be very valuable. But I think even I may be able to judge of Oriental music.

"There was one extraordinary creature, the first singer. He had thick red moustaches hanging down from the corners of his mouth, and shaggy eyebrows with colorless eyes. His jaw was shaped much like that of the 'Wild Boar of the Ardennes,' whom Sir Walter Scott describes in 'Quentin Durward.' Altogether he bore a most grotesquely ferocious aspect, and sang with hideous contortions of the face. He is just the kind of ogre that one might dream of in a nightmare. His next-door neighbor, the second singer, was a signal contrast —fat, jolly, peaceable-looking, and might stand for one of the sleek citizens of Liege whom Quentin Durward delivered from the Wild Boar's power. The requirements of the music were evidently too much for this personage. His fat cheeks shook with the exertion of beating the tamborine and singing up to time. The contrast between these two afforded amusement to all of us; for I had a select party assembled to hear the music."

On New-Year's Day, 1869, Shaw wrote: "The weather here is beautifully bright and clear, although quite cold enough to suit one's ideas of the season. To-day, the mean temperature of the air has been fifteen degrees Fahrenheit. Water freezes the moment it touches the ground, and all articles of food become as hard as stone. It is a curious illustration of the climate of Toorkistân that grapes grown in the villages round Yârkand now daily appear on my table, *hard frozen*. Yesterday I had some dipped into hot water to thaw, but as they lay on my table near a bright fire, they froze together into a mass, owing to the wetness of their outside. Cold pie has to be re-baked before it can be cut. Yet, with all this, I have not yet for one moment felt even chilly, such is the dryness and stillness of the air, and the warmth of the long Toorkee robes, or 'jâmas,' which I now wear. Besides, we have been acclimatized by the intense cold experienced on our journey, when wine froze into blocks, bursting the bottles, so that I had to break off pieces of claret to put into my glass, and the men used to go off to fetch *water* with a *hatchet* and a *rope*. There it was the fierce wind which chilled one's bones. By contrast, the present still cold is like paradise.

"To-day I heard an anecdote of the King, which shows the energetic nature of the man, and his disregard of the Oriental notions of dignity. The messenger who took the first news of my Moonshee's approach found him on the Artash Pass, beyond Kâshghar, personally superintending the erection of a fort to defend the road. He was covered with dust, and had just had his leg hurt by the fall of a stone. The messenger could not discover which was the King, but the latter perceived him, and called to him to bring his dispatches, which he read and answered on the spot."

By this time it was evident, from hints dropped by the officials, that Shaw would be received by the King, and would therefore be sent on to Kâshghar. This was a piece of good fortune which he could hardly have anticipated, on leaving Leh. The journey would enable him to see nearly all the inhabited part of Central Asia lying along the eastern base of the great mountain-chains which bound all this region on the south, west and north. On the third day of January, the permission came, accompanied with additional tokens of kindness:

"This morning, before I had breakfasted," he quotes from his journal, "the Yoozbashee arrived with a large packet of silks and brocades for me to give as presents to the King, &c., according to an arrangement which we came to yesterday. Nominally, these things are merely lent to me, and are to be replaced by my own things when they arrive. After showing me all the stuffs, he gave me the welcome news that I was to start for Kâshghar to-morrow. All this he communicated through my two attendants who talk Persian. After this, sending them both out of the room, he produced from the breast of his robe a packet containing eleven lumps of stamped silver (called 'kooroos') one full-sized one, and ten small ones, equal in value to another kooroos. The whole is worth about 35*l*. He whispered to me to put them away out of sight, and that the Governor had sent them to me, thinking I might be in want of ready money for use. Having said this, he ran away with his usual imitation of an English military salute, which I have taught him. I am evidently intended to suppose that this is a private act of friendliness on the part of the Governor. It is very thoughtful on their part, as I certainly was in want of ready money. They will not allow me to have recourse to my only source of supply, viz., the sale of the goods which I had brought for that purpose. I should have seriously felt the inconvenience had it not been that they supply me with every sort of food in quantities sufficient to feed a troop of cavalry, so that all the dervishes of Yârkand, in their tall caps, make my gate a daily place of call, and the families, friends, and horses of my attendant officers are entirely maintained by me. Besides this, I daily receive about seventeen shillings in small change (50 'tanga'). I have not yet mentioned that the chief money of Toorkistan consists of small copper coins, with a square hole in the middle [like the Chinese *cash*]. Of these, 25 make one *tanga* (about 4*d*), and they are ran on strings, containing 20 tangas' worth on each string. These strings are the common currency, from which smaller sums are detached at will. I receive two strings and a half every day" (about four dollars).

CHAPTER XIV.

THE JOURNEY TO KASHGHAR.

ON the morning of January 4th a handsome gray horse from the Governor's stables was brought to Shaw, and he was told to prepare at once for the journey to Kâshghar. All his servants were provided with horses, and there were others for the baggage, making twenty-seven in all, besides those of the Yoozbashee and his attendants. The first start is always accompanied by many delays, and they did not get away from Yârkand until noon. Shaw must be allowed, as far as space will permit, to describe the journey in his own words :

"We rode along part of one side of the new city, and the whole of another side. I thus had an opportunity of inspecting the defences. From the road there slopes up a small glacis to the brink of the ditch, which is about twenty feet deep, and of equal width, revêted on both sides with sun-dried bricks. The escarpe or inner side rises into a battlemented earthen wall, which is hidden from an advancing enemy by the glacis, leaving only the machicoulis along the top visible, from which musketry fire might be directed on to the slope of the glacis. Inside this wall is another ditch, from which rises the main wall of the town. Counting from the crest of the glacis, the main wall is about thirty or thirty-five feet high, and the same in thickness at that level. At intervals of about sixty yards, there are square projections to afford a flanking fire, while at the corner there is a regular bastion, surmounted by a fort two or three stories high. Near the gate the wall is immensely strengthened, being (at a guess) fifty feet thick there. An outwork protects the gate, being connected with the wall which divides the two ditches. Through this a second gate (not opposite the inner one) leads out into the space between the two cities. Pagoda-like buildings rise at intervals above the wall, especially over the gateways.

"We continued our march westward,—the small mosques constantly met with along the road form most convenient indicators of the direction, pointing out as they do the course towards Mecca, which, in Toorkistan, is made very slightly south of west. They use a small compass for this purpose, with an arm pointing west. Some three miles out, we halted for the Yoozbashee, and then proceeded with him through a thickly peopled country.

"However, about six miles from Yârkand, we suddenly entered upon a tract consisting of sand-hills covered with coarse grass. This tract we crossed transversely for eight miles, but its width straight across must be much less. It bears the appearance of having been brought down by some large flood of water, and so heaped upon the fertile plains. In the middle we crossed a wide depression, extending as far as we could see right and left, and filled with marshes and pools of water, with a small rivulet connecting them. This may have been the latest channel of the torrent which brought down the sand; as we often see, when a stream of water has been poured on to light soil of any kind, it carries a quantity down with it, heaping it up in front of itself and at its sides, leaving, when it dries, a raised ridge with a depressed channel down the centre.

"Emerging from this raised sandy country, we came out upon a plain sloping upwards to the foot of a range of mountains, which were now visible (about twelve miles distant, they say, to the west), apparently running north and south. As I write down this distance, I am forcibly struck by the contrast between the climate of this country and of India. For it is twelve miles from Kangra to the range of the outer Himâlaya, and at Kangra they seem to overhang the town. Every gorge and every rock could be counted, one would think, so distinctly are the forms visible. But here, at a distance of twelve miles, the Pamir Mountains appear to be a distant range, of which the outline only is distinguishable.*

"The sloping plain at their foot is dotted with villages, more sparsely, however, than the country

* On my return, I found that the real crest of the range is very much farther back than twelve miles.

round Yârkand. What secrets are hid among those mountains, which so few European eyes have ever looked upon! At this point they seem scarcely to deserve their appellation of '*Bâm-i-doonya*,' or, 'Upper Floor of the World.' A lower range is chiefly visible, a long, almost level line, while the giants of the range rise behind it, forming in appearance a higher and more distant chain. The Yoozbashee pointed to the mountains due west, and said, 'Beyond these lies Badakhshân; again, a little more to the right, Bokhâra; still farther, where the range disappears in the distance, is the road to my own country, Andijân; while to the north, where no mountains are visible from here, is Russia (Siberia).' I learnt from him that the King's dominions extend far up the valleys of this chain to the confines of Badakhshân; they are full of nomad inhabitants, and contain many villages. The only name which he could give me for the range was that of 'Kizil-tâgh'—'Red Mountain,' evidently a mere local appellation. Orientals, as has often been remarked, are bad at generalization. They will have a name for every part, but none for the whole.

"Turning N. N. W., after a halt for prayers, we rode about four miles further through fields, and then were met by the Beg of Kokh-robât, who, after dismounting and taking my hand, escorted us into the large village of that name. It contains two serais, the larger of which was full of two-humped camels and bales of merchandise. In the court-yards of the houses I here observed, for the first time, open carts used in fieldwork by the country people. I forgot to mention that we had met several 'arabahs' on the road with three or four horses a piece (never more than one wheeler, all the rest harnessed abreast as leaders, and driven with reins from the cart). Passing through the bazâr, at a distance of a few hundred yards farther we entered a large square surrounded by high battlemented walls newly built; thence into a second large court containing a garden, and having a range of buildings at one side. I was shown into a large room with carpets and a fire. My agent and the servants were equally well lodged. The Yoozbashee told me that this was a kind of royal rest-house, built by the present King for his own private use on his journeys. There are similar ones all the way to Kâshghar. They are called 'oorda.' Snow is lying in all sheltered spots, two or three inches deep, while the sloping plain and the mountains beyond are thinly covered with it. The cold is intense; the bitter wind made my agent quite ill, while even the Yoozbashee complained that his feet had no feeling left. Thanks to the Governor's fur-robe, I did not feel the least chilled.

"Our conversation during the day fell upon the subject of the Governor. He has the reputation of being immensely learned; my own acquaintance with him has shown me that he takes an interest in subjects which are utterly ignored by the majority of his countrymen. It appears that he was formerly chief secretary to the Khan of Khokand.

His fame has been great ever since the day when he wrote such a letter in his master's name to the Ameer of Bokhâra that none of the moollahs in that country could understand it! This seems to be considered the acme of learning in Central Asia; the fulness of light ends in darkness! When first my agent reached Yârkand, the Governor tested him in the same manner, though, I presume, with less severity, and put men to watch whether he read his letters with ease.

"The next day our course lay north-west, through a stony desert at the foot of the mountains. During part of the way we had a jungle of low scrub on our right, which is said to reach all the way to Aksoo, and to be full of wild beasts, tigers, &c. About halfway we stopped at a solitary 'serai,' with a mosque and two wells (nearly 100 feet deep). This had all been built by the present King, who seems to be doing a great deal for the good of the country. Several arabahs had stopped here to feed the horses, and the women were peeping out at the stranger and his party. They belonged to the better classes, and were extremely fair-complexioned, but with black hair. They reminded me of Rubens' women in shape, so different from the dark, almond-eyed beauties of India. Opposite this place the outer and nearer range of hills on our left began to trend away westward, while the higher chain behind was invisible in the haze. However, just before reaching our destination, we saw it against the sky rising into several very high peaks. Apparently it had continued in one straight line, although the lower range in front of it had receded westward.

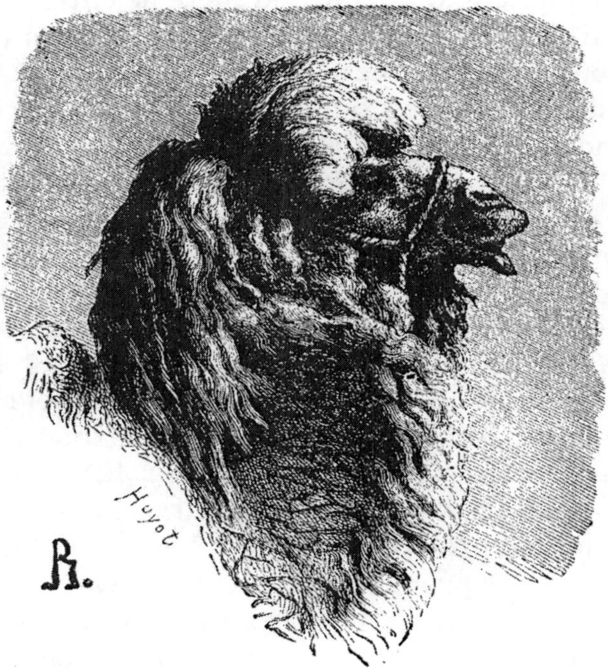

KALMUCK CAMEL.

"Before reaching our night's resting-place, we came upon a solitary ruined mosque, and a dry tank in the desert. The Yoozbashee took me off the road to see them, and told me that the mosque had been first put there by Chenghiz Khan while marching to the conquest of Toorkistân! The tank was such as he made at all his desert halting-places. Water sufficient for his vast hordes was carried on camels, and when they encamped, a tank was dug and filled with this water for the use of the men and cattle. Such is their tradition. They say also that he had a tent large enough to accommodate 10,000 men, and there he entertained hosts of guests, and had tea served to them in cups made of precious stones!

"While conversing thus, we came upon cultivated land, and presently entered the large village of Kizil. This word signifies 'red,' a name well deserved by the color of the soil. My surmise that there must be iron in it was speedily verified by the sight of several furnaces for smelting the ore.

"During the whole day there was a bitter wind from the north, almost directly in our faces. The Yoozbashee asked me whether I should prefer to put up in the royal 'oorda,' where the rooms are large and cold, or in a house in the little town, which would be warmer. I chose the latter, as I would not miss the opportunity of seeing as much as I can of the people. We were received by an officer whose features at once struck me as something different from the regular Toorkee type. He had a long aquiline nose and large round eyes, while his features were finer and his face less fleshy. Hearing him outside my door talking nothing but Persian as he gave his directions for procuring all he wanted, I inquired who he was. They told me he was a Tâjik from Andijân, one of the race akin to the Persians, who held the country before the Tartar invasion. I was very anxious to have a talk with him, as the first specimen of his race that I have seen, but could not get hold of him when I was at leisure.

"In the evening the village-boys amused themselves by sliding on the frozen tank, as in England. Starting, the next morning, through a large crowd of the inhabitants, assembled as usual to witness our departure, we travelled still north-west through a country of mixed cultivation and waste or pasture. The Yoozbashee pointed out to me a large barrow on the right side of the road, where he said were buried the Chinese dead who fell in a battle that took place here twelve years ago. The Mussulman soldiers of Wallé Khan, who were killed on the same occasion, are buried in numerous graves on the left of the road. One of our party, Sâdoo Khoja, an old soldier who was with me at Shahidoolla, had been present at the battle. Wallé Khan was defeated, and fled to Kâshghar, where he had built a house of human skulls, as also at Yanghissâr. The armies are said to have numbered 50,000 on each side; but part of the Chinese were stationed at places nearer Yârkand, and I cannot make out the actual numbers engaged. The Chinese were all infantry, the Andijânees cavalry.

"The mountains continued parallel with our route, which ran about north-west. After riding not quite three tâsh (say fourteen miles), we halted at a village full of ironworks. I was taken to a house where the large room was given up to me, the family retiring into some inner apartments. A bustling, good-humored farmer's wife did the honors, and was very grateful to me for interceding with the Yoozbashee, who wished to turn her whole household out of doors. A few presents of tea, meat and bread (from my dastar-khân), were received with numerous Allaho-akbers, and a return present of a melon. Later in the day, at the time of breaking the fast, her husband advanced, bringing me a basin of hot *macaroni* soup, while she brought me a newly baked cake of bread; both very good indeed. Basins of soup were also given to my Hindoo servants, who, although unable to eat of it, at a hint from me took the basins with a bow, and, going out, handed them over to the other servants. The household arrangements are quite as good as those of an English small farmer and his family. Neat and clean earthenware dishes placed on the shelves; large, well made, and ornamented wardrobe boxes—everything comfortable and well-to-do. The entrance is through a regular farm-yard, with sheds for the cattle on one side, littered down with straw, closed stables for the horses, cocks and hens strutting about, and all the tillage implements standing up in corners. The hay and straw are stacked on the roofs, while a door leads out into a walled orchard. To make the scene more homelike, snow is lying an inch or two deep over the whole country, and the roadside pond is hard frozen, with village boys cutting out slides on it in their hob-nailed boots.

"In the afternoon, I went a little way down the lane to see an iron-smelting furnace at work. It is just like a dice-box, four or five feet high, with a roof over it, leaving an exit in the middle for the smoke. Round the dice-box, under the roof, sit six boys and girls blowing skin bellows with each hand—twelve bellows in all. An opening shows the glowing mass with a stream of molten stuff slowly .oozing downwards. A pit two feet deep shows the bricked-up door of the furnace, through which the metal is extracted daily. The ore is broken up by a man with a hammer, who keeps throwing it in at the chimney, while another supplies charcoal through the same opening. No third substance. Twenty 'châraks'' weight (sixteen lbs. each) of ore, and the same quantity of charcoal, are used in the twenty-four hours, and the produce is about *four* 'chârakș' of iron. The metal is very good and fine-grained, looking almost like steel when made up into tools. In the hill-districts of India, where magnetic oxide of iron is found, the process is almost the same; but the blast is much less, only two people blowing one skin in each hand, or four bellows instead of twelve. The molten metal also is taken out hot, and hammered, while here, in Toorkistân, it is allowed to cool for a whole night before the furnace is opened. The ore is a black-looking stone (got by digging from the mountains fifteen or twenty miles off), which breaks square, or with straight edges. Returning from this furnace, we were amused at watching an urchin four or five years old who had brought a donkey to drink at the pond. Although his home was only twenty yards off, he would not walk; but his difficulty was in mounting the donkey. First he tried to swarm up its forelegs, but as that would not do, he took it to the wall, and then climbed triumphantly on to its back. Then seating himself almost on the tail (as one sees in England), he whipped him up into a donkey's gallop, and disappeared into a neighboring farm-yard. They begin their riding habits early in Toorkistân.

"In the afternoon, two officers of the Beg of Yang-hissar were brought to me by the Yoozbashee. They began by embracing me, and said they had been sent to welcome me. Presently they returned, bringing a dastar-khân and a fine sheep, and making excuses for not offering more, as nothing could be got in this village. My poor Yoozbashee is quite powerless here, being out of the immediate government of his relative, the Governor. He could hardly get anything for himself even, so I sent him half a sheep, &c.—a strange turning of the tables.

"The next morning (the 7th) I went out to examine the neighboring iron-smelting furnace which had just been opened in order to take out the pig of iron, the result of yesterday's smelting. All night the furnace had been allowed to cool, and about eight o'clock the hearth was opened, and the mass of metal, still warm, was removed from the bottom. The hearth slopes towards the front, where it terminates in a narrow neck. Before being charged again, it is lined with some sort ot fire-clay. The furnace itself is wider at the bottom, slightly diminishing in diameter as it ascends.

"Here again the villagers were full of curiosity regarding my habits. They asked my agent whether I did not get tired sitting up always on a chair! They are much struck, too, at the number of dishes and plates which I require at my meals. They themselves use only one large dish between four or five of them to eat from.

"I started with my party from the farm-house, and was joined by the Yoozbashee and his followers outside of the village. Riding still in a direction more west than north, and parallel with the range of high mountains on our left, we gradually converged towards the long low edge of sand-hills which had been dimly visible yesterday to our right. After passing through alternate grassy plains (now dry and withered looking) and village cultivation for two tâsh, we halted at a solitary 'langar' (or rest-house) on the edge of the sandy track. While sitting before a fire here, we were joined by a Mirza-bashee, or chief of scribes, who had been sent to meet me. With him we rode the rest of the way to Yang-hissar.

"First we crossed transversely the lines of sand-hills. Their ridges much resembled the waves of the sea when subsiding after a storm, as they come rolling in to the shore in long lines divided by broad spaces of almost level water. There was the same order apparent through the same confusion, and the size is about the same. These hills are composed of stratified sand, assuming in some of the ridges the consistency of stone, and dipping north. The spaces between were now covered with withered vegetation. After riding about five miles slantingly through this tract, we came to the fertile banks of a small river which had cut for itself a gorge through the hill. The regular bridge was broken, but we crossed on the ice, where a gang of laborers were employed in strewing earth on it as a road for us. They had also thrown a temporary bridge from the ice to the shore across a space where the current had not allowed the water to freeze. Our party was joined by the officials in charge of the work.

"Ascending the high bank of the river, we found ourselves in a well populated district, still, however, traversed by the low ridges of sand. Crossing the last of these, we saw at our feet a charming landscape which reminded me of the Vale of Cashmere, an illusion supported by the sight of the snowy mountains behind us and to our left. As far as the eye could see, there stretched a highly cultivated plain, to which orchards and groves of trees surrounding the numerous scattered homesteads gave almost the appearance of a wood. A little way out on the plain, the orchards and houses crowded more thickly together pointed out the town of Yang-hissâr. We reached this plain by a rapid descent of about fifty yards, and then rode through a country resembling the suburbs of a large city. In one house the walls were ornamented with drawings of steamers and railway trains! Before we entered the streets, however, we turned aside to the left, and rode along under the high mud walls of the old town. Leaving this, and preceded by the Mirza-bashee and the officials, I was led to one of the royal rest-houses, consisting as usual of a large walled enclosure, with court-yards and ranges of good-sized rooms. The 'new-town' or fort appeared about half a mile to our right and the same distance from the old town. In dimensions it resembles a large fort rather than a town. To me was assigned a room handsomely carpeted, with large cushion-mattresses covered with silk arranged along the walls, and near the fire, for myself and my visitors to sit on. My servants and the agent were lodged in other apartments of the same building, but the Yoozbashee had to take up his quarters in a neighboring farm-house, although there was plenty of room for him. Apparently it is only the King's guest who is allowed to lodge in the royal rest-house. Our acquaintance of yesterday ushered in a large dastar-khân, sheep, fowls, &c. I hear that he is one of the King's principal 'masters of the ceremonies,' sent to see the proper etiquette followed. At the Yoozbashee's suggestion, I gave him a 'khilat,' or robe, and another as to the secretary.

"In the afternoon arrived the officer to whom I had given a present on the first night after leaving Yârkand. I afterwards learnt he was a relative of the King. The Yoozbashee now brought him to pay me a visit. He said he had gone on to Yârkand on some business to the Governor in connection with the issue of warm clothing to the troops. The Governor had instructed him to join my party, and accompany me on, unless orders came from the King for me to delay at Yang-hissar. As to this, my agent was in the afternoon told by the master of the ceremonies that he had received orders for me to sleep two nights here, and go on the next day. So I suppose I shall have the company of my friend, the King's relative, during the rest of the journey. He seems a very good fellow, as hearty and good-humored as the Yoozbashee, and, as I told him, I hope to improve in my Persian by having him to talk to.

"The same afternoon, while strolling about the neighborhood, I happened to come across the Yoozbashee's temporary dwelling-place, and saw him standing outside. He shouted to me to come, brought me in, and made me sit down by the fire to drink tea while he washed his face and arms according to rule, and said his evening prayers. In the intervals of his devotions, after turning his head right and left to salute the two angels who are supposed to sit on each shoulder of a Mussulman, he interrupted himself to call for more tea and more sugar for Shaw Sahib, and then continued his chant of 'Bismillah-ar-rahmân-ar-raheem.' He made me stay, and join in his meal; first breaking the fast by dipping a finger in a cup of salt and water, and putting it to his mouth. Not till after this is done does it become lawful to eat other food. He gave me a bowl of soup containing little lumps of paste tasting like macaroni. He was very anxious that I should stay to join in the great pilao of rice and mutton that was preparing, but I with difficulty excused myself, saying it was getting dark, and I should not find my way home.

"On the morning of the 8th, my Moonshee was

visited by a moollah who said he had been present when Schlagintweit was killed. He came before Wallé Khan, who was then besieging the Chinese new town or fort at Kâshghar. Schlagintweit asked how long he had been so engaged. Wallé Khan answered, 'Three months.'—'Oh,' rejoined Schlagintweit, 'my countrymen would take the place in three days. There is no difficulty at all.'—'Indeed,' replied the chief; and, turning round, he gave orders to take the Frank out, and cut his throat. The moollah says that Wallé Khan was a regular demon, far different from the present King. Schlagintweit was taken to the banks of the Kâshghar River, and there killed. In his pocket were found a compass and a watch. The executioner offered them to the moollah, who says he refused them.

"To resume my day's report. In the afternoon I took a walk round the neighborhood. The fields are all covered with snow an inch or two thick, and the numerous ponds are all hard frozen. The water-courses (artificial) are very numerous, being led under and over one another to suit different levels. They are at this season nearly all dry, water being only let into them when required for irrigation. The stubble of the Indian corn appears through the snow, that having been the last crop in the fields round here. On returning I was shouted to by the Yoozbashee, while I was making my agent, to his own horror, walk across a frozen sheet of water, a thing he had never in his life before had a chance of doing. The Yoozbashee had a carpet spread for me outside his farm-house on a raised earthen platform, such as are common in the East for sitting on out of doors. He was examining the country through my opera-glass, which he had sent for.

"My servants visited the town during the day. From gate to gate it is over 1100 paces long, but the suburbs outside the wall double the size of the town. It was the weekly market-day, and crowds flocked in the streets. My servants found two fellow-countrymen (Hindoo traders) at the serai, and described with much laughter a long row of bullocks' carcases that were hanging just opposite their doors. Travelling subdues prejudices wonderfully; who would have thought of Hindoos making a joke of such a circumstance!

"The 10th of January we remained at Yang-hissar, and I took a long walk to the first ridge of the low hills. These hills I find run exactly east and west here, and appear parallel to the range of snowy mountains. I measured the ice of a tank; it was eight inches thick! In the afternoon it was announced that we should march next morning. Accordingly, on the 11th, we travelled about twenty-five miles, as far as the village of Yepchang. The country consists alternately of village lands under culture, and of grassy plains covered with cattle and horses. We crossed the River Koosoon by a wooden bridge at a narrow spot; above and below this place it was about fifty or sixty yards wide, and is said to be dangerous to cross on account of quicksands. Now it was nearly entirely frozen over. *En route* we met Mahammad Isâk Jân, the brother of the Governor of Yârkand. We dismounted, and embraced very cordially. As he was on his way back to Yârkand (having gone to Kâshghar since I have been on the road), I gave him many polite messages for his brother. About two o'clock we stopped for prayers at a cottage where they could get warm water for their ablutions. There was a child four or five years old whom the Yoozbashee amused himself by frightening, making faces at it, and clawing at it with his gloves, to the great disturbance of its mother. Riding on again, we had much conversation. He says the pay of a Yoozbashee (captain of 100) is 300 tillahs a year (150*l.*),. while that of a private soldier (cavalry) is 30 tillahs, or 15*l.* Their dress, accoutrements, and horses are all given to them. In war time the pay is more than doubled. He had heard of our Abyssinian war five months ago, but asked the Moonshee whether the Abyssinians were Mussulmans or kâfirs (heathens). He also related to me that last year he carried to Yârkand the news of the capture of Kooché, which is twenty-eight regular marches distant (about 560 miles), and he accomplished the distance in three days, changing his horse twenty-eight times. From the village of Yepchang he went to Yârkand in one day (121 miles). For this service he received forty tillahs at Yârkand=24*l.*, and on his return to the King's camp the latter gave him two silver yamboos (worth 34*l.*). Talking of riding, he remarked that my Moonshee carried himself in a peculiar way, while I rode in the same fashion as himself and his countrymen. The Moonshee's seat is of course that of Indian horsemen, with short stirrups and reins held high. I had myself noticed that the Toorkee seat on horseback is more like that of Englishmen.

"On reaching Yepchang, we were met at our night's quarters by the master of the ceremonies, who had come on in advance to prepare everything for us as usual. He ushered me into my room, and presently returned with the usual dastar-khân. His manner almost proclaims his avocation. Quiet yet decided in his movements, and handsomely dressed, he seems by a glance of his eye to put everybody in his proper place. You remember Steerforth's gentlemanly attendant who made David Copperfield feel so young. My master of ceremonies is a second edition of him.

"We left Yepchang in the morning; the master of ceremonies had ridden in to Kâshghar during the night to announce my arrival. He met us again about halfway. We passed through a populous and well-cultivated country, crossing four rivers during the day's ride. The first was about five miles from Yepchang, and occupied a bed a quarter of a mile wide with its numerous channels. We had some difficulty in crossing the nearest channel, as the ice was rotten, and the horses had to wade. Some of the loads got a wetting. The other channels were crossed on the ice or on temporary bridges. A broad dam retained the further waters at a level considerably above the rest, so as to form as it were two separate rivers. A broad artificial cut also conveyed water along the higher level. Leaving the bed of these streams, we passed in sight of two small towns right and left of the road. At the next stream, which we crossed by a bridge, an arabah was being dragged with great difficulty through the broken ice and water. On the banks of the last stream we stopped for the afternoon prayer. The fortress or new city of Kâshghar was here in full sight, in the midst of an open treeless country, covered, however, with cultivation. The defences, as we approached, were seen to be exactly similar to those of Yârkand New City, but the place is smaller. Passing several obtuse angles of the wall, we reached a gate on the E.N.E. side, before which, however, we were met by a Yoozbashee carrying a double-barrelled rifle of European make. He and the master of ceremonies preceded us in through the gate, past a *corps de garde*, where sat rows of soldiers (converted Chinese), through a second gate to the right past more rows of soldiers, and into a third gateway giving entrance into the New City. In front of these men were ranged their arms, consisting of huge muskets called 'taifoor' which are managed by four men a piece. These 'taifoor' were propped up in front on a forked rest, while their butts rested on the ground. At the third portal all our party dismounted, and we walked for two hundred yards through a broad avenue, crowded with men in bright-colored robes—all apparently hangers-on of the Court. Through these a way was kept clear for us by numerous ushers with white wands, one of whom preceded us down a street to the right to the house assigned to me. It is apparently a new building with numerous large courtyards, in the farthest of which are my own quarters. The rooms are smaller than at Yârkand, but to make up for this, there is a large covered reception-place with a verandah in front of all. Here an immense Khoten carpet is spread with rugs along the back.

"A 'dastar-khan' was immediately brought by an officer, and I was asked when I wished to visit the King. I answered that I should wish to do so at once, but that, if it were proper that I should present my gifts at my first visit, they could not be unpacked and got ready in time. They replied that the visit had better be to-morrow then. Aftewards they presented to me a Mahram, or usher, and a Dahbashee or captain of ten (a sergeant), who are appointed to remain night and day in attendance. The Mahram deputed for this office is the son of the former Mussulman Governor of Kâshghar, under the Chinese.

"We now began getting together the gifts which I had brought for the King, cleaning and putting the things in order. The Yoozbashee came in after dark and began asking me what I proposed to give, so I sent for my Hindoo agent to bring the list. Meanwhile the Mahram came in and sat down. When the list was brought, I observed that the Yoozbashee would hardly listen to it, but turned the conversation, saying : 'You may give just what you like to the King ; my task is only to conduct you in safety to his presence.' When the Mahram had gone out, the Yoozbashee told us in a low voice that he could not say anything on that subject in the former's presence, as it would be reported that he was telling the guest what he was to give and what not to give. I took the opportunity of asking his advice as to whether I should give a separate present to the King's son. Ascertaining that there were no listeners outside, he replied, 'Don't give a needle's value to any one but the King. He would be displeased if you did.' "

CHAPTER XV.

DETENTION AT KASHGHAR.

THE interview with Mahammad Yakoob, the Atalik-Ghazee or King, took place on the 12th of January, the day after Shaw's arrival. We give his account of it, entire :

"Early this morning all my presents for the King were set in order on trays, and about nine o'clock various ushers and officials came to fetch me. I started, escorted by the Yoozbashee who met me yesterday, my own Yoozbashee (whose name, by-the-bye, is Mahammad Yakoob like the King's), the Mahrambashee, &c., and followed by between thirty and forty men carrying the various articles forming my 'nazar,' or gift. From my door to the entrance of the palace, a distance of a quarter of a mile, a broad avenue had been formed in the crowd, whose bright robes of various colors had the effect of a living kaleidoscope. Entering the gateway, we passed through several large quadrangles, whose sides were lined with ranks upon ranks of brilliantly attired guards, all sitting in solemn silence, so that they seemed to form part of the architecture of the buildings, whose want of height would otherwise have given them a mean appearance. Entire rows of these men were clad in silken robes, and many seemed to be of high rank from the richness of their equipments. Those of divers tribes, and with strange arms, were mixed with the mass. For the first time I saw soldiers armed with bows and carrying quivers full of arrows. They were Kalmâks. The whole effect was curious and novel. The numbers, the solemn stillness, and the gorgeous coloring gave a sort of unreality to this assemblage of thousands. In the innermost court, smaller than the rest, only a few select attendants were seated. Here none entered with me except my conductor, the Yoozbashee of yesterday.

"Approaching a kind of pavilion, with a projecting verandah roof, elaborately painted in arabesques, I entered a side door. I passed through a small antechamber, and was conducted into a large audience chamber, or hall, in the middle of which, close to a window, was seated a solitary individual, whom I at once knew must be the King. I advanced alone, and when I drew near, he half rose on his knees and held out both hands to me. I grasped them in the usual Toorkee manner, and at his invitation sat down opposite him. Then, as is the custom, I rose again to ask after his health ; he would not let me do so, but motioned to me to sit, drawing me nearer to himself. He began inquiring after my health, and hoping my journey had been comfortably performed, to which I replied, excusing myself for my bad Persian, which, however, he smilingly declared was quite comprehensible. Then ensued a silence of about a minute, each waiting for the other to speak (this is a polite etiquette). Finally he commenced again by a remark about the weather (English-like). I responded and went on to say that my countrymen had heard with the greatest pleasure that the brothers of our friends, the Sultan of Room and his people, had established a kingdom in Toorkistân in place of the Chinese, with whom we had already had three wars. For myself I said that the Lord Sahib had not sent me, nor entrusted me with any letter; but I had come of my own accord, attracted by the renown of his name. He nodded and muttered assent to all that I said, and then replied that he had been delighted when he heard that Shaw Sahib was approaching his dominions with a friendly purpose. As for the Lord Sahib (the Viceroy of India), he was very great, and he himself was small in comparison. I answered, 'The Viceroy is very great, but our Queen, his mistress, is greater.' At this he stared.

"I continued that I hoped for the establishment of friendship between our nations, and that between friends there was no question of greater or smaller. He said, 'And you yourself, did you not send me a letter?' I replied, 'Yes; I sent one by the hand of my agent to Yârkand, but he had no opportunity of delivering it to you; therefore I have now presented it with my gifts.' I then said that I had brought a few specimens of

English rifles, &c., for him, and hoped he would accept them and pardon any deficiencies. He laughed, and said, 'What need is there of presents between you and me? we are already friends, and your safe arrival has been sufficient satisfaction to me.' With this he crooked his two forefingers together to typify our friendship. I said that I hoped to have some further conversation with him, but that on the present occasion he was probably not at leisure, and there was also no interpreter present to make up for my deficiencies in Persian. He replied, 'Between you and me no third person is requisite; friendship requires no interpreter,' and he stretched his hand over, and gave mine a hearty grasp. Then he added, 'Now enjoy yourself for a few days, and see all the sights; consider this place and all it contains as your own, and on the third day we will have another talk; you shall bring your agent with you, and talk with me for an hour; after that we will meet oftener, and so our friendship will be increased.'

"Then he called to an attendant, who brought in a pink satin robe, and the King dismissed me very graciously after the robe had been put on me. I rejoined my conductor at the gateway of the inner court, and returned home through the same brilliant assemblage. At each successive gateway my party was swollen by the accession of those who had been left behind there as not worthy to proceed farther with me. On reaching my own door, my conductors left me, each wishing me 'moobârak,' or 'happy,' to which I returned the proper answer of 'Koolligh,' or 'your servant.'

"Before starting for this visit, I had been much put out by my agent not being allowed to accompany me. The officials also told me that, whatever I had to say to the King, I must say now, as the King was very great, and I should have no further opportunity of speaking to him. I, however, determined that I would not attempt this, as it was impossible at a first visit to say properly all that I wished to say, even were an interpreter provided. I therefore resolved only to request a further interview, and as you see this was the proper course, and the King evidently expected it. Had I begun a long discourse, I should not have made myself understood to begin with, and, moreover, should have trespassed on the etiquette of a first interview. I cannot think what was the reason of my being told otherwise by the officials.

"During the day, we began to perceive many marks of neglect on the part of those who were charged with our entertainment. Supplies of all kinds were either not to be got, or were scantily furnished to the servants, after much asking. No official came to inquire after our wants. We could not help comparing this treatment with that of the Dâd-khwâh, and regretting our Yârkand quarters. Here we were all, masters and men, crowded into one court. Then *my* house alone consisted of three courts, and the agent and his servants had separate quarters. I was also annoyed by the constant running to and fro of boys and servants to a room full of stores at the end of the court. There was no privacy whatever.

"At last, my displeasure culminated when I saw one of my servants approaching with a tray full of bread, which had been served out to him instead of the usual 'dastar-khân,' presented by the proper official, and put before me with proper ceremony. Of course, the thing was a mere trifle in itself; but in the East, want of respect is a precursor of danger. I resolved to stop it if I could, and ordered the man to put the tray down outside my door, and to tell any one that asked about it that I did not want it. My Yârkand interpreter, Jooma (for it was he), stood aghast at the order, and told me he dared not do it, as it would be considered a dreadful insult by the King. I re-assured him, and made him do as I said. Then my Moonshee came with a scared face, and begged me to take in the tray. Jooma went away and hid himself in the kitchen, until the storm should blow over. Soon my move began to produce its effect. Officials went and came, looking at the rejected tray, and then hastening out. At last they approached and carried it off. Then arrived the 'Sirkar' (or comptroller of the household), an official in charge of all the royal stores. He went and sat down by my agent, and made a long apology, saying that on account of the great festival of the Eed to-morrow he had been unable to pay me proper attention, and those whose duty it was had neglected their charge. Then he entered my room and spread the cloth himself in front of me, putting on it a number of trays containing fruits and preserves of all sorts, brought by the attendants who remained outside. He then stood with folded hands until I broke and ate a piece of bread as a token of acceptance. No sooner was he gone than the bleating of a sheep was heard. It was a second one for my Moonshee, one having been given me in the morning as usual. Presently, although it was now dark, supplies of all sorts came pouring in in profusion, loads of wood, bundles of hay, rice, corn, in fact, all that had been before kept back.

"After dinner the Yoozbashee came in and begged me not to be angry at any apparent neglect; saying that the number of people collected for the festival created the greatest confusion, and that, if the King heard of any misunderstanding, it would cost the lives of several officials. I replied, 'I do not feel the least anger; on the contrary, I am very grateful to the King for all his kindness.' He said, 'I am only speaking about the future, and hope you will make allowances for any want of due attention. After further conversation, he went away, but I learnt that he had previously spoken his mind in strong terms to the culpable officials, telling them that he had not brought the royal guest so far with such care merely to be offended by their gross neglect, and that the honors bestowed on me by the King were not to be made of no avail by them. Later in the evening the penitent Sirkar came and sat down by my fire for a talk, begging pardon at the same time for the intrusion. I told him I was delighted to see him there; and now my point being gained, I was all smiles, gave him tea and sweetmeats, and dismissed him with friendly words.

"So ended my first and, I hope, my last encounter with the Atalik-Ghâzee's* servants. I have come to the conclusion that the King had given orders for every attention to be paid to us; but being engrossed by state affairs, he is not able to bestow that attention on details which the Governor does. Greedy officials are thus enabled to intercept for their own benefit the favors intended for the guest. Another explanation, however, may be the true one. The Shaghâwal may have exceeded the measure of honor and attention ordered to be paid to me by the King. Ambitious aims or the desire to secure a friendly place of refuge in case of necessity may have induced him to exhibit his own especial regard for the English. But this still leaves the fact unexplained that my public reception here is conducted with more *éclat* than it was at Yârkand, while in private matters, to which the King's eye cannot reach, my comfort is less consulted."

The next day Shaw began to reap the fruits of his victory. Everything was supplied in abundance, and twice in the day a hot dish (the first of macaroni soup, the second of mutton and rice) was brought to him from the royal kitchen. In the morning a present of half a dozen pheasants and

---

* Atalik-Ghâzee is the title assumed by the King Yakoob Beg. It means Tutor or Leader of the Champions of the Faith.

wild duck arrived from the King. In every other respect, however, Shaw was restricted, and, under the circumstances, he did not venture to make any protest. On the 14th he writes :

"I am settling down into the former prison life that I led at Yârkand. Although the King told me to go about and amuse myself, yet I am halt afraid that it was only a figure of speech, and at any rate it is wiser not to excite suspicion by being too anxious to take advantage of the permission. But you can fancy that it is rather difficult to get through the day without books (for all mine I have read through a hundred times). The talk of my Guddees is amusing ; Choomâroo, especially, has a hundred anecdotes to relate, with shrewd remarks on every occurrence. Every one that goes out brings in some news of the outer world, which he contributes to the common stock of conversation. The discovery of a new row of shops, or ot a fresh gateway, furnishes talk for an hour, while a meeting with one of the Indian sepoys who have taken service here, is hailed like the periodical arrival of the mail steamer in some dull colony. We linger reluctantly over each topic ; we wring out of it each drop of subject matter which it will afford. We return to it again and again, like a dog to a bone which he has already gnawed clean. Meanwhile, I pace up and down the verandah, the only exercise that I can obtain. At any sign ot animated conversation, a raised voice, or a laugh, half-a-dozen faces peer out of as many doors all round the court, like marmots at their holes. To

KING YAKOOB BEG.

the Mussulmans their devotions are a great resource. The washings of face, arms, hands, and feet, the undressing to do this, and the dressing again afterwards, the spreading a cloth to prostrate themselves on, and, finally, the varied postures required during the prayers—all these help to pass the time."

The next day he received a message to the effect that the King had inquired very kindly after him, and had said: "Go and tell Shaw Sahib that I am loaded with business at present, but hope, in a day or two, to have time for a long talk with him. Tell him not to be impatient at the delay, for I look upon him in the light of a friend." Shaw sent back word that he was much obliged to the King for putting off their interview until the latter had more time, as what he wished to say could not be said in a hurry. He added that he was ready to wait any number of days, so that in the end there might be full leisure for all his business.

Shaw's subsequent experience showed him that his answer was accepted literally, and with all the Oriental disregard of time. We quote from his journal, January 20th: "During the visit of the Yoozbashee and the master of ceremonies, the hot dishes arrived from the King's kitchen. I invited the guests to join us, and we made an impromptu meal, *à la* Toorkee. The three commenced operations on the huge dish with their fingers, while I sat on my chair, and used a separate plate and knife and fork, to their great admiration. Their delight is to use one of my spoons to stir their tea with. When they had finished, I had some grapes put before them, but they raised cries of horror, saying, 'How can we eat them now, after meat?' They seemed as much astonished as English people would be were the soup served after dessert. I explained our custom in this respect, but they thought it quite barbarous. They explained their theory on the subject. Put into European phraseology it was this: that eating meat before fruit was like sending a heavy goods train down a line in front of a fast express; the fruit being more quickly digestible than the meat, and therefore proper to be eaten first.

"Hitherto the servants have been allowed to go out of doors at will. To-day most of them were turned back, and told to stay within the four walls. My agent asked me the story of the prisoners in Abyssinia, apparently considering ours a parallel case. I cannot say that we feel much anxiety, however, though this kind of imprisonment is annoying, as well as ridiculous.

"I learn that the price of cotton here is about one tanga per jing, or three tangas for four pounds, which equals 3*d*. per pound!

"*Wednesday, January 20th.*—For several days past the Yoozbashee has not come to see me. To-day I sent to inquire after him, and he sent me back many salâms, with a message, saying that he was most desirous of visiting me, but these rascals (meaning the King's officers in attendance) kept such a watch on him that he was afraid to come.

"*January 22nd.*—This morning the Governor arrived from Yârkand. He was received, as I was, by soldiers lining the gateways and approaches, and went to pay his respects to the King at once. At the same time he presented a nazar, or gift, consisting of 100 'koors' of silver (1700*l.*), and thirty horses, mounted by as many slaves, fully armed and equipped from head to foot, with four changes of clothing a-piece. Besides these, there were numerous minor gifts. He himself rode a splendid horse, with housings mounted with turquoises, and saddle-cloth of gold brocade. The Yoozbashee rode out as far as Yepchang to meet him, and came to see me about one o'clock, after being dismissed by the King. He said he was famished, having started long before daybreak without any food. I made him stop and join me in a huge pilao, a great part of which he devoured.

"The Governor sent me many kind messages of inquiry, and said he had heard how tired I was of confinement (for yesterday, sick of this life, I had poured forth my complaints into the sympathizing ears of the Yoozbashee, who tried to pacify me by saying that I was too great a man to go about the place like a common person ; but at the same time he evidently thought my desire for a little open air only reasonable). The Governor told me to have patience for a little longer, that everything should be arranged to my satisfaction, and I should go back with him to Yârkand when he returned. The Yoozbashee affects mystery, and does not mention the Governor's name when the other attendants are present. Whether the Governor's friendliness towards me is in excess of the King's orders, and concealed from his knowledge, I know not ; but he evidently wants me to believe so.

"I have had some Indian dumb-bells made to pass the time with. To-day the Yoozbâshee saw them, and asked their use. He was much pleased with the exercise they afford, and said it was fine training for the arms. He tried them himself, in imitation of me, but never having handled them before, of course could not keep up the play long. I then showed him some other tricks and exercises, such as rising from the ground on one leg, without help from the other, &c. He tried them all, and showed great activity in these novel amusements.

"He says they have earthquakes at Yârkand and Kâshghar two or three times a year ; but last year, at Yepchang, for eight months together, there were shocks two or three times a day. All the houses were shaken to pieces, and have had to be rebuilt. The shocks did not extend beyond the immediate neighborhood of the village."

Shaw's account of his life in Kâshghar is given in the form of a journal. The entries of many days are simply notes of what occurred in his household, and are of no general interest. We will therefore only take such particulars as relate to his intercourse with the King and the chief authorities, or which give some information concerning the country and its people. On the 29th of January, he says : "My Tibetan servant Jooma has confirmed an opinion which has been strengthening in my mind ever since I have been in Toorkistân. He declares that, until this year, the people of this country, and its rulers, had no idea of the British dominion in India. The name of Frank was not even mentioned, except as belonging to a people who had been fighting with the Chinese, and who had some possessions far away in the south. The Maharaja of Cashmere was the great potentate whom they heard of on their borders. Every trader who came from Ladâk was reckoned a Cashmere subject, and was put under the authority of the Cashmere Akskal, or consul, Ahmed Shah. The Indian merchants dared not give any other account of themselves, partly from fear of the Yârkand authorities, who might have detained them, but chiefly on account of the Cashmere authorities, by whose favor alone they had access to the Ladâk market. The reduction of duties last year at Ladâk was such an unusual thing for a native sovereign that it attracted attention, and it was rumored that the English had taken Tibet. My arrival this year, and afterwards that of Hayward, and the accounts given regarding the Maharaja by myself and my servants, who are under no restraints, have convinced the authorities here that the English power is paramount in India. Until last year, they do not seem to have known of its existence there, but sent an envoy to the Maharaja of Cashmere *and Delhi*. So new is the notion to them that they now call all British subjects Franks. The mistakes occasioned by this are amusing. First came the original report that *five*

Franks had reached Shahidoolla, when I and four Indian servants arrived there.

"A few days ago the Sirkar came officially to tell me that another Frank (politely rendered by 'Sahib') was approaching Kâshghar with Mahammad Nazzar, and the King wished to know whether I was aware of his business, or the purpose of his coming. I said that I only knew of Hayward, and did not even know a third Sahib had come into the country. The next day the Sirkar came back to explain the mistake. The Frank, he said, was not an 'Inglish,' like myself, but a Mussulman; in fact, it was my friend, the old mutineer. A day or two after, the Governor of Yârkand arrived. News was brought in that Hayward Sahib had arrived, also, that day. He had been received by the King, and his lodging was appointed in a house outside the walls. Next day came the further reports of his sayings and doings. He had said to the King, 'Why do you bring in your water for this fortress *under* the wall? I can bring it in *over* the wall.' They also said that he was quite an old man. This puzzled us; but we came to the conclusion that the color of Hayward's beard, being light, had been mistaken for the grayness of age, as I have several times known to be done in India. A couple of days afterwards, Jooma inquired for the officer who is in attendance on Hayward, and then it came out that neither he nor Hayward had left Yârkand."

During the greater part of February, Shaw's principal occupation consisted in trying to distil some authentic news out of the rumors and stories which those of his servants picked up who were allowed to frequent the bazârs. He was by this time satisfied that his own imprisonment (as it really was) indicated the intention of the King to send him back to Leh ; since, if his death had been resolved upon, there could have been no objection to his temporary liberty. One of his servants, Sarda, met a native official, who stated to him that the King was much pleased with the Englishman's visit. He said that it was a most unusual mark of favor for the King to keep a stranger so long near him ; the most were sent away after two or three days. Sarda remarked that Shaw was annoyed at being kept so long in the house ; whereupon the official replied : "The Sahib must not think anything of that ; it is the custom of the country, and is universally practised with strange visitors : they are never allowed to go about at will, and even so are rarely permitted to stay more than a day or two at the King's headquarters."

On the 25th of February, Shaw says : "The other day our horses broke loose, and made their way up the ramparts on to the wall of the fortress. They were caught after making half the circuit of the town. I pretended astonishment at their not falling over, and thus got a description of the wall from the Yoozbashee. He paced out a distance which on measurement proved to be twelve feet, and said : 'The wall has a roadway on the top of that width ; on both sides are battlements nearly a man's height.' This would make the total thickness of the top about sixteen feet. As the wall is nearly forty feet high (as far as I can judge from seeing it twenty yards off), and slopes inward on both sides from the basement, the width at bottom must be over twenty feet. Near the gateway it is much thicker.

"To-day there is a little news to write. First came the Sirkar with a present from the King, consisting of a chest full of pears from Kooché. We had some talk about my departure. I impressed on him the fact that the road becomes almost impassable when the streams are swollen by the melted snow a few weeks hence. He replied that the King was occupied in preparations for my departure.

"In the evening the master of ceremonies was very communicative. In reply to questions of mine (brought in naturally, after I had led the conversation round about from crickets on the hearth to crickets in the woods, and thence to forests in general, and the forests of the Kâshghar mountains in particular), he told me that the range north of this is called Kakshâl, and that to the south, Kizilzé. The continuation of the Kakshâl range east is called Moostagh, and farther east Thian-Shan. This, of course, we knew already. At the foot of the Kakshâl range is the ancient town of Artash, about twenty miles from Kâshghar.

"Ascending a very winding gorge, where the road is barely wide enough for a horse, a precipitous peak called Moostagh (not the range of that name) is reached. Here the road is compressed between the torrent and the mountain, and this place has been chosen for a fort lately built by the Atalik-Ghâzee. One of its sides abuts on the precipitous mountain, and it commands the only road with its ten guns. The roads from Kool and from Almatee unite shortly beyond it, and continue in one. All other paths across the range have been rendered impracticable. A few months ago the King went in person to inspect the progress of the work. One wall was already built, but he had it thrown down again, as it gave no access to the water. With his own hands he labored at the work, and was perforce imitated by all his officers and nobles. The master of ceremonies complains pathetically of the toil he then went through, carrying huge rocks on his back up and down steep hills. This is the time referred to by Mahammad Omar at Yârkand when he took the news of my approach to the King. The fort is strongly built of stone, and encloses a safe supply of water. The present garrison consists of 500 converted Chinese, 200 Toongânees, and 300 Toorks. The fort, which has been called the Moostagh Tashkoorgan (Ice-mountain Stone Fort), is three days' ride from Kâshghar. Seven or eight days beyond it are the plains of Issik-kül and of Almatee. The Russians, however, are posted in advance of these places.

"The King apparently is a most plucky soldier. He has eleven wounds on his body, five of which are from Russian bullets. While besieging Yârkand, he was hit in the side and in the thigh, and had several horses killed under him. He bound up his wounds with scarfs, and mentioned them to no one, bearing a smiling face when any one approached, but writhing with pain when unobserved. The master of ceremonies was there as usual in personal attendance on him with nine other Mahrams who accompanied him to the field. 'While the King was thus concealing his wounds,' says the master of ceremonies, 'I, who had received a scratch on the face' (of which he showed us the mark), from a Toongânee spear, was lying groaning night and day in my tent. When no one was near, I sat up drinking tea, but when any one came in, I was rolling on the floor with pain. As fast as the wound healed, I tore it open again, and if the siege had lasted two years, I believe I should have kept it open all that time. I had no mind to go out again among the bullets. One had struck the high pommel of my saddle, and another had broken the clasp of my belt. I reflected that if it had been one of these instead of a spear that had struck me in the face, I should have been a dead man. My death would have been reported to the King, and he would have said, "Allaho-akber"' (God is great), 'and that is all! Ah, your bullets are bad things. If it were not for them I should be a brave man. The King does not care for his life, but I care for mine. While I lay there wounded, I had *two* hearts' (which he illustrated by holding out two fingers). 'One said, "Go out to fight;" the other said, "Lie here in peace!"

At night the former heart' (pulling his fore-finger) 'was victorious, but when morning came, I always listened to that which told me to lie still. The King gave me a *koors*, and a brocade robe for *my* wound, but he did not heed his own at all."

On the 1st of March, the orphan boy, whom Shaw had brought with him from the Himalayas, was sent for to be given into the care of Nyaz Beg, Governor of Khoten. The King sent many messages of thanks, &c., and the boy and his goods were carried off by the Sirkar. They said the boy will be kept under the charge of the Governor till he grows up, when his goods will be given to him. Meanwhile, his brother is to be allowed to see him occasionally, but not to touch his property. He will be brought up with the two sons of the Beg, who are about his age.

On the 6th of March, Shaw was officially informed of Hayward's arrival in Kashghar, and on the 11th he writes as follows: "As usual, much time was spent in listening to rumors and scraps of information, furnished by my servants and the officials, out of which I try to build up some grounds of hope for a speedy release and leave to depart. Some say we shall be kept another month; others that we shall start in three days. I told the Yoozbashee to-day, that in my country even prisoners had their complaints forwarded to the proper authorities; but that here, no one would even take a letter for me to the King. In reply he, as usual, invented a number of stories—all lies—to explain the conduct of the King.

"To-day came a long and interesting letter from Hayward. The account I heard of his warlike demonstration at Yârkand appears to have been a great exaggeration. In the first part of his letter, written at Yârkand, he praises the hospitality of the Toorks, and says he shall carry away pleasant recollections of the country; in the second part, written at Kâshghar, he is inclined to think the King the greatest rascal in Asia. Apparently, he made a very laborious trip up and down the Yârkand rivers with valuable results.

"I am more than ever convinced now that the Atalik-Ghâzee is 'exploiting' me for the benefit of subjects and neighbors as an English envoy. He knows perfectly himself that I am not so, as I have repeatedly told both him and the Governor of Yârkand that I am not sent by Government, and they have assented, saying that they knew this before. But for all that they wish the world to be misled on the subject. Hence all this parading of me about the country, and the assembling several thousands to line the approach when I went to visit him. This also, I believe, is the reason why my letter sent by my agent, asking permission to come, was detained till I could deliver it myself, a dreadful solecism otherwise, for the favor which it requested had already been granted. But the parade of the gold casket and ornamented papers presented in state was what they cared for.

"The master of ceremonies says some years ago the Russians asked the Chinese to sell them a few acres of land in a desert at the foot of a mountain.

The Chinese were glad enough to get 500 yamboos for such a spot, but within a year they saw a fortress rising on it. From this centre the Russians have extended in all directions, while the Chinese watched them with their fingers in their mouths! The fortress is Almatee or Vernoje."

On the 20th of March, Shaw's Moonshee, or agent, was taken to see the King, who received him in a cordial but condescending way, and said, 'Sit down, and pray for me.' Thereupon the Moonshee repeated some formal prayers in Arabic to the effect that the King's rule might be to the profit of himself and Islâm; and the King replied, 'With God's blessing, with God's blessing!' After a few more civil words, he was taken into another room, and presented with a robe and 'dastar-khân,' and afterwards led to the inner gateway to make a distant farewell salutation to the King. It is the custom of the country, after receiving a robe, to wear it outside the rest of one's clothes for three days; and, after receiving a turban, to wear it without tucking up the ends for the same period."

Towards the end of March, Shaw received a smuggled note from Hayward, in which the latter expressed his fears that they would both be put to death. Shaw still retained his first impression, that their confinement denoted an ultimate release, and sent back a letter in which he explained his grounds of belief. The servants were no longer confined to the house as at first, and the bearing of the officials was still very friendly and encouraging. One of the men, Jooma, was even allowed to visit the Old City of Kâshgar, which he reported to be larger than Yârkand, and crowded with inhabitants. It has five gates : the stables for animals are underground, and all the houses have upper stories.

On the 1st of April, Shaw writes : "The Chief Jemadar says that the King will start for Yang-hissâr in six days' time. He has been ordered to follow three or four days later, bringing us with him. The Jemadar added, 'Many other officers could have brought you along, but I fancy he thinks you will be under less restraint with me.'

"I hear from other quarters also that the Atalik starts in six days.

"The Yoozbashee propounded a theory, that at this season a great part of the strength of men goes into the trees, to enable them to shoot and bear leaves and fruit. After the first season the strength leaves the trees, and comes back into men. Hence men at this present season are languid and limp."

Two days later, "The Yoozbashee was talking about everything being God's work, and why was I impatient? I replied, 'My impatience is God's work also.' This he seemed to consider a poser. I also said, 'What I regret is this, that out of the fixed number of years which God has appointed me to live, I have just lost entirely three months, which are as it were wiped out of my existence, and cannot be replaced.' He replied, 'No, no, they are not lost ; you will see that your residence here has been productive of very important results, and then you will look upon these three months as one day.' "

The period of deliverance was really at hand. After so many rumors, and three months of close detention, there was a sudden change in his treatment. " On the afternoon of the 5th of April," he writes, " the Sirkar came and announced that either a big officer would be sent to communicate with me or else I should be taken myself to see the King. I answered, 'I am pleased with either course, whichever the Atalik-Ghâzee orders.' After a few minutes, the Sirkar said, 'Get yourself ready, for you will be sent for this evening.' I suppose his first announcement was intended to try me.

" When he was gone, I got ready two guns (the only ones I had left), to present as a 'nazar,' by the Yoozbashee's advice. I know they had coveted these two guns ever since I have been in the country, as they knew they were those I kept for my own use. English-made fire-arms are not so common in this country that they can let any leave it.

" About eight o'clock in the evening I was fetched. They took me to the opposite corner of the great square before the palace, and then by a side street to a big gateway, with a row of guns standing on each side. Opening the gate, we passed through the *corps de garde* and into a square, lighted with Chinese lanterns. Opposite was a kind of pavilion, with walls of open work, which, lighted up from the inside, had a pretty effect. My conductor left me at the foot of a flight of steps leading up into the pavilion. I went up alone, and entered the room. In a corner was sitting the Atalik-Ghâzee, close to an opening in the trellis. He held out his hands to welcome me, and placed me opposite him, telling me to sit down comfortably (for I had, of course, taken the excruciating sitting posture usual in Toorkistân). After the usual inquiries after health, &c., he called for an interpreter, a Hindoostanee Jemadar, who came and stood below the window at which we were sitting. I cannot attempt to give the whole of our conversation, for I sat there more than an hour talking and being talked to. But the chief points are the following:—The King began by saying that he felt highly honored by my visit to his country; that he was very inferior in power and dignity to the English; only so big (showing the tip of his little finger) in comparison with the Malika Padishah (the Queen).* I replied, I hoped there might be friendship established between the two countries as there is between the Sultan of Room (Turkey) and the English, and that between friends one does not consider inequality (you will say this answer of mine was a stale one, having been given before, but remember the statement which drew it forth was stale also). He said, 'God grant it,' and then went on to say that I was his brother, that all his subjects were my servants, and that when neigh-

* I noticed that now he seemed to know all about the Queen; whereas in my first interview it was all the "Lord Pashah," or Viceroy of India. He has profited by his lessons.

boring nations heard of my coming to him (he mentioned Russia and Khokand by name), his honor would be greatly increased. I answered that I had not been sent either by the Queen or the Lord Sahib (the Viceroy), but had merely come of my own accord, hearing his renown ; that the only use I could be of was by giving him information as to my own land and sovereign, with whose affairs I was, of course, acquainted. (I noticed that the interpreter sank his voice almost to a whisper in translating all this.)

"The King replied that I was his brother, &c., and paid me many compliments, saying he had never seen an Englishman before, though he had heard much of their power and truthfulness. He added that he was convinced that from them could proceed nothing hurtful to himself, but rather good. He then said, 'I consider you my brother ; whatever course you advise, I will take. I am thinking of sending an envoy to your country. What is your advice?' I said, 'Your intention is most excellent, and it is most desirable that an envoy should go.' He then replied, 'I will send the envoy, and give him a letter to the Lord Sahib, asking him to send him on to the Queen.' I replied, 'That is the very best plan.' He said, 'Well, now about the time ; when should he go?' I said, 'That is as you please ; either send him with me, or before me, or after me, but I advise that what is done should be done quickly.' He said, 'Of course ; my envoy will go with you, and as you think he ought to go soon, I will only keep you here three days more, then you shall go to Yârkand, and I will put him under your charge either at Yang-hissar or at Yârkand.' I said, 'Very good; and if it is your order, I will then explain to him all that he may expect to be asked, and other things which you probably have not leisure to hear from me, and he can then obtain your orders on these subjects, lest when he gets to the presence of our rulers, he should find himself unable to give an answer.' He replied, 'Do so, by all means. We will have another talk together to-morrow evening, and again at Yang-hissâr, where I shall go after visiting the Mazâr (a Mussulman shrine). I will also send a man' (I caught the word 'pisar,' or *son*, but the interpreter did not say so), 'who shall come and go between you and me, and through whom we can communicate; when he comes, let no one be present but your two selves. Send all your servants out of the way, and whatever passes between us, keep it secret till you re-enter your own country.' I promised to do so. He said, 'The Queen of England is like the sun, which warms everything it shines upon. I am in the cold, and desire that some of its rays should fall upon me. I am very small—a man of yesterday. In these few years God has given me this great country. It is a great honor for me that you have come. I count upon you to help me in your own country. Whatever services I can render you here, you may command, and you must do the same for me. Come, what report will you give of me when you get back?' I said, 'I shall tell them that the renown of you that has reached India is but half of what I have found the facts to be.' He laughed, and stretched out his hand to shake mine. Then he said, 'You must keep on sending a servant of your own with merchandise to Toorkistân. Whether the Malika sends me an envoy or no, that she will decide, but your own special agent must come and go. Will you send one yearly?' I replied, 'If I have your permission, I will certainly do so.' He said, 'That is right. Send all sorts of merchandise by him, and send a letter to me, asking for whatever you want. You may always command me, and the arrival of your letter will be as wealth to me.' I said, 'I trust by that means I shall be able to receive frequent intelligence of your well-being and prosperity. That will be my greatest pleasure. I trust that your kingdom may be established for hundreds of years.'

"After more of this style of conversation, and drinking my tea, he called for a robe to be put on me; but after I had received it, he again made me sit down, and repeated some of his previous speeches, saying, 'Az barae Khooda' (Before God), 'I mean all that I say. I am a Mussulman, and will not stir from my engagements.' Finally I was let go, and the King's son appeared, and conducted me as far as the outer gateway. Towards the latter part of the time, the interpreter apparently thought I did not appear grateful enough for the honor and compliments bestowed on me. He kept on saying, in Hindoostanee, 'Consider what this great prince is saying to you;

he has never said so much to any one before.' I don't know whether he expected me to stand up and say 'Allaho-akber,' or perform any other ceremony of that sort; but the King evidently did not, for he stopped the interpreter, and told him to say only what he was ordered.

"On coming out I was assailed with wishes of 'Moobarâk' by all my attendants, who all came and sat with me, to hear the result of my visit to the King.

"The next morning the Sircar brought me as a parting present from the King bags of gold and silver yamboos, and some gold-dust in paper, saying they were for my private expenses. I estimate their value at about £690. Presently he reappeared, with about £45 of silver for the agent. Again, he brought me a robe of crimson satin, gorgeous with gold and embroidery, and a high velvet cap, and other robes for myself, the agent, and all the servants. Soon after arrived a horse, with handsome trappings, whose bridle was put into my hand, while blessings were invoked with outstretched arms. This evening I have again been taken to see the King. Everything as before, except that my agent was allowed to come into the court after I was seated, and say a distant salâm, to which the King responded from his window, with a muttered 'O aleikoom as-salâm,' stroking his beard, and adding, 'He is a good man, poor fellow' ('bechâra,' a patronizing term of friendship). As before, his conversation fell chiefly on his own insignificance compared with our Queen,

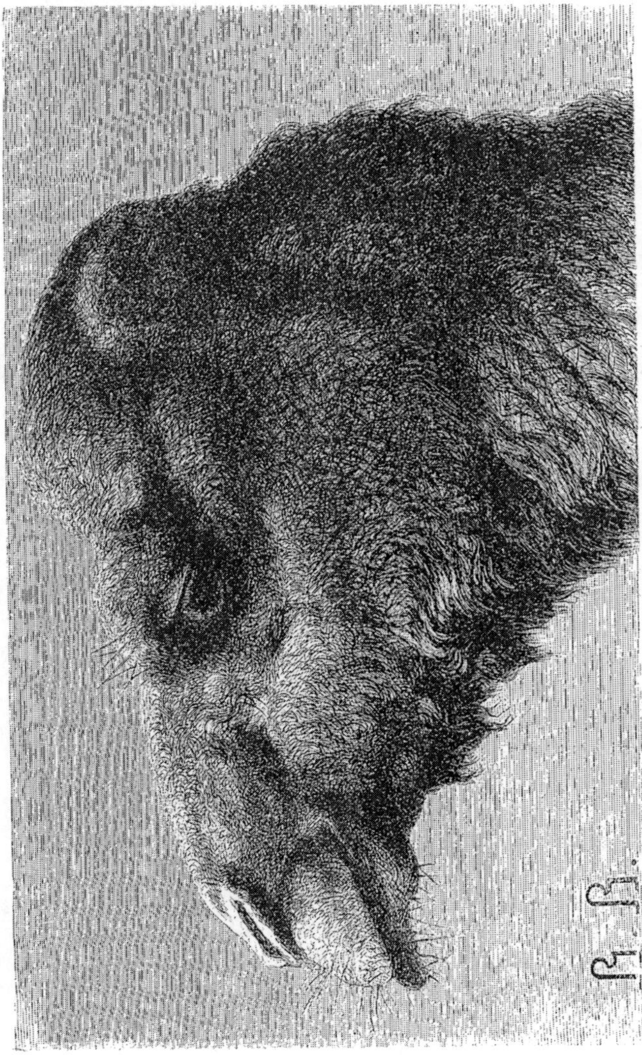

'Ruler of the seven climes,' as he called her. He enlarged on his desire of friendship with England, but chiefly on his special friendship for me, saying that, when he saw my face, God put it into his mind to take it for a good omen for himself.

"I replied that his kindness was overpowering, and that as I myself was too insignificant to deserve it, I took it all as meant for my Sovereign and nation. He took me to refer to the presents he had sent me in the morning, and said, 'No, no, it is all for yourself in particular, on account of the private friendship I have formed for you. For your Queen I mean to prepare some fitting gifts, and as you are my friend, and I am ignorant of the customs of your country, I count on you to tell me what is proper to be sent to her. She is very great, and I am very little ; I conceal nothing from you ; you know the state of my country ; it produces nothing but felts, and such like things' (laughing, and pointing to the matting of the floor), 'so you must give me advice.' I said, 'Friendship is the most valuable gift that kings can give one another ; but if I can be of any use in giving advice, I am at your service.' He said, 'I count on you for this. When we meet at Yang-hissâr, we will arrange all. Here I am oppressed with business. There are people here from Russia (?), from Khokand, from Bokhâra, and from all quarters. But I purpose to go to Yang-hissâr, and throw off business like an extra robe, and then we will talk much together. Whatever advice you give me I will follow down to the least point' (showing the tip of his fingers), 'whether about writing letters, or sending envoys, or doing anything.'

"I replied, 'The plan of sending an envoy proceeds from your own counsel and wisdom; but if in the execution of it I can be of the least service, from my knowledge of English customs, &c., that is what I most desire.' Then, counting on his fingers, he said, 'To-morrow is Char-Shamba, next day Panj-Shamba, and the day after Friday. I shall start for Yang-hissâr, leaving my son here. Stay with him a couple of days (my country, and all my subjects are yours), and on Friday come to meet me at Yang-hissâr. I have a great affection for that place, as it was the first town I took in this country, and I intend to pay my devotion at the shrine there. We will arrange all matters there, and I will send with you two or three men of rank and wisdom. They shall carry you in the palms of their hands till you leave my country, and then go with you to your own country.'

"After further talk, he said, 'I feel great shame because an Englishman once before came to this country, and was murdered by a robber, one Wallé Khan, who was then here.' I replied, 'We know that you had no hand in it, and do not throw the blame on you. The traveller you speak of was not an Englishman, but a German; but still we felt much grieved at his death, for he was a guest of ours in India, whence he came to Toorkistân.' He went on to say, holding up six fingers, 'There! that is just the number of years that I have been in power; before then I was nobody.' I answered,

'Those kings who succeed to thrones by right of birth obtain their power by no merit of their own. But those who, like Timoor and Sikandar (Tamerlane and Alexander), obtain great kingdoms by their own deeds, are looked upon with admiration.' The king clutched his robe (*à la* Toorkee), and said, 'May God make your words true.' (You will say I am wonderfully sententious, but that is the custom of the country. Tupper would be a great literary character here.)

"Again, the Atalik said, 'Another Englishman came to Yârkand; do you know who he is?' I said, 'I met an Englishman in Tibet, who asked me to take him with me, but I told him that I could not do so, as I had only asked permission of the King for myself alone to enter his country.' He answered, 'Well, whatever Englishman comes, he is welcome to me.'

"After this I was allowed to go, being nearly stifled, from having to wear three heavy robes, one above the other, the gift of the King this afternoon; such is the custom of the country. I forgot to say that, when I entered, the King wished me 'Moobârak' (or happy) on putting on the new robes.

"I tried to give a robe of honor to the Sirkar who brought me my presents, but he resolutely refused to receive anything, saying the King would cut his throat if he accepted the smallest present from a Mihmân (guest). I told him to try and get permission from the King."

On the 7th of April, the King left Kâshghar for

Yang-hissâr, and the same afternoon, says Shaw, "came a note from Hayward, saying that, as I am being allowed to depart, while nothing is said about his going, he anticipates that they mean to keep him. I am sorry to say this was rather confirmed by an ugly rumor that one of my servants heard to-day. He was told that I should now be sent back to India with an envoy from the Atalik-Ghâzee, and that Hayward would be kept as a hostage for his safe return.

"I immediately gave orders to Jooma to go to the Jemadar Dâd-Khwâh, who seems to have some influence, and is also sensible and friendly. Jooma is to explain to him that, as long as an Englishman is kept here against his will, it is quite useless to expect any good to come from sending an envoy; and that, if they are not going to allow Hayward to depart, they may save themselves the trouble of entering into any communication with our Government."

The next day the answer was returned that Shaw would leave Kâshghar on the morrow, and that Hayward would be allowed to go at the same time.

CHAPTER XVI.

THE RETURN TO YARKAND, AND SECOND RESIDENCE THERE.

ON Friday, the 9th of April, 1869, Shaw was escorted out of the gates of Kâshghar, on his return journey. He says: "We started about ten o'clock. Most of the servants and all the luggage came in two 'arabas' (country carts). A nasty windy day, storms of dust and drizzling rain at intervals. The Sirkar rode out with me a little distance from the fortress, and then got off his horse to take his leave of me. I am accompanied by the red-robed Yasâwal, and by the Sirkar's deputy, besides the Yoozbashee and his party. We breakfasted on getting to Yepchang, where we put up at the old place, a master of ceremonies having been sent on to prepare it. The house belongs to the head-man of Yepchang. I went out with Sarda to some sand-hillocks about a mile off, where we had a splendid view of the Kakshal and the Karantagh mountains to the north, and the gigantic snowy range to the south-west. We could see Kâshghar fortress plainly, and took bearings till interrupted by fresh storms of dust. On returning, I found the arabas had arrived: they are tilt carts, with a pair of enormous wheels, one horse in the shafts and two leaders attached by long traces of rope running through iron rings on the shafts, and fastened to the axle under the cart. Each horse has a separate pair of traces all the way back, also separate pairs of reins to each. On the horses' necks is a kind of yoke (two parallel sticks), which are kept from the shoulder by large pads; the whole effect being that of a horse collar, except that the yoke is thrown off with the traces, leaving the pads on the horse.

"Afterwards, the weather having cleared, I made another excursion to the sand-hills, and got more bearings, and a sight of the mountains all around. The wheat and the barley were both sprouting, a couple of inches high. Ploughing for some other crop was going on, with pairs of bullocks yoked very wide apart. I saw a pair of horses, too, employed in harrowing, or rather clod-crushing. Gourds with holes in them were stuck up in the trees, near the houses, for a small kind of blackbird with yellow beak to build in. These birds sing well, and are said to turn dark blue in summer. The Toorks call them *kara-kooch-kach.* I was told that Indian corn here produces sixty-four measures of produce from one measure of seed; wheat and barley less. I noticed also some Tartar wheelbarrows, very light and handy.

"Some of the trees were almost in leaf; all were shooting. The rivers are very empty, being drained by the canals for cultivation. Great work is going on at the third river, where a bridge is being built by the Atalik's order. They have made two piers in the middle of the stream (with noses both ways). They consist of a casing of planks riveted together with iron, and filled up with great stones. Less elaborate piers, or rather breakwaters, have been erected to protect the banks above the bridge from the action of the stream, and the spaces between the breakwaters and the bridge have just been planted with willow cuttings, to strengthen the bank by their roots.

"The whole way the ground is cultivated, excepting the basin of the last river, which is left in pasture. Farmhouses are dotted over the whole country, their orchards and plantations hiding the view beyond a few hundred yards. There were a great many 'arabas' on the road.

"The next morning was cloudless, with white frost and a thin coat of ice on the wayside pools. I made another excursion to get a view of the mountains. A perfect view all round. There are enormous mountains to the south-west with snow extending at least three-fifths of the way down from their tops. The northern and the southern ranges trend away to the westward, where there is an apparent opening (a little north of west) occupied by lower spurs, and where no snowy range is visible. Thus the ranges form a deep bay of which we cannot see the end. Almost immediately south of us the southern range culminates in a gigantic knot of peaks, and then turns off southward out of sight. But the northern range continues far away to the eastward till it vanishes from mere distance; a long wall of snowy mountains (called first 'Karantâgh,' and further east 'Mooztâgh') from which long lines of lower ridges run out into the plain. Over these lower ridges, and parallel to the higher range runs the road to Aksoo, crossing as many as eight several 'cols,' or small passes.

"The Yoozbashee fell ill, and came part of the way in an 'araba.' We stopped half-way at a village, and had a dastar-khân and pilao. A hot ride afterwards into Yang-hissâr. The country is even more cultivated than I had thought it in the winter. There are a few tracts of pasture.

"Before reaching Yang-hissâr, they made me put on a crimson satin robe and velvet cap; so I rode in in triumph! I am lodged in a mosque near the fort, and opposite the camp of the Envoy from Kolab (one of the small states of Western Toorkistân).

"My master of ceremonies, Ala Akhoond, met us half-way, and rode in with us. Numerous officials seem to float in front of us, though we appear unable to grasp them, as it were. They disappear as soon as seen, and finally rejoin one's party mysteriously and are found in one's train. They prepared everything, and ushered us into our lodging.

At Yang-hissâr, on Sunday, the 11th: "I have spent a much pleasanter day than for several months past. We seem to have re-entered the world again, after our long seclusion. We are living in a mosque just outside the gate of the fortress, and between it and the town, which is about a quarter of a mile off. Our mosque is raised some height above the ground, and, sitting on a kind of covered platform at one side, one can see a long way over the country. On one side this platform is left open, but the side opposite the door of the mosque is shut in with silken screens, of the kind called in India 'kanâts' (which are generally used as the side walls of tents). Other 'kanâts' enclose a small open space, of which the fourth side is formed by a row of small chambers, running at right angles from the end of the mosque. Tents for the servants are pitched outside, in a little garden by the side of a tank which belongs to the mosque.

"The gate of the fort is about 100 yards off, and the road leading thence to the town has been thronged all day with people, forming a good noisy boisterous crowd, collected to see the distribution of the King's bounty to a lot of poor people, the maimed, the halt, the blind, and the professional beggars, who have gathered from the surrounding district. After gazing at nothing but bare walls for nearly three months, it is indescribably pleasant to watch this scene of life and activity: the crowd swaying to and fro, the small boys skirmishing round its skirts, and making themselves a nuisance to the steady-going sightseers, as they do all over the world. Not content with the dust stirred up by the movements of the multitude from ground where it lies three or four inches deep, they swept it about with their boots, and pelted one another with it, and when a 'devil' (a small *whirlwind*, common in India as well as here) raised its revolving column of sand, they made common cause with it, rushing after it from all quarters, and struggling to throw their caps into the vortex, for the pleasure of seeing them whirled up into the air.

"Then there are the 'faqueers,' or dervishes, in their tall conical caps, carrying a gourd by their side. More than a hundred of them sat down in a row, waiting for their turn in the distribution of money. Stragglers of these would come periodically to the foreigner's camp to ask for alms, and when they received their allowance of bread or rice, would repeat an Arabic prayer, with outspread hands, finishing with an 'Allaho-akber,' as they drew them slowly over their face, down to the tip of their beards. One of them, with long elf-locks (a rare sight here), came and addressed me in Persian, begging, not for himself, but for his horse, an uncommonly good-looking one, which he was leading by the bridle. I had before heard of beggars on horseback, but had never seen one. Indeed, they are proverbially said to ride in another direction. Among the rest I recognized a most amusing young beggar whom I had seen at Kâshghar, a small boy of four or five years old, with only one eye, who lisps out Arabic prayers in a most voluble manner, chattering away in Toorkee in the intervals, and interrupting himself to pick the big

THE RETURN TO YÂRKAND.

lumps of sugar, or the most tempting 'pistachio' nuts, out of the things which are being poured into the skirt of his coat, held up for the purpose. His parents seem to wind him up before they send him in to beg, for nothing stops him in his voluble, but incomprehensible, invocation of blessings.

"A separate crowd is formed by the women, with their round blaek-rimmed pork-pie hats (their winter head-dress), and white head-kerchiefs. When they pass in front of my abode, they drop their small net veils over their faces. The respectable men and local dignitaries, when they pass, make me low reverences with folded hands, adding the usual salutation, 'As-salâm aleikoom,' never suspecting me to be an unbeliever, but taking me for some swell Mussulman, in my silk robes and turban. There is a never-ending stream of horsemen going in and out of the fort gateway: the officials in brilliant garments with silver-mounted belts and swords, their guns slung over their shoulders; the moollahs in loose, sober-colored robes ungirt at the waist, and huge white turbans; grooms in high boots, taking their masters' horses out to exercise or water, riding one and leading another, both in their stable clothing, which covers them up to their eyes, much like that of English horses.

"On the other side of my dwelling are some men at work making a vegetable garden, throwing up the ground into ridges and furrows for irrigation. No Englishman could labor harder, or do more work. When I sent them out some bread,

&c., they made low bows, and sat down together to make a meal, bringing out their bottle-shaped gourds full of water, which had been covered up by their overcoats from the heat. But they made no long business of it; they ate the bread, and immediately got up again to work, only interrupting themselves twice in the afternoon to say their usual prayers, prostrating themselves on the newly-turned earth.

"In the same direction also lies a walled enclosure, occupied by barracks, from which issued a company of red-coated foot soldiers, led by a captain in blue. Their uniform has a very Oriental look: long robes, reaching below the knees, turned up with black at the edges and round the cuts at the sides; wide trowsers, the same; and a conical cap, blue with a red tip; a curved scimitar at the side, hanging from a belt crowded with pouches and flasks. They have no idea of marching in any regular formation, but come straggling after their captain.

"In the afternoon a horse with fine trappings came for the Moonshee, and he was taken away into the fort to say 'Allaho-akber' to the King for it; which he did from a distance, as before. The saddle-cloth is of the Chinese silk-embroidery on cloth.

"The next morning (the 12th) I had a parting interview with the King. I was taken into the fort, and through a wide street, bordered with blank walls, to the gate of the 'Oorda.' Entering this, at the end of one court-yard I saw the

King sitting at the window of a room. As usual, I was made to sit down opposite him, and he told me to make myself comfortable. The interpreter was called for, and after mutual inquiries after health, we had another long talk, which it is impossible to reproduce entirely. He said he was going to send an envoy with me, a Sayad of high degree. We should go as soon as the young fruits of the apricots were formed, which was the time when the passes were open. (I must interrupt myself to notice that, as the Mussulman lunar months run through the four seasons in a space of thirty-two years, they are unable to denote seasons by the names of months, but have to take some operation of nature as a guide and a sign, either the time of harvest, or the ripening of certain fruit, or, as in the present case, the setting of the fruit.) He informed me that he would have messengers sent back from Yârkand, fsom Shahidoolla, from Tibet, and from Cashmere, to bring news of me, and of our progress. He then asked me, 'Shall I send a letter to the Maharaja of Cashmere? what do you advise? and he leant forward to scrutinize my face for an answer.

"I tried to excuse myself from giving one, but as he pressed me, I replied, 'It is, of course, just as you wish; but my own opinion is that great Kings should not condescend to send letters, &c., to tributary chiefs.' He turned off this subject at once, saying, 'That is all I wished to know: I shall send with you a man who will be under your orders, to send him back from Cashmere whenever you think fit.' He then asked whether he should keep a merchant as a news-writer at Cashmere, as he had done hitherto. I answered, 'By all means, and I hope you will soon have a representative at Lahore also, through whom mutual intelligence may reach.' All this I only said after a great deal of restiveness, telling him first that these were matters beyond me, and that his own judgment should guide him. But he put it all upon private friendship, saying, 'You know all about Hindostân, &c., and what is the use of having a friend if he will not give his advice about matters that he knows?' Then there was more talk about the greatness of the Malika Sahib (the Queen), and her being like the sun, which warms everything that its rays fall upon (here the interpreter got into a mess, his Indian ideas of the sun being that it is an *enemy* to be avoided, and *shade* the chief blessing of life; and he entangled himself in a metaphor about the sun casting its shade upon people!). The King went on to say that he was unworthy to be the friend of such a great sovereign, but he hoped he might be allowed to bask in her rays. He desired friendly relations with us, as he was surrounded with enemies and jealous powers.

"Again he came to the subject of his friendship for me. I responded, telling him that my heart was knit with his, and that I should tell my countrymen of his kindly feelings and kind treatment. He said, 'Be sure to send some servant of yours, some Moonshee or other, often to me.

Write me word how you are, and I will send you news of myself; also, ask me for whatever you want from this country, it is all at your service.' I said I would be sure to do so, &c. During all this conversation he was still more friendly than usual, wearing a continual smile, and leaning over familiarly to talk to me himself in easy Persian, saying at every phrase, 'Mâkool, Shaw Sahib?' ('Do you understand?') His whole manner to me is most *prévenant* and friendly, putting aside all affectation of dignity or reserve. Finally, after tea, a robe was put on me, and he took quite an affectionate farewell, taking my hand in both of his, and holding it while he wished me safe home, putting me under God's care. Then, with outspread hands, he repeated an Arabic prayer for my safety and success, drawing his hands over his face down to the beard, with an 'Allaho-akber.' The interpreter, Ghoolâm Kâdir, was sent back with me to my temporary abóde, to write down hints for presents to our Queen, which he had made me promise to write for him.

"I stated, vaguely, that things peculiar to this country, and not very bulky, would be most acceptable and proper to send. So he wrote down a list of productions of these regions—jade, silk-stuffs, &c., &c. He went off, promising to be back as soon as he could, if possible before I started. But he did not reappear, and we took our departure almost immediately. We rode through the Bazâr of Yang-hissâr and so on to Toblok. I went out in the evening and took bearings of the mountains; there is a remarkable depression visible from here, through which, according to Jooma, a pass leads to Kolab and Badakhshan."

The further journey to Yârkand occupied only three days, and was made without incident. The country through which they passed was like a garden, all the orchards being in blossom and the hedgerow trees in full leaf.

On entering Yârkand, Shaw relates:

"I was led to my former house, and there again had to eat of a dastar-khân, followed by nearly a dozen hot dishes. After this I went to see the Governor, and had a most friendly meeting. The Governor met and embraced me most cordially, with many expressions of joy at seeing me again, and of sorrow at not seeing me at Kâshghar. *A propos* of my visit there he related a fable.

"Solomon, who understood the language of every creature, overheard the King of the Worms warning his subjects against him (Solomon), and telling them to keep clear of him or he would crush them. Solomon summoned the Worm-King to his presence, and asked the reason of this misrepresentation. The King of the Worms replied: 'If they went near and saw thee, O Solomon, they would never again reverence me!'

"At this parable, which was given without any interpretation, I laughed and answered that although the Atalik-Ghâzee had shown me much friendship and kindness, yet he (the Governor) was my first friend, and therefore had the precedence in my affections.

"In the evening I had a talk with the Panjâbashee Dâda-Khan about a relic of antiquity which is said to exist on the road from Kâshghar to Khokand. He says it is situated at a place called 'Arawan,' three tash (fifteen miles) beyond Oosh, and consists of a flight of ancient steps hewn in the rock, and leading up to the mouth of a cave, with a very narrow and small entrance. The cave is very extensive, and appears to be a regular labyrinth. These steps are known by the name of 'Chihil-Sitoon,' or 'the Forty Steps.' The natives have no traditions regarding them, except that they are very ancient."

For several days nothing of any importance occurred. Shaw was anxiously expecting news of the goods which he had left behind in Ladak, and concerning which such contradictory rumors had reached him during the winter. Ten days later, two of his servants who had been left in charge of the goods arrived at Yârkand, and reported that they had been misled by guides the previous autumn, some of the horses died, and the goods had finally been left at the foot of the Karakoram Pass. The hospitality of the Government fortunately prevented Shaw from being seriously inconvenienced by this neglect and delay; yet it was now desirable to obtain possession of the goods, in order to repay the advance made to him by the Governor of Yârkand.

On the 27th of April Hayward arrived, and soon after managed to send a private note to Shaw, in which he spoke highly of the King's kindness to him, on leaving Kâshghar.

On the 11th of May, Shaw writes: "During a visit from the Yoozbashee, I asked him about my going, and represented the anxiety of my friends at my long absence. He replied that the road was still impassable on account of the waters, and besides, a visit to a great King of the Deen-i-Islam (Mohammedan faith) could not be hurried over so; it was their custom to do things deliberately with 'maslahat, maslahat' (consultation and counsel). They could not send me back at a season when I should lose all my horses on the road. He then drew a picture of the delight of my friends at seeing me back safe, the joy of the Lord Pashah, and concluded with representing a kind of war-dance by which they would celebrate my return! He made me laugh too much to continue my complaints, which was of course his object.

"This morning also the Panjâbashee came and said he had just been told that we should start in a month's time, and he would go with me as far as Shahidoolla. We had some further talk about the horse that had been given me in the morning. He said the Governor wanted to know whether I wanted another. I answered, 'My mouth is shut, for when I ask leave to *buy* a horse, the Governor *gives* me one instead. There are several other things I wanted to buy, such as mules, a few horse-loads of silk as a sample, &c., but I am in a fix. If I buy them without asking, the Governor will be displeased. If I ask him, he will make me a present of them. So shame keeps me silent.' He said, 'If you will trust to me, I will arrange all that before you go. As for the mules, I will get them for you as if they were for carrying loads. You can give them light burdens as far as Sanjoo, and then take them on empty.'

"I do not think that I have yet described the Toorkee manner of treating horses, which differs in many respects from ours. As a rule, they are kept saddled and tight-girt both by day and night, and many Toorks will not allow their horses to lie down at all ; saying that, if they do so, the corn settles in their legs and feet, and makes them lame ! So they tie them up short by the head. At the beginning of the day's march before the sun is high, they are allowed a full drink of water at the first stream, but are given no more during the day, or until they have been in several hours. On coming in from a journey or ride, the horses are first walked up and down for two or three hours by small boys ; after which, without unsaddling them, or even loosing the girths, they are covered up from head to tail with several thick horsecloths, even in the hottest weather, and tied up as I have described, merely taking the bit out of their mouths, but leaving it hanging under their chins. After some hours they are taken to water, and a little hay is given them, and afterwards their corn ; but unless it is still early, they are not cleaned till the next morning, as far as I have observed. At any rate, they are not touched till at least five or six hours after they have come in.

"In cleaning, a curry-comb is used, but afterwards, instead of a brush, they employ a small broom of twigs similar to the birchen switch formerly so familiar to schoolboys. With this they switch the horse all over by quick motions of the wrist ; first of all, the reverse way of the hairs, and then the proper way. This little instrument is most effective, and leaves the horse with a beautifully clean and glossy coat. The Toorks are most particular about this, thrashing their grooms heartily if they detect the least neglect. The master will often test the cleanness of his horse with the cuff of his white under-robe or shirt. He wets this a little, and rubs the horse's coat ; nothing will satisfy him but to be able to do this without leaving the least mark on the white sleeve. As a rule, horses here are not shod except for journeys in the mountains. But I need not say there are no macadamized roads to batter their feet—the whole country, roads included, being very soft earth, ready to fly into dust."

Shaw succeeded in having an interview with a man who had some of Schlagintweit's property in his possession, but the latter refused to give it up, promising to deliver it in Ladâk, at some later time. As the month of May wore on, there were signs of preparation for the return journey. On the 20th, Shaw reports : "This morning the Yoozbashee came to bring me a message from the Governor, that our time was now near, and our horses should be got ready for the journey. Everything I wanted to buy I must make haste and get. He concluded by appealing to me to mention what presents I should like the Governor to give me, as he was my friend. I replied that, according to our customs, it was very improper to ask one's friends for presents, and I could not do so. He cried out at this, 'You are not in your own country now, and you must here do as we do.' I had some difficulty in silencing my agent, who began enumerating a lot of things to be given to me. However, the Yoozbashee declared that the Governor would be offended if I did not mention my wishes, and started off, saying, 'Well, the Moonshee shall do 'maslahat' (deliberate), and tell the result afterwards.'

"He afterwards met Jooma, and told him to get fifteen horses ready at once, as we should go in ten days. The merchants are having their goods taken to Kargalik by relays, ready for their start. The reason the caravan men give for this is that in four or five days the river (Yârkand) will come down full of water, and will then have to be crossed in boats.

"Two days later, the Yoozbashee took me to see the Governor. We began to talk about the heat of the weather; he said what made it worse was that there was no rain to cool the air, whereas in Andijân, though it was very hot, yet frequent showers made it more bearable. I said, 'I fancy the climate of Andijân is not unlike that of my own country, England. I hear there is plenty of snow there in winter, and plenty of rain in summer, as with us.' 'Just so,' he replied, 'England is probably due west from Andijân, and opposite it, which makes the climates similar.' I explained that England was still farther north than Andijân, nearer the pole-star, which, seen from my country, is higher in the heavens than from here. 'Indeed, he replied, with an interested air, 'I did not know that. Which of the seven climes is your country in? What is the length of the day there, sixteen hours?' I answered that we had not the same division into seven climes, as they had, for we divided the earth into five zones, so I could not tell which of the climes we belonged to. But on the longest day we have about eighteen or nineteen hours of daylight out of the twenty-four. He held up his hands at this, and exclaimed, 'You must be on the extreme verge of the fifth clime.'

"I then told him that still farther north, where our ships went to catch big fish, the sun did not descend below the horizon night or day, during the summer. He asked me what kind of people lived there, explaining that, according to their theories, such a climate must influence the juices of the body in such a way as to produce great strength. I told him of the Esquimaux, who were no higher than my breast; upon which he remarked that they must be stunted by the cold. I told him our Government had sent many vessels to explore those regions, with learned men and 'hakeems,' to report on the natural phenomena. He replied, 'That is the part of a wise government to obtain information on every subject.' I continued, 'We English have a great liking for such inquiries. Among other things, we are much interested in Central Asia, because we believe that most of the nations that now inhabit the West originally came from these regions. Our learned men, therefore, are very curious regarding the past history of these countries.' He said, 'I will either get you a book which shall tell you all about this or else write it out for you myself.' I thanked him very sincerely, and said, 'I talk of these things to you because I see that you take an interest in such matters, just as our own learned doctors do.'

"He then said, 'You are the first Englishman that I have ever seen, and I am the first Andijânee that you have seen. I trust we shall be firm friends, and our two nations as well. You have opened the door of intercourse between us ; may it never be shut.' I replied, 'That was the purpose for which I came, and as the Atalik-Ghâzee bid me send my servant every year to Toorkistân, so I hope by that opportunity to hear every year also of your prosperity and good health.' He answered, 'Al-hamd-ool-Illah' (Thank God) 'the door is open, and I trust it may be as you say.' I then told him that I had now been absent a long while from my country, and my friends would be anxious about me ; therefore I should be glad to get leave to depart as soon as he and the King thought fit. He replied, 'You are our guest, and we cannot say to you, "Go ;" on the contrary, we should wish to keep you with us altogether. For a short time longer the passes will detain you ; but the time is near ; probably towards the end of this moon the road will be open. The merchants came and asked me to let them start and go as far as Shahidoolla, to wait for the proper time to cross, but I would not allow them. It is not fitting that any one should go before you.'

"I then motioned for the dastar-khân to be removed (which had been put before me as usual, as also repeated cups of tea, both to the Governor and myself). The usual robe was then brought in (two this time, one above the other), and the Governor, rising up when I did, said, with a laugh, as I put on the robes, 'We have made quite an Andijânee of you; you have taken our dress and our manners.' I answered, 'We have a proverb, that "When you are in Turkey, you must do as the Turks do."' This proverb delighted him, as he, of course, applied it to the Central Asia Toorks. As usual, he accompanied me to the door, and parted from me with a dignified and courteous bow.

"I note this conversation about the climes, as showing the intelligence and knowledge of the man. For an Asiatic to be aware (without European learning) that greater distance northward is accompanied by greater disparity between the lengths of night and of day is very unusual in my experience. His division of the world into 'climes' seems to be regulated by the length of the longest day, and is therefore purely a division according to latitude, although arbitrary as to the number fixed upon."

On the 27th of May, Hayward secretly sent

Shaw his maps and manuscripts, as he heard that the latter would be sent off before him. But the very next day Shaw writes, in great joy :—"The Yoozbashee came to state that we should start the day after to-morrow ! A note fromHayward saying he goes the same day. Tumult of preparations.

"I went to see the Governor after the second prayer of the afternoon. On my asking whether there was anything he wished me to send him from India, he said he was a mere soldier, and what should he care for but *guns !* but he desired my happiness, and after that he wished for guns. I sounded him about the proposed envoy who was to have gone with me :—but he ignores him altogether :—he says I have opened the door, and my name and friendship is engraven in his heart as on stone—that neither wind nor rain can efface it, and only death can destroy the inscription."

And finally, on the 29th : "I am busy in preparations. Concluded arrangements with an Argoon for nine horses to Ladâk. The Yoozbashee brought presents—two pieces of silk, a pair of boots, sugar, &c. He said that the Governor would be engaged to-morrow morning, so I had better wish him good-bye through the Moonshee now. The latter went, and gave the Governor my revolver as a parting gift. In return the Governor said he was my friend, and therefore desired as keepsakes my own pocket-knife and *my compass !* I sent them at once ; of course the object was to get hold of my compass. He does not know that I have another !

CHAPTER XVII.

CROSSING THE KARAKORAM PASS, AND END OF THE JOURNEY.

ON the 30th of May, 1869, Shaw was dispatched from Yârkand, not having been allowed to see more of the city than on his first visit. The horses were not ready until the middle of the afternoon, so only seven or eight miles were traversed. The road led southward through a beautiful green country, dotted with large farm-houses, surrounded by orchards. In one of these, which had a court-yard covered with vines on trellis-work, they camped for the night. Half an hour after their arrival Hayward and his escort were announced, but the latter was lodged in another part of the building.

The next morning, however, the two travellers were allowed to meet, and thenceforth they formed but one party. Hayward informed Shaw that he had not been permitted to enter Yârkand either going to or returning from Kâshghar, but was taken around the city outside of the walls. At the little town of Poskyam, where they stopped after a short day's journey, they were furnished with lodgings inside the walls: In the evening a man possessed with a devil was brought to Shaw to be cured !—but he declined to undertake so serious a case.

For several days the road lay through a green and fertile country, very beautiful to the eye. The marches were very short, to accommodate the convenience of the native officials who still accompanied the travellers, but as the camping-places were usually farm-houses, with gardens and shaded court-yards, and Shaw and Hayward now took their meals together, the journey was very agreeable. The cultivation was rather rude, but there could be no doubt of the fertility of the soil and the favorable character of the climate. The vine grew luxuriantly everywhere, and the walnut and mulberry trees were of very large size.

At Kargalik, where they halted three days, the Yoozbashee gave them an entertainment of music and dancing, the band consisting of guitar, violoncello, dulcimer and tamborine. At this place, on the 4th of June, barley was ripening, and wheat in full ear, though still green. Early nectarines and apricots were brought to the travellers. The whole country is irrigated from the mountain-streams, as there is very little rain-fall.

On the 6th, they advanced to Besharik, only one hour's ride, over a stony desert. The next day, however, they made 22 miles, to Bora, crossing another stony tract, covered with rounded pebbles and sand, like a sea-beach. The valley-oasis of Bora was beautifully green and fertile : maize was already two feet high. The valley is watered by a small stream, flowing through deep banks lined with reeds. Shaw thus records his journeys, on the 8th and 9th of June :

"We ascended from the fertile valley of Bora to the barren plains which slope down from the mountains, and through which the several streams have cut their way, each forming a sunken oasis down its course. These sloping barren plains, at the foot of the mountains, form a peculiar feature of the country; they are found also on the western side, when we passed through them from Kokhrabat to Yang-hissâr.

"After winding for twelve miles through the sand-hills, which cover this plain, we reached the brink of another oasis, into which we descended to the village of Ooee-Taghruk. It is only about a mile above the village that the little ravine or valley begins to sink below the level of the plain, gradually increasing its depth till it runs between cliffs 300 feet high, being itself about half-a-mile wide and beautifully cultivated. The plain is formed of water-worn stones (including pieces of granite) and sand, suggesting the idea of its having been the beach of some inland sea, which may have covered Eastern Toorkistan up to the base of the mountains which surround it on three sides. The edges of this sloping beach, towards the lower plains (or the bed of the imaginary sea), are cut into ravines and broken ground. These ravines, for the most part, contain only brushwood; but such of them as extend far enough back, and have their source in the mountains, form the lovely fertile oases of Bora, Ooee-Taghruk, Koshtak, Sanjoo, &c. It is decidedly much cooler here. No fruit is ripe, and the barley is still green.

"The next day we rode on to Sanjoo. The last five miles we came through sandy hillocks gradually ascending to the brim, whence a descent of 800 or 1000 feet leads down into the valley of Sanjoo. We were met half down this descent by our old friends the Alam Akhoond (chief-priest) and two Kirghiz headmen. Dastar-khâns were spread for us at the entrance of the cultivation. We rode two miles through houses and fields, down the valley, crossing the river. Hayward was shown to a place prepared for him in a garden. I was taken on to the house of Mahammad Bai (the old man of Sanjoo), where I was shown to a kind of daïs, with carpets and a raised seat, and a tent-roof overhead. Tea was poured out for myself and the Yoozbashee by the son of old Mahammad Bai, the Kirghiz chiefs sitting on the edge of the carpet and receiving tea also. Afterwards I had a visit from the Beg of Khoten, Mansoor Khoja, a jolly fat man, formerly Governor of Yârkand city, who fell into disgrace and was imprisoned for a year. He was only let out about six months ago. The house I lived in at Yârkand had been his. He has been newly appointed to Sanjoo, and seems to think such an office rather below his dignity. On my saying (in order to console him) that his district was of high importance, being the door of communication between India and Toorkistân, he rejoined, 'Then I am the Ghoolam-i-Darwâzah, (Slave of the Gate). He came and sat with me several times, and when the Yoozbashee was not there, he broached his grievances (begging me not to mention them). 'However,' he said, 'I do my best in my present position. The late Beg, (Shereef Khan, whom I had seen when I passed through Sanjoo before), 'was dismissed and imprisoned for his tyranny. The peasants were half ruined,' continued the Slave of the Gate, 'so I have been trying to set them up again; borrowing money and advancing it to them to buy cattle, &c., with.'

"At Sanjoo we halted a day to prepare for our journey and load up provisions, &c. My host (old Mahammad Bai) and his sons were very polite. He is a rich old farmer, with a very pretty daughter. I saw this damsel several times when she came out of the house with a jar on her shoulder, and accompanied by a female servant or slave, to fetch water for the household. She seemed to fetch far more jars full than could be necessary, and made little opportunities of lingering about the doorway and looking at the English stranger and all his wonderful arrangements. I learned, afterwards, that my Yoozbashee was in love with this young lady (I quite admired his taste, nothing could be prettier than her dark eyelashes, rosy cheeks, and dimpled chin). He had asked old Mahammad Bai to give her to him in marriage, but the old man said he wished his daughter to marry a man in his own station of life, who would

A TURKOMAN WEDDING PARTY.

settle down near him, and not a soldier who was always on horseback, at one moment on the Pamir and the next on the borders of China. The Yoozbashee hopes to persuade him, and I was astonished to see the alacrity with which my highly connected guardian got off his horse and ran forward to embrace the old farmer. But love levels all distinctions apparently, in Toorkistân as well as elsewhere."

Leaving Sanjoo on the 12th, they took a new route to the southward, to avoid going up the Sanjoo river, which was still much swollen. The first day's journey was along the valley of a smaller stream, between sandy ridges, to a camp at a solitary farm-house. "On starting the next morning, the Yoozbashee called for the old moollah, to whom the house and orchard belonged, and said to him '*dua kilip*' (say a prayer)! Upon which the old man went down on his knees, with outspread hands, every one else outspreading theirs also, while he prayed, after which we all stroked our beards, and the Yoozbashee cried 'Barak-allah, barak-allah' (with God's blessing); and so we rode away.

"Still following up the stream, while it enters the higher mountains, we came in sight of the crest of the range at the head of our valley. It was covered with snow, below which some bright green grassy slopes extend, a great contrast to the barren mountains around. We camped at the junction of a valley leading away westward, at the head of which is the small pass which we were to cross the next day, and which will lead us back into the valley of the Sanjoo stream, but at such a point that we shall no longer have any difficulty on account of its swollen state.

"On the road, Hayward often stops behind to take observations. The Yoozbashee seems to have got quite accustomed to this now, and says to me, 'There he is, off again after some new road.' They have an idea that his sole object in exploring is to find some easy road into their country.

"The Yoozbashee is redoubling his attentions as the time approaches for us to part. To-day he gave us some cold breakfast on our arrival, as our things were not up. He tells us that the Toorks are lovers of horses (ashik).

"On the 14th we crossed the Choo-choo Pass. First up the side valley six miles, then an easy climb up to the Pass, which leads across a spur of the range. The descent is chiefly down a narrow gorge, emerging into a more open valley, which leads to the Sanjoo Stream. We turned up this stream, crossing it three times, passed the old ruined wall which used to guard the valley, to a patch of cultivation and the few huts of Tam. We arrived about 2 P. M. Presently the river rose suddenly so as to become impassable, thus cutting off all our baggage from us. We had to sleep in one of the huts without bedding, on the ground, and with our saddles for pillows. The Yoozbashee and his man were firing at a mark; also a Shikaree (or hunter) who lives here. This man is said to be able to shoot an apple off a man's head, and to have done so the other day at Khoten before the king, who gave him a considerable reward.

"Our baggage rejoined us the next morning when the stream had diminished sufficiently. It was still quite high at 5 A. M. We rode a few miles up the stream, and encamped on a grassy spot to consult with the Kirghiz about our future movements.

"On the 16th we pushed on to a place called Kichik Yelâk, the 'small pasture.' At five miles a valley joins from the right; at eight miles the road begins to ascend long grassy slopes, occupying a broad valley. At the junction of a valley from the left we came upon a Kirghiz camp, four akooees pitched separate for myself, Hayward, Moonshee, and Yoozbashee. Yoozbashee told me a story of a small Russian force near Chimkend being surrounded, and agreeing to become Mussulmans (!) in three days' time. At the end of the three days it was found that they had strongly entrenched themselves, and declined to come over to the true faith.

"All the Kirghiz came out to meet us. Numerous greetings from old acquaintances. The Kirghiz here consists of twenty-two households, which were called a *yürt;* he says that the latter word is not applied to the felt tents, which are called *akooees.* There were no camels at this place. A Kirghiz *akooee* which I measured was 51 feet in circumference, 8 feet high in the middle, and 4 feet at the sides to the springing of the dome."

On the 17th of June, Shaw and Hayward halted

at the foot of the Grim Dewân, or Sanjoo Pass, which the former had crossed on his way to Yârkand, nearly seven months previous. Some of the servants were sent on in advance with the baggage, which was taken over the pass on the backs of Kirghiz yaks. The next morning, the travellers started on yaks also, after taking an affectionate farewell of the Yoozbashee, who embraced Shaw almost with tears. Several officers remained, to cross the pass with them. "First," says Shaw, "we went up slopes of grass, surrounded on three sides by snow mountains,—a kind of bay; then we turned off to the south up the ridge. There was no snow until the very summit, though off the road it was lying 1500 feet below the top. We found more on the southern descent, which was slushy for 1000 yards. We rode to the very top, and found the baggage on the other side. Here we took leave of two more of the officials, and went on with fifteen yaks and five or six Kirghiz. We went down the bed of the stream, which was much swollen, to a camping-place on the former journey.

"The next morning (the 19th) we descended to the Karakash River. Then we breakfasted, and then walked twenty minutes up-stream where deep water runs against the rocky side, and everything has to be carried by men for fifty yards. The horses were sent round above. The Kirghiz drove their yaks through the stream, here about forty yards wide, averaging two feet deep, running four miles an hour, by experiment. Another twenty minutes' walk to rejoin the horses, then one hour further to camp in grass and bush jungle.

"Here we halted for a day, waiting for the baggage to rejoin us from the last stopping-place. We also shod the horses. An old Kirghiz, seeing me with this very Diary Book, asked whether it was the Koran. I said it was a Kitab (book), upon which he reverentially touched it with his finger, which he then kissed.

"I had a conversation with this old Kirghiz. He says this tribe first lived in Sarikol, but were so persecuted by the Kanjootees *(yaman kâfirs*, evil heathens he calls them), that they migrated to Sarikeea* twenty years ago; they consisted of thirty families. Since the Atalik has been in power, the security now enjoyed in Sarikol has induced a fresh immigration of Kirghiz from the Alai plains (in Khokand), and they now number 200 tents. It is ten or fifteen days' ride from Shahidoolla to Taghdoombash† in the Sarikol district, and about as far onwards to Andijân across the Pamir. The passes are low. There is no lake called Sarikol, but one, twelve days round, called Karakül. The Pamir is covered with grass, and abounds in wild animals, among which are the big-horned 'arkar' (*Ovis Poli)*, and its female, the 'goolja;' they are very shy. The Kirghiz asked me whether I had any '*Frang* miltek,' or Frankish

---

* Sarikeea is the name given to the pasturages on the upper course of the Karakash River.

† Taghdoombash means "the head of mountains." It is the upper part of the Sarikol district.

gun, by which he means a rifle (as I found by his description); he said he and the other Kirghiz were mad upon them, and would perform any service to obtain one.

"On approaching the Fort of Shahidoolla, on the 21st, we were met by five soldiers under a Panjâbashee about two miles out. They made complimentary inquiries after our health, &c., and rode back with us. We crossed the river twice, and camped near the Fort. There was a little spitting rain in the evening: the snow was down to 1000 feet above the valley.

"On the 23d I started with a few light loads, leaving my heavier things to follow. Hayward did the same. I took my own five horses and three of Jooma's. The Panjabashee and four soldiers escorted us for a mile out, and then took leave respectfully. There is plenty of grass at the evening's camp, under an immense old moraine descending from the snow mountains to the east of the valley, and plenty of shrubby wood also by the stream.

"The next day's march, to Chibra, was eight and a quarter hours, or fifteen miles. Our Pass of Souget wound up the stony bed of the valley, first one mile south-west, then half a mile west. (Here a nullah joined from the west by which one could get over into the Khirghiz Pass Nullah.) After a couple of miles more S.S.W., we emerged from the stony nullah, and entered on an almost flat country bordered on both sides with rounded mountains, leaving a broad, open valley between.

Here we continued S.S.W. for a couple of miles more, approaching a snowy range of rounded hills which ran right across our front. Approaching the foot of these we found one open valley running down from the right, and another from the left, forming one straight line, and having their exit by the road we had come. To the left we turned S.E. towards the pass at the head. The opposite valley having a similar but snowless pass at its head, N.W. For six miles we gradually ascended the open valley to the foot of a short and rather steep ascent covered with snow. A quarter of an hour placed us on the top of it. From the pass a gentle slope in a broad valley for three miles S.E., after which it turns round S.S.E. for half a mile, when we reached a dry nullah with a few stone enclosures and many dead horses. Here we halted. Valleys with easy passes through low snow mountains leading about N.E. to the Karakash.

"On the 25th we went on from Chibra to Châdartâsh. For six miles we went down the broad valley south, the mountains on either hand gradually diminishing in height till they sank into the plain or high tableland through which an almost-dry river-bed cut its course, twenty or thirty feet deep. Thence turning S.S.W. we had a full view of the high snow mountains opposite (Karakoram), of which we had been seeing more and more peaks ever since Chibra. Ascending the level of the table-land on our right, we saw a cut in the range S.S.W. This leads to the Karakoram Pass. Further to the left, snowy mountains come round (bordering the upper Karakash), getting more and more rounded, though still snowy; till they meet the Kuen Lun or Sooget Range behind us. This range, a high snowy one, faces the Karakoram, being about parallel and more regular as we see the actual range, while of the Karakoram we only see the snowy buttresses, not the actual watershed: one is an army in line, the other is an army in parallel columns, of which we can only see the heads. The whole space to our left is a high irregular table-land, sloping up for thirty miles or so to the mountains to the east, which bound the Upper Karakash.

"Through these mountains a pass is visible southward, between a rocky peak to the south and a high double snowy mountain to the north. This high table-land which I have mentioned is called the 'Dubsa Sergot or Sertkol;' it appears utterly barren. A broad almost dry river-bed issues from it and unites at our feet with a similar one from the Karakara Pass opening, and with the one we have followed down from Chibra. The three go off together north-westward, forming the Yârkand River (which here has but little water, scarcely flowing, so gentle is the slope of the broad shingly bed). Further on this appears to sink deeper, and to become a kind of ravine between the barren spurs sent out from the Sooget snowy range to the north, and one from the Karakoram on the south. Then the character of the country seems to change from the open plateau on which we now are. Here one is reminded of views of Iceland, so close does the snow of the mountain sides come down to the plains. These mountains, although probably none less than 18,000 feet, seem mere hills, so high is the plateau from which they rise. The contrast between the view east and the view west is remarkable.

"Descending into the shingly bed again, we turned towards the Karakoram, though the difference between our former descent and our present ascent was scarcely perceptible. After a couple of miles from the turn S.S.W. we cross the shingly bed from the Dubsa Sergot. Here it was evident that it came from the pass of the Karakash, which hence bore S. E. The furthest point to which we could trace the Yârkand River bore hence N. W. by W. Four miles further, a few dead horses, in a side bed, marked the halting-place called Malikshah. Here, on the table-land to the left, we saw six *white* bucks (Tibet antelope). Beyond this the river-bed became entirely dry, and we marched up its interminable plains for eleven miles, till some low spurs from the Karakoram formed a kind of portal, through which we entered the mountains again: this is Wahabjilga. Thence, through a broad mountain valley three miles S.W. by S. to a solitary rock in a grass-plot standing in the middle of the shingly bed, which here has a little water in it. The slopes near have a little Tibet spiky grass: this is Châdar-tâsh (tent-stone) where we camped. No water or grass between Malikshah and this.

"The next day we made only one and a half

hours = 5 miles. To the east of Châdartash a broad valley plain leads to án apparent Pass through snowy downs about fifteen miles off. This Pass bears S. E. by S., and probably leads to the Upper Karakash also. Hayward means to try this route, so here we part. Starting I passed one of those large ice-sheets which are common in these parts, formed by the repeated floodings and freezings of the stream in flat parts of its bed. At a mile from Châdartash I obtained a view of the Sooget Pass through an opening. Halted on a slope with a little grass at a place where the bed of the stream forms a little plain of shingle surrounded by red hills, just before the entrance of some valley among big snow mountains. They say there is no grass further up, and the Pass is still distant. Went up a ridge three miles, to get a better view.

"On Sunday, June 27th, we made a halt. In the morning the mule and the gray horse (Yoozbashee) were missing. I sent out in all directions. Yoosaf on the other gray, after hunting about for the tracks, was suddenly seen to go off straight down the valley like an old hound that has found the scent. I found the two tracks leading that way, after vainly searching all the other directions myself. I sent two others after Yoosaf on horseback with nosebags, and food for the men. Presently comes Hayward's Argoon, saying Hayward's white horse is dead, and my two went past Châdartash at daybreak! I scolded him for not turning them (Hayward suggested in a note that I should give him a flogging). I also gave him a few spare nails, Hayward not having a sufficient supply for his horses' shoes.

"The following day I was still obliged to halt, as neither men nor horses have turned up. It was a frightful trial of patience. I counted remains of eighteen horses lying about the camping-ground within a radius of 100 yards.

"All along the road at every few hundred yards you find a skeleton, while the halting-places are crowded with them. At night we hear the howling of wolves who haunt this road. They are probably now expecting the opening of the horse season.

"The boy Abdulla came back at 3 P. M., saying he had followed the tracks of the mules, &c., nearly to Chibra. Yoosaf had evidently, from the tracks, tried several times to catch her, but in vain. They must all have gone over the Pass, where they will come across my caravan, &c. I determined to start to-morrow in any case, if possible."

"Here ends my diary, for the difficulties of the road left me no more leisure, even to jot down a few lines at night.

"The Toorkee boy, Yoosaf, who started on the tracks of my mule and horse which ran off from Kiziltagh on the 27th, followed them most pluckily over that high desert plain. It was not till the next day that he rode in, half famished, to the camp of some of my servants, sixty miles back at

Shahidoolla, who were coming after me, and who had already caught the horse and mule.

"I have mentioned the parallel ridges of mountains about the Karakoram Pass, which are like an army in column. As you progress through them by the broad valleys which separate them, you find that they diminish in height, and gradually sink below the lines of perpetual snow, with the exception of isolated peaks which rise above it. The valleys keep on rising, but never at a steeper gradient than you could drive a carriage up. At last you come to a ridge barring the way, and looking no higher than a railway embankment, though it may perhaps be a couple of hundred feet high. This ridge constitutes the Karakoram Pass, which seems rather like a *lip* by which some ancient lake may have discharged itself, than what we understand by a mountain pass. The so-called Karakoram *Range* might better be described as the raised edge of a basin, or the culminating part of an irregular plateau, than as a chain of mountains. The descent on the south side is greater, but you can hardly believe yourself to be on the watershed between the great river-system which flows into the Indian Ocean and that which runs eastward towards China. The heights on either side nowhere rise beyond the dignity of hills, and there is no perpetual snow at hand, though the Karakoram is 18,000 feet above the sea. The road is marked with skeletons of horses; the rarity of the atmosphere and the absence of grass for many days' journey causing a mortality among the beasts of burthen which hardly seems to be justified by the amount of inconvenience which the traveller himself experiences.

"At the distance of a day's march south of the pass, you come in sight of a range of real glacier mountains. The Shayoh River, one of the sources of the Indus, rises in a perfect ocean of ice, far more worthy of that name than the Mer de Glace of Chamounix, which is rather an ice *river* than a *sea.* Two glaciers, coming down from stupendous peaks, unite and overflow a large plain with their blue waves. It is worth a journey from England merely to see this place. The plain, barren as it seems, is frequented by Tibetan antelopes, with their slender lyre-shaped horns, the most elegant of their species. Terraces and other marks of the former existence of a lake extend to a height of 200 feet up the sides of this plain and of the gorge by which the stream escapes. There are the marks of a lake which has repeatedly been formed here by the glaciers blocking up the ravine below, and which caused such devastation by the cataclysm of 1841. But I think the marks are too considerable to have been formed during the short existence of recent lakes, and rather point to repeated phenomena of the same sort in earlier times. This, if true, is very interesting.

"But directly after this you leave the high plateaux and rounded downs which are the characteristics of the country, and follow the river down into the narrow gorges of the mountains. You have reached the broken edge of the table-land.

So narrow was the ravine we entered that the river had to be forded and re-forded at every turn, the way being constantly closed by its windings.

"The most difficult of these fords was caused by a huge glacier called Koomdan, whose nose protruded from a side valley, with pinnacles and seracs, some of which were quite 200 feet high, glistening like sugar. I had ridden half across the stream when my horse seemed to fall, as if he had broken through a sheet of ice. I was soon on my legs in the bitterly cold water, and on looking round saw all the horses floundering for their lives, like a shoal of fish in shallow water. We had got into a quicksand! Most of us reached the shore with a little difficulty, but two of the horses had got more involved; their loads were washed loose by the torrent, and they themselves lay exhausted and panting on their sides (for the actual water was here not more than two feet deep), with their heads gradually sinking below the stream. The sand which engulfed a horse was firm enough to support a man, and we were able with some trouble to hold the horses' heads above water, while they were being released from their loads and dragged ashore. Even when on dry land, they still lay exhausted on their sides, with their teeth firmly closed, blood oozing from their noses, and trembling in every limb. I have frequently noticed the presence of quicksands in proximity to glaciers which reach a low-level, and of the ice-beds described above.

"Some three miles below this, another glacier

blocked the way. After careful examination we discovered that the passage was entirely closed for horses, as the ice had in the last three months* advanced as far as the opposite cliffs, tremendous lime-stone precipices, while the river forced its way under it through a kind of tunnel. To make matters worse, it began to snow, and my servants, already wet through in fording the ice-cold water, sat down like natives to bemoan their fate and die. Moreover, night was coming on; so there was nothing for it but to halt. No grass could be discovered, and our supply of grain for the horses would only hold out another day, by which time we had hoped to reach a pasture ground. Now, however, this was impossible. The baggage had all to be left on this spot to be fetched hereafter, and the next day horses were sent round by a five days' *détour* over the mountains, dependent on a little of the men's rice for food. Being anxious to reach an inhabited place, so as to send off news ot my safety, after eight months' silence, I started with two men to cross the obstacle, leaving tents, bedding, cooking things, and everything else behind.

"After passing the glacier, we had again to ford the river, but this time on foot. It was coming down full of huge blocks of ice, which fell from the roof of the glacier-tunnel, alternately blocking it up, and again being swept away by its force. Choosing a moment when the tunnel was blocked

* Since the passage of one of my guides, three months before.

and the water shallow, we pushed in to the water. Before we were half-way across a rushing sound made us look round, and we saw a mighty ice-laden flood sweeping down upon us. A rock in mid-water formed our only refuge. We scrambled on to it and were but just in time, for Tashee was knocked on to his knees by one of the foremost blocks as I was helping him out of the water.

"The rock was but a low one, and as the waters raged around us, piling up blocks of ice on each side and gradually rising higher and higher, I foresaw the moment when it would be sweeping clear over our place of refuge! We spent a '*mauvais quart-d'-heure!*' When the level of the stream was not more than a foot lower than the highest part of our rock its rise was stayed, and presently it began to abate, the ice blocks ceasing. I roused my companions, and we hurried through the remaining stream. Before we had left the spot another flood came down, and this time we saw our friendly rock hidden under a surging tide of huge ice-blocks. Some of them must have been over a ton in weight!

"Drenched in the icy waters, we had to spend the night lying on the least windy side of a large stone, under the shadow, as it were, of the huge glacier cliffs, whose pinnacles and 'seracs' shot up 200 feet against the sky. The next night, at an elevation of over 16,000 feet, I found a hole in the rock in which I could curl myself up, while a waterproof sheet spread across the entrance kept out the falling snow. The next day we crossed the

Sasser Pass, over vast fields of yielding snow, in which one sank up to the thigh at every fifth or sixth step. Here my guide gave in, being struck with snow blindness, and I had to lead the way by compass. We had eight hours of this work through snow, and the night was falling as we left it behind us. Misled by the guide, and hoping to reach an inhabited place, we held on till midnight, when we had again to lie down on the leeward side of a stone not three feet high. But this time we had no food at all.

"Starting again at dawn with our throats feeling like iron, and our feet like lead, we reached a Tibetan shepherd's hut after ten miles' walk, and thought the milk and barley-meal which he gave us the finest food in the world.

"We had here arrived in the British dependencies, having crossed the Karakoram and Sasser Passes, first explored by Dr. Thomson. The country beyond this is known to our surveyors and our sportsmen, though the latter seldom penetrate to the Karakoram. I will now, therefore, close this account of my journey, for I considered that I had almost reached home when I crossed that imaginary *red line*, which, after at first modestly surrounding a few factories on the coast, has now reached its farthest extension among the snows and high plateaux of the Karakoram, the watershed between India and Central Asia."

Early in 1870, after his return to England from this most daring and successful journey, Mr. Shaw was appointed by the Government as one of a commission to be dispatched on a friendly mission to the Atalik-Ghazee. He therefore immediately returned to India, joined the other members of the party in Tibet, and in company with them made a second visit to Yârkand. Mr. Forsythe, formerly British Resident at Leh, was one of the party, and his observations of the latitude, longitude and elevation of various points in Central Asia, together with those made by Mr. Hayward, have materially corrected our former geography of those regions. The map accompanying this volume is copied from one drawn by Dr. Petermann, the distinguished geographer, according to Hayward's and other recent measurements, and is therefore entirely to be relied upon, so far as the explorations have extended.

Some reports of the second expedition, both by Mr. Shaw and Mr. Forsythe, have been published in the proceedings of the Royal Geographical Society; but no narrative has yet appeared. Mr. Hayward, from whose reports so much was expected, was murdered early in 1870, at the foot of the Darkot pass, in Chitral, a region hitherto unvisited by any European, lying beyond Gilgit, towards the sources of the Oxus, not far from the point where the Belor Dagh, the Hindoo Koosh and the Mag Dagh (or Karakoram) chains unite and form the great table-land of Pamir.

[illegible]

POSTCRIPT TO CENTRAL ASIA.

THE CONQUEST OF KHIVA.

THE early months of the current year (1873) witnessed the successful invasion of Western Turkestan by the arms of Russia, as predicted in Chapter I. Though the territory thus added to the dominion of the Czar lies without the region to which this volume is devoted, the importance of the conquest, as regards both the present political and social condition of Turkestan, and the future development of Russian policy in Central Asia, fully justifies the addition here of a brief chapter touching its conception and conduct.

Russia's method of absorbing the territory of her Asiatic neighbors is well known. It is the old story of the wolf and the lamb and the muddied stream, only in this case the lamb is a wolf, and the wolf a bear. The stronger disturbs the stream, blames, then devours the weaker.

Professedly seeking only a peaceful and civilizing influence among the half-civilized tribes along her borders, Russia persistently advances her power, chiefly under the cover of commercial treaties, which, if rejected or broken, are speedily followed by more stringent measures for the protection of trade. By such tactics the Khanat of Kokand, in the rich valley of the Syr Daria, has lately been brought under the dominion of the Empire ; while Bokhara and even more distant states have been forced to reconcile themselves to "friendly" intercourse with her. Khiva, however, had persisted in maintaining a hostile attitude. It preferred robbery to legitimate commerce, and would not abandon its predatory habits. Bands of marauding Khivans overran their Kirghes neighbors who were under the protection of Russia. Khivan emissaries enticed the Kirghes to rebel against their protectors ; and in the diplomatic intercourse which ensued the Khivan government was capricious and disrespectful in its treatment of the Governor-General of Russian Turkestan.

For these and other similar reasons Russia claims that it could not do otherwise than take vigorous measures to bring the contumacious government and people to reason—in other words, make a new attempt to carry out certain designs against Khiva which Russia has cherished for nearly two centuries.

The first essay toward the annexation of Khiva was made as early as 1717 by Peter the Great, in response, it was said, to repeated application made by the Khivan rulers, Shah Niaz and his successor, to take the Khanat under Russian protection. An expedition well planned but badly commanded was dispatched from the mouth of the Ural, and after a successful march almost to the gates of Khiva, was entrapped by specious professions of friendship and submission, and every man treacherously put to death.

The great events which agitated not only Russia but the whole of Europe during the ensuing century gave the Khivans a long respite from Russian vengeance.

In 1839 a second expedition was sent against the Khanat, but it proved a disastrous failure.

The campaign just ended by the fall of Khiva was projected toward the close of 1872. The following spring three columns of invasion were organized; one to start from the south-eastern extremity of the Caspian Sea, near the mouth of the river Atrek, and attack the Khanat from the west; another to march from Orenburg around the northern shore of the Caspian, across the country by the sea of Aral to Kungrad, and enter the Khanat from the north; the third, under the command of the Governor-General of Russian Turkestan, to leave the neighborhood of Tashkend and assail the Khivans from the east; the several detachments to unite before Khiva and pass under the superior command of General Kaufmann, the leader of the division from the east.

But two of the three armies took active part in the campaign. The column which left Tchikishlar near the Atrek made a gallant but vain struggle with heat and thirst for several weeks, but men and animals succumbed to the burning climate, and too weak to return to the place of starting, were taken to Krasnoodsk, near the ancient mouth of the Oxus, where they arrived in a miserable condition toward the last of May. Though defeated by the elements, this detachment contributed not a little to the successful issue of the invasion by preventing the Khivans from recruiting their ranks from the warlike tribes of the south-western steppes.

The Orenburg detachment arrived at Kungrad in the latter part of May. The Khivans made a stand at Chudjeili, but were defeated and fled southward, hotly pursued by the Russians, until they reached the fortress of Mangyt. They were again defeated on the 1st of June, and were retreating toward their capital when it fell before the successful advance of the division under General Kaufmann, which after a severe march and much fighting had crossed between the deserts of Kyzyl Kum and Batkak Kum, and entered the Khanat from the north-east.

As the victorious Russians approached the capital, the Khan sent messages announcing his intention to surrender both the city and the entire Khanat, but fled without waiting for a reply. The gates of the city were thrown open and the Russians entered, on the 10th of June, without giving a shot.

The next day being the anniversary of the birth of Peter the Great, divine service was performed with imposing ceremony on the public square of the conquered city, in honor of the great Czar, the first to attempt the conquest then completed, and in memory of the Russian soldiers fallen in the several Khivan campaigns.

Soon recovering from his fright, the Khan returned to his fallen capital, accompanied by his chief ministers, and formally tendered his submission. In accordance with Russian usage he was restored to his position as ruler, a Russian council of administration being appointed for the period of Russian occupation.

Khiva fallen, the question at once arises, What will Russia do with it ?

From the inception of the campaign the Russian government has protested that the permanent occupation of the Khanat was in no way contemplated ; that the country would be promptly evacuated as soon as the offending people had learned the lesson the expedition was intended to convey. The history of Russian conquest in Asia shows how such professions are to be understood. As observed by an English military critic, while the expedition was yet toiling over the burning steppes, Russia does nothing hurriedly. Having captured Khiva, she may remain there for years, always professing her intention to retire in a short time, but busily occupied all the while in preparations for an advance. This has been her strategy all along ; and thus her frontier has been steadily pushed forward.

Already the semi-official papers of the Empire are taking pains to show that the objects of the campaign will be only half achieved so long as the disorderly tribes of Khiva are allowed to hold their place. The remedy suggested is a wholesale transplanting of them to Siberia, and the substitution of some more orderly and industrious people, who will turn the natural riches of the country to better account. This is Russian strategy also. Certainly the occupation of the valley of the Oxus by a colony of trusty Russians would be of immense advantage to the Empire in the prosecution of her designs upon Central Asia. If the Khivans are intractable, they will have to give way; it is probable, however, that they will prefer to submit to the relatively liberal administrative system applied to all the states recently annexed, and gradually learn a more civilized style of living.

The Khanat of Khiva occupies the region around the lower valley of the Amu Daria—the ancient Oxus—the principal river of Turkestan. Very little is known of the country, and for that little we are indebted chiefly to the adventurous Vamberg, who visited Khiva in the disguise of a dervish. Wherever watered by canals from the river, the soil is extremely productive; beyond, on every side are barren steppes, traversed by few lines of travel, and overrun by fierce nomadic tribes. The people of the towns are degenerate followers of Mohammed, ignorant, bigoted and brutal.

Next to a debased religion, the heaviest curse upon the people of this region has been an atrocious system of slavery, the cause of endless warfare, poverty and misery. This, thanks to Russian conquest, is at an end. The Russians were scarcely established in Khiva when the Khan, "as a mark of gratitude for the consideration shown him," promulgated a decree abolishing slavery forever. Many thousand Persian captives were thus set free from the worst of bondage, to remain as Khivan citizens or return at will to their own homes.